the **ART** and **BUSINESS** of professional **GROOMING**

the ART and BUSINESS of professional GROOMING

BY
DOROTHY WALIN

TM

1986
Alpine Publications, Inc.

IV

Design and layout: Mary Harding
Typesetting: Hope Guin, Artline
Photos by Oster: All photos, unless otherwise noted, have been furnished through the courtesy of Oster, Division of Sunbeam Corporation, an Allegehaney International Company. All Oster grooming photos were taken of work done by Dorothy Walin and Paul Bryant at the Velvet Bow, Hinsdale, Illinois.

First Edition

Library of Congress Catalog Card No. 85-52450
ISBN 0-931866-15-4

Printed in the United States of America.

Dedication

It would have been difficult to complete this work without the total support of a patient husband, and the constructive and enthusiastic input from the rest of the family.

A special "thank you" to groomers, manufacturers, distributors, and other industry representatives, whose enthusiasm for this project helped to keep me going.

Acknowledgements

I am grateful to many owners of champions for their willingness to supply photographs of their dogs for breed illustrations in this book.

The following Champions of Record are shown to illustrate correct Breed Profiles:

Champion Kady-J Editorial (Schnauzer) Owner, Paul Bryant

Champion Sno-Built's Puzzle (Westie) Owner, Jodine Vertuno

Champion Dana's Sunday Edition (Scottie) Owner, Nancy Fingerhut

Champion Lily Gatlock Of Druid (Bichon) Owners, Betsy Schley & Betty Keatley

Champion Illsan's Brandy Alexandra (Wirehair) Owner, Sandra Bamberger

Champion Suchan's Cinnamon Candy (Poodle) Owner, Dorothy Walin

Champion Cliffspride Black Baron (Poodle) Owner, Dorothy Walin

Champion Cliffspride Contessa (Poodle) Owner, Dorothy Walin

The following dogs were photographed at The Velvet Bow in Hinsdale, Illinois, and are used to illustrate various functions of grooming shown in this book:

"**Bambi**" Iverson - Standard Poodle
"**Hank**" Vilardo - Miniature Poodle
"**Colby**" Dashevsky - Toy Poodle
"**Shadow**" Butler - Miniature Poodle
"**Dusty**" Webb - Miniature Poodle

"**Sieri**" Walin - Miniature Poodle
"**Taffy**" Walin - Toy Poodle
"**Schmity**" Gaul - Miniature Schnauzer
"**Gretal**" Malecki - Miniature Schnauzer
"**Angel**" Schafer - Westie
"**Scamp**" Bartley - Cairn
"**Happy**" Effinger - Cairn
"**Clancy**" Ortmann - Welsh
"**Clancy**" Fuller - Lakeland
"**Ginger**" Haffner - Wirehair
"**Marcus**" Garvy - American Cocker
"**Buffy**" Zemke - American Cocker
"**Clancy**" Murphy - Lhasa Apso
"**Dubbie**" Dewey - Lhasa Apso
"**Sake**" Milligan - Shih Tzu
"**Truffles**" Schlesinger - Bichon
"**Tiffany**" Tallberg - Bichon
"**Charlie**" Whiteford - Maltese
"**Midget**" Thomas - Yorkie
"**Minnie**" Spitzer - Mix
"**Rocky**" Finnegan - Mix
"**Christmas**" Chimenti - Mix
"**Taffy**" Raffl - Mix
"**Pepper**" Kennedy - Mix
"**Sandy**" Schmidt - Mix
"**Desiree**" Jozwiak - Mix
"**Starr**" Krupka - Mix

Table of Contents

I. The Business

II. The Art

VIII

Preface

Recently I asked a fellow groomer what happens in our profession when hands become arthritic, the neck and back ache, knees don't work too well, and feet develop bunions. Her answer to me was so simple... "You should teach!" Taking her advice, I would like to share my experiences with those of you who follow in our footsteps.

You have decided to become an artist—a sculptor if you please. The professional groomer must be an artist in the true sense of the word. Though your medium is a wiggly, unkempt mass of fur, your final product will be a clean, skillfully clipped and scissored dog presenting a pleasing picture. The true *professional* groomer *always* has the finished picture in mind when working on *any* dog.

The professional groomer may be an individual shop owner, or a lone groomer working out of her home. Many young groomers find the pressures too great and turn to other occupations. They become disillusioned with long hours, difficult dogs, cramped working quarters, or myriad other problems. Few other workers must give as much personal care, endure as many headaches or suffer the losses the individual groomer/shop owner must face. The groomer/shop owner works long hours, sometimes foregoes vacations, and worries about customer relations and personnel needs. The home groomer, on the other hand, has difficulty managing home, family and a job on the side. Insurance may be more difficult to obtain for a home business unless certain conditions are met. Neighbors and zoning laws may also present problems.

On the other hand, you will feel a great sense of satisfaction if you can look at a well run business operation. When you have built your business step by difficult step and have become successful, your rewards will be abundant. You may go home tired, but you will have a smile on your face. You'll know you've done a good job *and* you'll have the profits to show for it.

This book has been written in the hope that by sharing many years of experience, our profession will enjoy greater satisfaction and profit for our efforts. Often professional groomers do not understand such terms as money management, cash flow and other business language. Tested ideas are presented on many aspects of our profession—to help you understand what succeeds and what does not.

Greater recognition of the groomer as a true professional will help in the marketplace. There is still too much hesitation in the area of fair pricing for the type of grooming done. This in itself is a great part of the failure many groomers experience when they first open their own businesses. You will be helped in evaluating your work and determining its monetary value.

After reading this book, you will find greater pride in being a professional groomer. We keep expanding our horizons, learning about new products, new techniques, and new ways of handling our problems. We share *together* the burden of making the general public aware of what *good* grooming really is.

Dorothy Walin
Spring 1986

I

the

BUSINESS

1
The Successful Groomer

Commitment is the one word that spells the difference between success and failure for the professional groomer. Webster defines commitment as "a promise or pledge to do something." As a true professional, you have committed yourself to the proper handling, grooming, and care of the dogs or cats that have been entrusted to you. The preparation and training for this task takes many hours of diligent work, but the rewards come with financial success and pleasure when you hear the words "thank you" for a job well done.

The same principles of *fine workmanship* and care apply equally to the professional grooming salon, the pet shop with a grooming facility, the groomer in a veterinary clinic or boarding kennel, or to the home grooming shop. It is vitally important for the groomer in each situation to have basic skills in business practices, as well as excellent grooming abilities, or the venture is destined to fail.

Grooming is an *art.* Just as the sculptor must carefully chisel the stone to the shape he envisions in his mind, so must the groomer be an artist, sculpturing a wiggly mass of fur into an attractive, clean, and correctly profiled dog. It must always be the groomer's best effort.

Groomer's hours may sometimes be long, the body crying out with tiredness long before the groomer is finished for the day. However, it is hard to describe the satisfaction that comes from turning a smelly, unkempt dog into a pet that is attractive and well groomed. If the job is well done, the customer should have no cause to complain about pricing, particularly if time spent can be substantiated.

PERSONALITY OF A SHOP OWNER

Certain strong personality traits are evident in the person who is successful in a business venture. Analyze yourself, and ask the question "Am I a leader or a follower?" If the answer is "yes" to the latter category, your best bet is to find an opening in a good shop that pays adequate wages based on skills, and let someone else have the headache of running the show.

Let's examine the traits common in a successful shop owner, and how they apply. Do you like to take charge of a project and see that it is properly carried out? Good leadership traits such as this are important for the successful business person. So are responsibility, dependability, and the ability to deal with people. Grooming is a people oriented business where diplomacy comes into play. For example, when the client comes to pick up an unruly dog, it may be necessary to smile and say, "We had a few problems but we worked them out." Do not unduly criticize the behavior of a client's dog as it may cause loss of a client. There is always the option to refuse any future service for a dog that bites or cannot be controlled.

What about work habits? Most shop managers find it important to go to work early and organize the day's schedule. Also, there are times when a grooming shop owner has to stay late to take care of a problem that one of the other groomers has neglected to finish. An owner or manager usually has to be in the shop until the last dog has gone home.

The ability to work with and supervise others is another important consideration. It is important to be able to delegate authority to others. Don't feel you have to do everything yourself to make sure it is done correctly. Perfectionism has a place. There must be pride in the work your shop turns out. But, if your desire for perfection makes you so picky that your groomers quit in disgust, you defeat yourself, so strike a happy medium.

Determination and persistence are also needed. There are times when depression hits and the groomer has to be willing to stick with it. Groomer burnout is a very real problem.

Another prerequisite is good health. Can you work even though you have a cold or other mild illness? A high energy level is a definite plus in this business. Allergies are a frequent problem. Some groomers develop allergies to dog dander or grooming products. This can make working a miserable task.

In addition to the above factors, many long hours of training are necessary, with a considerable outlay of money involved. By far the most important consideration is the commitment to and love for the animals that are entrusted to the groomer's care.

People who enter the grooming profession strictly in hopes of making money quickly, soon realize they might be happier in some other occupation. Quality of work should not be lost in order to turn out quantity for a greater dollar return.

FINDING A LOCATION

The groomer contemplating opening a shop in an urban area can minimize the chance of failure by finding a productive location, then seeking the help of professionals in that locale.

Begin by contacting the local veterinarians. Ask them what types of dogs they service, primarily mixed or pure breeds, large or toy breeds? Keep in mind what dogs you enjoy and are best equipped to handle. It would be difficult for a tiny, 5-foot, 100-pound person to lift a 150-pound dog without the aid of someone else or some specialized equipment.

Next, canvas the area where you want to locate. You can learn a great deal in an afternoon of traveling around in your car, analyzing the size of the homes in the area, and the types of cars the people are driving. This helps determine if the kind of shop you want and the prices you plan to charge are in line with your proposed service area. Visit

the site of your proposed shop location. Is it an area that would get "walk-in" trade? Would you have a free-standing shop on a busy thoroughfare? How much parking is available for your customers? All of these factors are important considerations if you plan to incorporate a merchandising area.

If you are only interested in grooming, with no product sales, 500 square feet would be ade-

Figure 1. The Velvet Bow is located in the business district of Hinsdale, Illinois. The door on the far right, painted a bright green, is the entrance. Other business entrances were also painted bright colors, one red, the other yellow. (Photo - D. Walin)

Figure 2. "Dog Patch" is the catchy name of a pet shop and grooming salon in Marietta, Georgia, an affluent suburb of Atlanta. (Photo - Karen Walin)

quate for as many as four grooming stations. In that case, do not locate in a shopping center mall. Rent and shared tenant expenses for parking lot maintenance, and various other charges, may escalate costs too high.

Some veterinarians have boarding facilities, and/or adjacent areas for grooming services. These are either rented to the groomer or the veterinarian receives a percentage of each grooming done in return for supplying space, utilities, and perhaps some or all of the needed grooming equipment. Boarding kennels may have grooming services performed by the kennel help, or by a professional groomer usually hired on a commission basis.

Groomers working as independent operators must observe current laws governing such work, and should consult a lawyer in order to protect their independent contractor status.

A grooming shop usually does well if located in a well established area of other boutique type shops independent of an enclosed shopping mall. Other area shops, especially craft oriented ones, give the grooming customer a place to browse

Figure 3. The Montrose Pet Hotel is located in Marietta, Georgia. Attractively styled, scrupulously clean, this establishment has an inviting interior waiting room. (Photos - Karen Walin)

while waiting for the dog. This is especially true if the client comes from a considerable distance.

Contact real estate people to find possible location sites. You might want to locate in one area, but an agent might be able to steer you to another location that would be more suitable. The groomer cannot usually find a building that is precisely suited to grooming needs unless built to specifications. The groomer may be allowed to completely gut an area and start from scratch. Pay particular attention to plumbing needs. Make sure there is easy access to tub traps and drain pipes. There will probably be periodic hair blockage that will require removal. Check to see that there is adequate ventilation for both winter and summer.

Always check local zoning laws. If they do not permit the location of a grooming shop in the area which interests you, contact a lawyer to find out if there is a possibility of changing a zoning law. Be prepared for considerable expense if you should choose to go this route. You need documented evidence to prove to the zoning commission that your shop can be an asset to the community. Be prepared to present picture proof of other well run shops that exist in a similar situation.

Make sure there is room for future expansion as your business grows. This is sure to come if you do a fine job, and have taken into consideration all the other aspects of owning a business. As you find your clientele coming from an ever widening area, expansion will be necessary. Clients of my shop, The Velvet Bow, came from areas as far as twenty miles away; a few came from out of state, and two Westies were flown up from Florida for their beauty treatment when their owner was in the area for business! We were particularly proud of this loyalty when we considered the number of groomers located in our area.

CONTRACTS

Rental contracts can be tricky business. From experience, I recommend taking any rental or purchasing contract to a lawyer who specializes in business law. Find out if there are any legal loopholes that are unduly biased in favor of the person who owns the premises that you plan to rent or buy. Examine the contract to determine what your obligations are as to maintenance of the area. If there is more than one store in the building, ask what percentage of the utilities will be your responsibility. Also, ask that it be clearly defined who is responsible for such things as roof leaks, hot water heater replacement, defective wiring, etc.

MONEY MANAGEMENT

One of the quickest ways for a groomer to run aground is poor financial planning. Some grooming schools or apprentice situations don't adequately teach the need for financial stability when first beginning a new enterprise. A groomer desirous of opening a shop would do well to work for someone else for a year or two to become familiar with the day-to-day problems of cash management that plague this profession primarily because of unsound pricing structures.

In addition to locating in an economically stable area, the groomer must have either considerable financial backing, or have saved up enough money to pay all of the operating expenses for the first six to nine months. (Don't plan on a rich uncle to die and leave his estate to bail you out of financial trouble.) However if the groomer *can* get family backing, lower interest rates may be obtainable.

Financial planning is an accountant's area of expertise. If the groomer has not had training in marketing and business, he/she should rely on the ability of an accountant to help advise how to plan for the costs of set up and operation during the "shake down" period. Later in this book, I list the equipment needed to open shop. That information plus a cost estimate for such things as plumbing, wiring, lighting, and decorating costs, help evaluate opening costs.

For many reasons, obtaining the services of a reliable accountant is a must. When looking for

Assets
Petty Cash
Cash in bank
Inventory - grooming supplies
Inventory - products for resale
Equipment
Auto (if any)
Accumulated Depreciation
Accumulated Amortization

Liabilities
Sales Tax Payable
State Wage Withholding
Federal Withholding & FICA
Unemployment Tax Payable
Notes payable (if any)

Capitol
Owners Investment
Owners Withdraw

Expenses
Cost of products sold
Salaries
Commissions
Contract labor
Payroll tax
Employee benefits
Accounting
Office expense
Bad debts
Bank charges
Interest expense
Income tax expense
Licenses & tax
Rent expense
Utilities
Phone
Misc. Expense

Income
Grooming sales
Product sales
Breeder sales
Misc. Income
Cash short & over

Figure 4. A sample chart of accounts for a grooming shop which also sells retail supplies. Accountants use this as the basis for setting up a bookkeeping system.

Monthly Sales and Grooming Income Summary
(Two Groomers) & Retail Sales

Date	Invoice Numbers	Grooming Amount	Product Sales	Breeder Sales	Misc. Income	No. of Dogs Groomed	Daily Income	Deposit Amount
08 01								
08 03	66192 - 66209	215.00	72.91	8.42		9	296.33	296.33
08 04	66210 - 66220	214.00	15.26			9	229.26	
08 05	66221 - 66230	141.50	Refund 6.32			6	135.18	364.34
05 06	66231 - 66247	202.00	34.21			9	236.21	
	(Monthly Total)	4824.50	1061.25	151.09		205	6036.84	6036.84

Figure 5. Many groomers prefer to operate on a strictly cash basis to avoid complicated double-entry bookkeeping. This easy-to-use record of cash receipts has proved adequate. This information plus your check book should be given to an accountant, who can provide a monthly profit and loss statement.

someone to help with all the necessary government forms, check for an accountant who is licensed to appear before the I.R.S. on the client's behalf in the event of an audit. Honesty in dealing with an accountant goes without saying. The groomer is required to keep daily records of grooming income and retail sales.

The accountant should provide the groomer with a monthly profit and loss statement so the progress of the business can be charted and, in the event of selling the business, there can be an accurate evaluation of a fair selling price.

The groomer must figure real and hidden expenses, plus wages, plus profit to have a sound business venture. How do you arrive at these figures? First, list the following expenditures: Rent, set up costs (equipment and supplies), estimated utility costs, insurance, taxes, advertising, interest and principal on borrowed moneys, maintenance, attorney and accountant fees, a reasonable salary for yourself, and all other wages. If you are opening a new shop, some one time expenditures will also be on the list. They include such things as permanent fixtures, remodeling, costs of installation (plumbing, electrical, etc.), deposits for public utilities, local licenses or professional fees, the starting inventory, and printing and art work for a logo. This knowledge should determine how much to charge per hour for grooming and what percentage of markup is needed on product sales. (Pricing of grooming and product markup is discussed in another chapter.) Your own living costs must also be budgeted to determine your minimum necessary salary during the first year or two of business.

It is impossible to give an accurate estimate of costs of set up for a shop or home situation. Much depends on how much equipment you may have already purchased in school or in a work situation. In addition, rents vary greatly depending upon the area of the country in which you are located.

If you are lucky enough to be able to do some of the set up jobs such as building cabinets for storage or doing the decorating, you can discount some of the costs. Check local building codes on any of the jobs you attempt to do yourself. If you are a "klutz" like me, you will need lots of help.

I cannot overemphasize the importance of establishing good credit habits from the beginning. Groomers are not known to be good credit risks! Be prepared to pay for goods C.O.D. at the time of delivery until you have established a reputation for prompt payment.

Financing

How does the groomer go about finding the needed financing? Before anyone will undertake to assist you financially, you will need to prove that you have the ability to do your work well and have some business sense. You must have a reasonable amount of your own money to invest. You may have collateral that you do not realize. For instance, if you own your own home, and it is worth more than your mortgage, you may have equity on which to base a bank loan. If you have any savings in a credit union account, the company may be willing to underwrite a small business loan. If you have tried to obtain financing through three or more

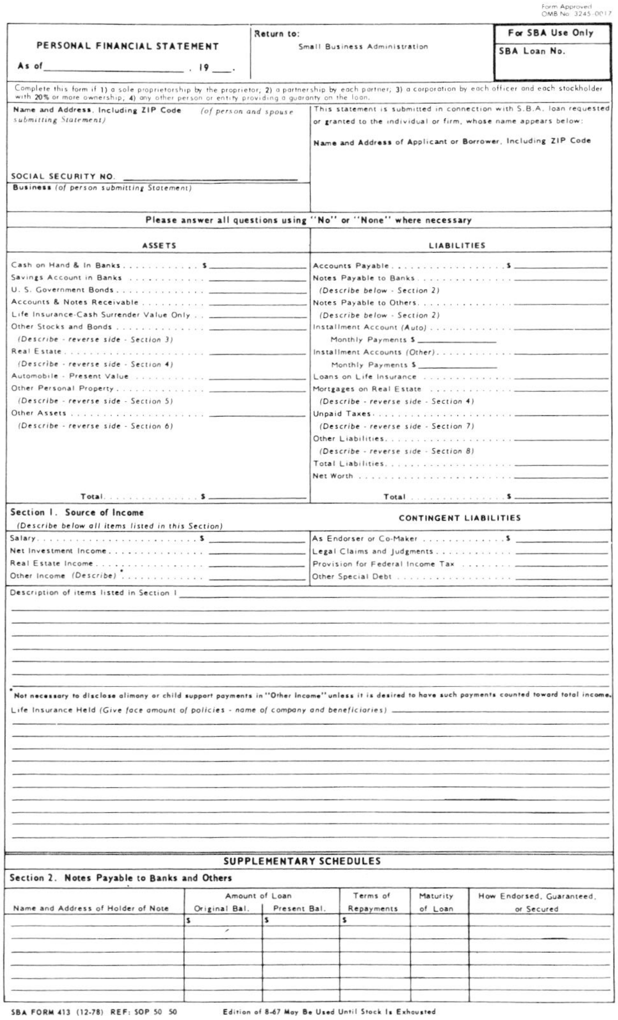

Figure 6. A personal financial statement helps your banker or financial consultant assess your ability to handle business risks. Pictured is a standard bank form for listing personal assets and liabilities.

financial institutions and have been refused, you can try through the Small Business Administration. Stocks and bonds can also be used for collateral, but jewelry cannot.

It is a sad fact that some 25 percent of groomers who attempt to go into business for themselves fail in the first six months. This indicates that there is a tremendous lack of education and business sense within our ranks. Perhaps the sad, but true reason for this failure ratio is the lack of proper *preparation* both in *education* AND *abilities*.

CASH FLOW

As business increases, definite patterns emerge showing the months of higher and lower cash flow. Regardless of whether yours is strictly a grooming business, or also includes retail products, you will find a rising trend in gross income during the months of March, April, May and June. July and August are sometimes slow because of vacations, but there should be a pickup again in late September and early October. November can be rather dull, but WAIT TILL DECEMBER! I can remember dreading December when everything seems to go bonkers. You push yourself to the very limit every day, squeezing in another dog because a good customer forgot to make an appointment. Bone weary, you think about the fact that you haven't had time to write Christmas cards, or shop for presents. After a few years in the grooming business you will remember to do these things in October and November.

During this month of high activity, money seems to flow in. . .then comes January! If you groom in a cold climate, snow may force you to close down for days at a time when older clients are unable to drive on snowy roads. Cancellations are common because of the high incidence of illness and the plague of bad weather.

In all parts of the country many regular clients will want their dogs done for Christmas, so there will be a natural decline in the number of dogs done after Christmas for about a month and a half,

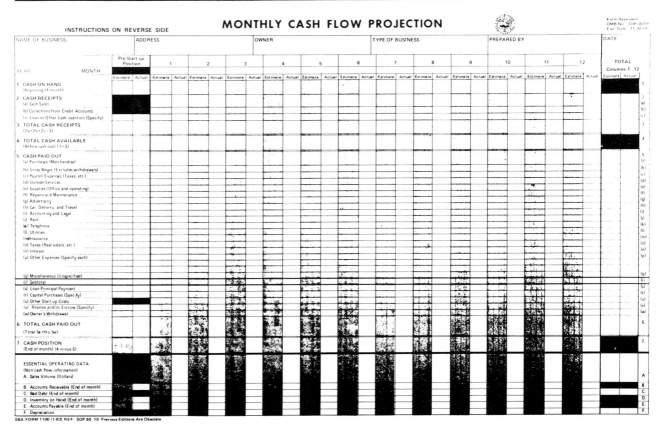

Figure 7. Applicants for a bank loan or groomers who need to project income and expenses during the first year of operations will find a cash flow projection sheet such as this helpful. Projected income and expenses are entered in the shaded columns. Actual expenses may be entered later for comparison. Cash flow projections are extremely useful when planning for peak and low periods in a business.

after which things begin to pick up again. At this time of year, you will be particularly grateful to the clients that bring their dogs to you on a regular basis.

Groomers in warm southern areas of the country have a more even flow of customers, but their business may slow during the hot summer months when clients and their dogs are off to cooler areas of the North.

Therefore, when you are in your busiest time of the year, grooming your heart out, remember, you have to eat and pay bills just the same when the going gets slow. Set aside enough income from your busy period gross to take care of slack season bills and salaries.

If you are planning to have a retail merchandising area, you need to be aware of seasonal trends. Such items as coats and sweaters must be ordered in the middle of summer. Flea repellent products are ordered right after the Christmas holidays. It must be emphasized that the wise groomer plans ahead, and does not live from hand to mouth.

Bill Payment

Every groomer and retail merchant must have supplies and merchandise with which to operate. If you neglect the prompt payment of your bills as they come due, you soon find yourself without the wherewithal to continue business.

Businesses that are under-financed just can't make it. Distributors will not ship supplies or product if you are behind in payment. If this should happen, you will be forced into a "cash only" basis. It is not enough to just be an excellent groomer, because it usually takes a year or more to reach a break-even point, or make a profit.

Gross income represents all moneys that flow into the cash register, whereas, income after all bills are paid is your take-home pay (net income before taxes). Sometimes the two are a long way apart. When you look at your gross income for the month, your first concern must be paying legitimate business expenses. (This does not include taking "lunch money" out of the till...you may be eating a lot of peanut butter and jelly sandwiches your first year in business.) In addition to everyday operating expenses, money must be set aside for hidden expenses such as insurance premiums, workman's compensation premiums, and quarterly social security and withholding payments.

After you have projected a schedule of expenses, plus your salary and a reasonable yearly profit, you can more clearly see the amount of operating capital needed. If you can survive the

first year of being in business, you are usually over the hump. If for some reason, you cannot pay a bill, don't just ignore it. Contact the company or utility to make arrangements for partial payment. As difficult as it may seem, you should take NO SALARY until bills have been met.

SHOP DECOR

Your shop decor offers your client the first impression of your professional abilities. A well lighted, clean, attractively decorated shop or grooming area immediately inspires confidence and establishes a professional atmosphere. Colors influence moods, not only for the client but for the groomer who must spend long hours in the working area.

Figure 8. A clean, attractive, well-lit shop inspires confidence in your professional ability and creates a first impression for your customer. In this photo, notice that the grooming area is open for public viewing. Carpeting in the front of the shop is of tightly woven nylon—easy to clean and vacuum. The grooming area floor is covered with easy care sheet vinyl.

Cool colors, such as pale shades of blues, greens and violet are more soothing to the spirit than bright shades of red, orange or yellow. Restaurants have played upon this psychology to great advantage. Fast food shops are usually done in bright shades of the hot colors to hurry you along, while the more expensive restaurants with an extensive menu will use soft shades of color and lighting. Attractive scrubbable wallpaper combined with matching shades of paint will make your "home away from home" a pleasant place to be. On the other hand, grooming in a dark, unattractive room is demoralizing to the spirit. Drab, dark, or cluttered surroundings cause mental fatigue and impatience.

Soft music to groom by helps keep tempers of both dogs and people in check. We experimented with this in our shop by trying the "easy music" station in our area for one whole day and the next day we left the rock and roll music on at a little higher decibel. The second day, we were all at each others' throats and the dogs were agitated and barked all day. Guess where our radio was tuned from then on!

As your client enters your shop, there should be no unpleasant odors to assail the nostrils. Stale tobacco smoke, dog odor, or any other offensive odor should be eliminated. Groomers should not be permitted to smoke in the grooming area for the sake of fellow groomers, dogs who may have congestive heart problems, or the client to whom the smell of tobacco smoke may be offensive. Good housekeeping habits will take care of other odor problems.

SHOP LAYOUT

The ease with which your shop functions can be helped by careful attention to the original layout. If you are working in makeshift quarters, this may not always be possible, but certain rules must always apply.

Grooming stations should be set up so that whether a groomer is standing or sitting while grooming, he or she has adequate room to move around the grooming table with ease, especially if stationary grooming tables are used. To the right or left of each grooming table should be a cabinet or island for tools and electrical outlets for clippers and dryers. A four-outlet box per station should be enough to satisfy power needs.

Voltage entering the building should be checked to see that it is within correct range. If it is too low, clippers overheat and run too slowly to clip quickly and efficiently. This is a problem sometimes found in older buildings. Volt ohm meters are obtainable at the hardware store, or if you suspect a problem, ask your local utility company to put a meter on your incoming electrical meter for a few days to make sure there are no great fluctuations in power. Each piece of electrical equipment has the necessary voltage requirements stamped on the equipment itself or included in the care and maintenance instructions.

Whether the shop owner supplies all the equipment, or commissioned groomers supply their own, it is important to insist that groomers hang or rack their clippers when they are not in use. There should be either a rack for the clippers to stand in, or a series of hooks along the edge of

Figure 9. Part of the grooming area at The Velvet Bow. Both groomers have stools with back rests. Removeable mats make grooming tables easy to clean. Notice placement of telephone. Hooks on the front of the cabinet next to the grooming table make it easy to hang up clippers when not in use.

a cabinet on which to hang them. Clippers should never be left lying on the grooming table where they might accidentally be knocked to the floor. Clipper and blade prices have risen to a point where breakage must be kept to a minimum. Clipper cords can be shortened to minimize the danger of catching a foot and falling.

Overhead lighting as near to daylight intensity as possible, should be hung in a arc arrangement to eliminate shadows. This can be done by hanging the center set of two or four florescent bulbs parallel to the ceiling and then slightly tipping the sets of lights on either side of center so their light is directed at an angle toward center instead of directly downward. This causes light to shine under the dog as well as on top. Long florescent bulbs in six- or eight-foot lengths hung in groups of two or four bulbs effectively light an area.

If grooming and retail areas are next to one another, softer lighting in the retail area blends the colors of the product containers to greater advantage. The brighter light of the grooming area gives it a professional appearance. Think of the lighting in a hospital examining room, or a dentist's office. Intense lighting using daylight-type florescent bulbs, helps keep down the bacteria count because the ultraviolet rays emitted by such lighting is helpful in germ control.

Holding crates for the dogs are best arranged adjacent to the grooming stations so if any dog is in trouble, it can be noticed immediately by the groomers. Dogs that are chewers occasionally get their teeth caught in crate doors. Escape artists lift certain types of latches and need closure hooks to keep them properly contained. Nervous dogs may vomit and choke or have bowel problems. Heat prostration should have immediate attention. The alert groomer is aware that problems *can* and *do* arise!

Crates are available in many styles and types of materials. Stainless steel units with individual stalls are the most expensive, are easily disinfected, but never need replacement. Most veterinary clinics use this type. Plastic air line-type crates may also be used, but cannot be stacked as closely as metal wire crates and cannot be cleaned as easily. These fiberglass crates have a fiberboard flooring

Figure 10. Stackable wire cages are enclosed in specially constructed cases. Cages of various sizes are neatly contained and dogs are separated which helps to prevent the spread of infectious viruses. Compartments are painted with washable enamel for easy cleaning.

that should be replaced with individual towels or some other material that can be washed and sterilized. Wire crates with metal, removable floor pans are probably the most popular. They usually have interlocking brackets on the bottom so they can be stacked two or more high depending on size. They can be obtained in many sizes and are more reasonably priced. Distributors at most major dog shows, large grooming conventions or industry trade shows have various crates on display.

The groomer contemplating opening a shop, whether at home or in a business location, should make a list of needs, then attend seminars and conventions, and contact distributors to obtain catalogs and price quotations.

WORKING OUT OF YOUR HOME

The groomer with an area set aside in the home must work and exist under the same rules and guidelines as those practiced in a shop situation. Figure expenses prorated according to the amount of heat, light, water and space used for business purposes. Keep accurate records of every utility bill paid, so your accountant can take proper deductions. If you don't do this, you are cheating yourself. The area you claim for business use must be clearly defined and used exclusively for your business.

One important consideration for the home groomer must be the type of liability insurance obtained. You may have a problem if any injury to a dog groomed on home premises is not covered by insurance. You might be sued and settlements are frequently in favor of the client, unless you can prove the dog had a previous problem.

Groomers in a shop usually find it easier to obtain insurance. Certain professional grooming groups offer insurance packages that are tailored to the specific needs of the groomer. If there is a large enough groomers' association in your state, you may be able to work through a reliable insurance broker to offer your association members an adequate insurance package. Some state groups already have this available.

As we proceed through this book, groomer problems are examined in detail. When you are finished studying, it is my hope that your confidence and knowledge will be enhanced so that you may be a SUCCESSFUL professional groomer.

2
Groomer Professionalism

Professional—the word brings to mind many images; doctors in white smocks; technicians in hospital laboratories; a nurse at the bedside; a lawyer pleading his case before a black-robed, dignified judge. This type of professional has earned the right to his or her respected image by spending many years in the educational process. Almost every field has some type of professional labeling, be it the trained technician who fixes your car, or the person who lays your carpet.

Dog groomers no longer want to be called just a "groomer." There are many groomers who feel completely justified in attaching the prefix of "professional" when speaking of ability. The question before us is "Just what does it take to be a *Professional Groomer?*"

Grooming will never receive the recognition due from the general public until *all* groomers are serious about the necessary educational background, and show a constant striving to upgrade their image in the community.

HISTORY

There are many fine accounts of the history and grooming of various breeds. Often, grooming was merely combing or brushing out weeds from the coats of the hunting dogs or clipping back the nails with crude plierlike scissors. We have seen pictures depicting early circus dogs resembling Poodles, whose hair had been clipped in bands or bracelets on various parts of the body. A 14th century picture by Pinturicchio depicts a clipped Poodle. Can you imagine doing that kind of work using a straight razor or a pair of common scissors?

Then, someone discovered that the dead hair of certain breeds could be plucked out using the fingers or a rough blade and the coat would come back in dense and of proper texture. Notched blades in a handle evolved into our present-day stripping combs. Hand held clippers probably evolved in the same manner. Then came clippers powered manually by one person turning a wheel while another did the clipping. Grooming has come a long way from those first crude tools to our present-day array of fine grooming equipment.

The people involved in breeding, handling and showing fine specimens of the various breeds were the first to become experts in the field of grooming. They realized the cosmetic beauty of the dog would go a long way in the winner's circle. As the Poodle became *the* dog to own, grooming began to come of age. Breeders had to find an outlet for Poodles that were less than fine enough to qualify in the ring, and these were sold as pets. Veterinarians specializing in small animal practices, found it lucrative to groom these pets on the side. People who were skilled in cutting human hair began to experiment with clippers and scissors on their Poodles. They would set up a table in the kitchen or basement and go to work on their own dogs or those of relatives and friends. The art of grooming began to accelerate.

Veterinarians soon found themselves too busy to continue this work on the side, and people began to realize that perhaps it was not wise to bring healthy dogs into contact with dogs that might transmit disease. At that point, veterinarians began to set aside a special area that was used only for grooming and hired a technician to do the work. If that was not possible, they sent their grooming clients to those skilled in the art, and the grooming business was off and running.

More and more home groomers appeared. Boarding kennels and breeders also had grooming services. In the middle 1950s and early 60s there were no grooming schools. Most people acquired their skills by trial and error, or from helping someone else. Groomers apprenticed to professional handlers found themselves busy servicing pets also.

When the *Complete Poodle Clipping And Grooming* book, written by Shirlee Kalstone, appeared in 1968 it was a boon to those interested in grooming. Anyone with a little talent could buy the book, a clipper, some blades, a comb or two, and set themselves up in business. There were no controls, no standards by which to judge what was right or wrong. I can remember seeing some atrocious grooming jobs back in those days and this is still a problem in some areas of the country.

Figure 1. Grooming schools now exist in many countries. Fish, Fur & Feather is a grooming school located in London, England and owned by Jill East. (Photo courtesy of Val Penstone).

It wasn't long before some of the finer groomers began to open shops in towns and cities as the Poodle craze continued to grow. Soon we began to see cross-breeds of Poodles and various other breeds. These dogs needed as much care as the Poodles, so the field grew even more. As Schnauzers became popular, those who did not want to spend the time doing tedious hand stripping of their dogs, or the expense of having someone else do it found an alternative in having the coat removed by clipping. With the advent of more apartment dwellers came an increase in the small dog population that needed frequent bathing and brushing to keep them presentable in smaller living quarters.

Today, the person desirous of becoming a professional groomer can choose from schools specializing in teaching grooming skills. An alternative is to apprentice with a professional groomer whose skills are top quality and whose background qualifies her* as a skilled teacher.

No matter which route you choose remember, our profession is now one in which high standards of find work and responsible care of the animals is primary. We are responsible and *liable* for the safety of the pet from the time it enters the shop until the door closes behind it as it leaves.

GROOMER EDUCATION

Past statistics for the grooming industry tell some interesting facts. The greatest percentage of groomers are women. Most groomers of the past have been in the 30- to 45-year-old category, but at present this statistic is showing a much younger trend. In the past, college education was seldom a part of the groomer's background, but we are now seeing many more groomers with advanced educations. Most groomers previously came from home grooming backgrounds and were self taught, but now most young groomers have grooming school or apprentice shop experience.

We can liken our industry to the past history of many of industry's corporate giants. Many men who currently enjoy the seat of chairman of the board started with the company as a stockboy. However, future giants of industry will need to have undergraduate, masters, and advanced degrees on their resumes.

---

* In the interest of clarity, when referring to the professional groomer I have used the feminine pronoun. This is *not* to imply that all professional groomers are female.

Professional grooming has come of age. Schools, conventions, seminars, and workshops are stressing professionalism. The general public is being educated by magazine, television, and newspaper articles on what to expect from the professionals who care for their pets. People are being encouraged to inspect kennels and grooming shops and to question their veterinarian in order to enter into a better health care relationship for their pet.

Which Route To Take?

Before you decide what route to follow in acquiring the necessary knowledge and skill to enter the field, you should do some research. If you are thinking of going to a specific school, spend some time and money to investigate the facility. Training is costly and your research will help prevent the mistake of choosing a poor school. Take the time to travel to the facility. Go to the person in charge and ask to see classes in session. Watch the work being done by the students. Are they *cautioned to be gentle* to the dogs, or are they allowed to pull and tug at mats without any consideration for the animal? Are advanced students producing quality work?

Is the facility clean and well cared for, or are cages rusty, the bathing area moldy and unkempt? Is the enclosure around the bathing area well maintained, or is it cracked and conducive to bacterial growth? Schools should be maintained with the best possible equipment. Try to determine if the major objective is *quality education* or if it is teaching the largest number of students for the greatest possible revenue.

Accreditation of grooming schools is awarded by the National Association of Trade and Technical Schools (NATTS) for those schools that maintain high technical standards for education and function under ethical business standards. Check for NATTS accreditation of any school you may consider.

Another area of concern is whether the instructors have adequate credentials. It is *not* sufficient for the school to allow a talented, new student graduate to assume the role of teacher, unless there has been sufficient background training to ensure the understanding of the role being assumed. If you see students teaching one another instead of working under constant supervision, there may be a problem.

All teachers in the field *must* have a reasonable knowledge of the correct visualization of the breed standards. If they do not, there is no way they can

properly convey what the finished product should resemble in order to portray the correct breed profile.

Examine the credentials of the teachers, whether in a school or apprentice situation. How did they enter the field? Do they have breeder/exhibitor experience? Have they worked as a veterinary assistant? Have they groomed at seminars where their work could be evaluated by other professional groomers?

Many teachers are experts in the correct techniques of scissoring. The problem may be the difficulty of translating that technique into words. Unless a skilled *groomer* is also a skilled *teacher*, the student will not be able to "see" with his mind's eye the lines and proportions the teacher is trying to convey. A teacher can instruct in proper starting and stopping points, but it will have to be *your* mind, *your* eye and *your* hands that translate instruction into a properly finished dog. If the teacher cannot instruct verbally, but must always "show" with a "hands-on" demonstration, the groomer will have difficulty understanding why a particular line must be done a certain way.

Some teachers are not psychologically suited to the art of teaching. Also, the teacher/student ratio has a great deal to do with the student's ability to grasp the knowledge. A teacher may have less tolerance if the class is too large, and might not be able to give individual help and explanation time for problem areas.

Good schools are aware of changes in grooming styles or breed profiles that may require new directions in grooming expertise. Good school directors and teachers attend any large grooming convention or seminar in their area, and encourage their students to do the same. Furthermore, a reputable school emphasizes proper handling to prevent injury or unnecessary trauma to a pet. Training should include such things as how to handle older or infirm pets, or those who may have bone or tissue problems. Abusive handling of a pet should never be tolerated in a learning situation. If a student shows any inclination toward abuse, or a great deal of impatience with the actual grooming procedure, he or she ought to be advised to find some other occupation.

The curriculum should also include the basics of good business practices. The time and effort spent in such areas as bookkeeping and accounting, can spell the difference between success or failure for someone who plans to manage or own a shop.

No matter how fine a school may be, there is one area that cannot be covered. Day to day problems of scheduling and unexpected interruptions, can throw the best laid plans into chaos. I feel that every groomer entering the field should spend a minimum of one year in an apprentice situation. The everyday time spent working with a good team is invaluable, and the importance of groomer cooperation with difficult dogs cannot be over-emphasized.

Good groomers never cease to learn! Every time the groomer attends a seminar, lecture, or convention, there will be new methods of product usage, and new tools that make the job easier. Visiting the dog shows keeps the groomer abreast of current ''styles'' that might show slight deviations from former breed profiles. Veterinarians bring information to seminars and conventions on ways in which the groomer can recognize the problems that make grooming difficult.

THE GROOMER LIBRARY

Groomers of the past had only a small amount of printed material from which to build their grooming skills. In more recent years, grooming information and publications designed for our industry have increased to the point where there is no excuse for the groomer to be uninformed. Monthly periodicals cover every aspect of the pet-related industry.

Every groomer's library should contain *The Complete Dog Book*, which is the official publication of The American Kennel Club. It presents a picture visualization of all breeds recognized by the AKC, with the complete breed Standards for each breed. You may question the wisdom of purchasing this book by saying, ''I am only interested in pet grooming, not grooming for show dogs.'' However, the true professional is aware of the need to know the CORRECT profile for each purebred dog that is serviced, and then, knowledge of blade and scissor usage helps the groomer achieve that look.

One or two good all breed grooming books should be in every groomer's library. Every seminar and convention that I have attended has had at least one distributor present with a fairly complete selection of grooming books.

We must also have some basic knowledge of dog behavior to help us cope with problem dogs we may have to service. A number of authors have written excellent studies of behavior problems. (See Reference section for specific suggestions.) Most

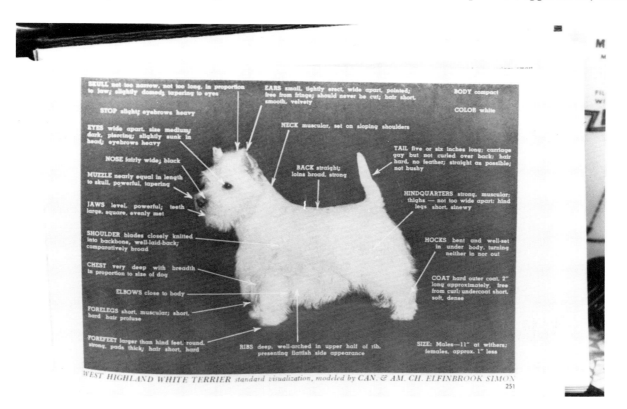

Figure 2. The groomer's library should include books which give the visualizations of the various breeds to help the groomer learn the correct breed profile.

of the current pet-related magazines contain advertising from various publishing houses. Groomers can find numerous interesting and informative books to help in the grooming profession.

PROFESSIONAL IMAGE

In your mind's eye, think of someone you admire. What is it about that person that really appeals to you: personality, dress, speech, mannerisms? If you are adequately prepared for work, you generally appear at ease and professional. Tension is quickly projected to dogs *and* people, and is sometimes the result of improper preparation and knowledge for the task at hand.

The first impression your customer will have of your shop and your general ability will be *your* appearance. If you wear a fresh, clean smock or a smart looking uniform as you step out to greet the customer, you will create an impression of professionalism. I would never allow a beauty operator with a slovenly appearance to do my hair, nor would I leave my dog to be groomed by someone with an untidy appearance.

A groomer should always dress to portray the image of a professional in the community. One of the most disgusting things to see is a groomer dressed in dirty jeans, with a nondescript t-shirt, and bare feet. I have witnessed this in past years at several shops and even in the grooming contest ring. Fortunately, at least in the contest aspect, things have improved greatly. Most contestants are now wearing nicely tailored slacks and a pretty smock or tailored grooming jacket. They have also learned to wear comfortable shoes. I have often wondered what would happen to bare toes if a groomer were to drop a pair of scissors, point end down!

Smocks and slacks or uniforms are appropriate for women; while male groomers may choose lab coats or jackets. If you color coordinate your grooming outfits to the decor of your shop the whole atmosphere takes on a professional air. When shopping for grooming clothes, check the local uniform shop. Try to find hard-finish fabrics that will shed, not attract, hair. Most double knits collect hair. Once the dog hair penetrates the fabric, it is impossible to remove. Some groomers have gone into the business of making shop aprons and smocks of hard-finish fabric to sell at conventions and seminars around the country. Another tip: set aside special undergarments to use just for grooming because you will find the dog hair gets into the darndest places!

Figure 3. First impressions can literally make or break a business. With this in mind, pay special attention to creating a welcome, pleasing, professional environment for your customer to enter. Think of it as a kind of insurance that doesn't require monthly premiums but *does* require planning and upkeep. (Photo-McKinney)

UNDERSTANDING ONE ANOTHER

Criticism and bickering have long been a problem in this industry. For too long groomers have been suspicious of one another. The general attitude has been, "I will keep my grooming secrets to myself." Openness and sharing of our abilities can only help all of us. We have all started somewhere, and thanks to the ability of someone else, either as a teacher or a resource center, have arrived at the status now enjoyed.

RECORD KEEPING

An important aspect for any business is close attention to proper record keeping. An accountant will take care of the monthly statements, but the professional groomer is the one who *must* keep detailed records of every pet that is serviced, and all retail sales.

There are now special documentation cards available to the industry that provide special areas for the medical data needed for each pet. There is also space for the client's signature, giving permission for the shop to use the services of a veterinarian, should the need ever arise. On the reverse side of the card are spaces for time documentation of each function performed. Use of a professional document inspires confidence from your client that you are truly interested in the best possible care of their pet.

Some type of duplicate receipt should be used. If there is a discrepancy in your cash drawer at the end of the day, it helps to have documentation of every grooming and retail sale for that day. In states requiring sales tax on all retail sales and on services rendered, you must keep proof-of-purchase receipts and documentation of services.

THE HOME GROOMER

Many groomers have thought of grooming only as a way to supplement other income. With very little preparation, they have set up an area in the basement, kitchen, garage, or patio. It seemed enough to set up a homemade table, hang up some tools, buy a cage or two, read a "how to" grooming book, and begin to advertise in the area. Many old timers in the business admit to such early beginnings. Most groomers who have been in the business for years are self taught. They acquired their expertise from trial and error, a book, or perhaps from caring for their own dogs. I have even spoken to some former beauticians who are now grooming dogs instead of people, and having much more fun.

My own beginnings in the industry were much the same. In 1963 we purchased a Poodle for a son who was allergic to all other breeds. As the puppy matured, our son decided it would be nice to try obedience training, but insisted his dog had to be "pretty" whenever she went to class. Lots of baths, (she was white), with face, feet and tail trimmed each time, became routine. I soon learned to scissor body, legs, tail, and topknot, too.

Eventually our daughter wanted her own Poodle, and soon we were traveling almost every weekend to various show sites to earn obedience "legs." While the children were busy in the ring, I would wander into the professional handler areas and watch with utter fascination, the dexterity and ease with which the handlers would prepare the Poodles for the show ring.

After a couple of years of traveling with the children, I began my search for MY conformation quality puppy. I found a lovely, sable brown Toy Poodle and began to practice the difficult techniques of show grooming. The years of observation, questioning and study paid off, she went on to become Champion Ch. Suchan's Cinnamon Candy. Her triumphs included many Best Of Breed and Group wins, and she became a top producer as well.

By this time I was grooming full-time and had opened a shop. Veterinarians in the area were sending me many customers who had had difficulty

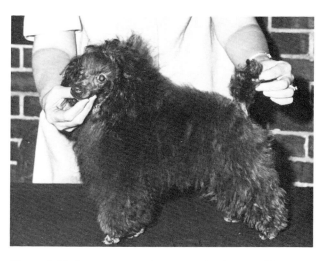

Figure 4. My first attempt at show grooming in 1967. Notice the ragged, uneven scissoring showing my inexperience as a beginner in the show ring. (Photo - Ritter)

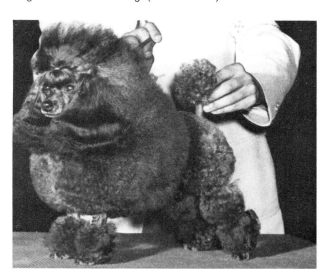

Figure 5. By the early 1970s, show grooming had begun to lose the bulky look with better proportions for the various parts of the trim. Time and experience had helped me in preparing our dogs for the ring. This photo shows a definite improvement in scissoring technique over that shown in Figure 4. (Photo - Lloyd W. Olson)

with previous groomers. Finally, my family rebelled at eating food generously sprinkled with dog hair seasoning. They gave me an edict: either quit grooming at home or open a shop! So my "midlife crisis" course was set.

At this time, I realized that my experience only with the Poodle breed left me woefully inadequate to groom the Terrier group correctly. I was fortunate in having a friend who contacted Bob Baker, (now deceased) at Leash and Collar Kennels in Deerfield, Illinois. Arrangements were made for me to apprentice with him one day a week for an entire year. I learned to admire his desire to produce *only* quality work, and to strive for the same quality in my work.

I have shared this experience to demonstrate how education is acquired by working with and observing many different experts in the profession. Many other home groomers have had the same growth of business as I had, and have had to face the decision of whether or not to open a shop. Some have been satisfied to stay small and limit the types of pets they service. Others found that a shop situation was a satisfying career choice.

Home Grooming Considerations

There are some definite pluses for the home groomer. First, if you are in a rural district zoned for farming, you should have no trouble setting up business in an area of your home or in another building on the premises. The farm dogs which you will service require expertise in stripping coat, since many of these animals may come in only once a year for their annual ''spring do.'' Most of these may be mixed breeds that will need their own unique design. The more you know about the correct profiles of purebred dogs, the better you will be able to design the nicest finish for a mixed breed. Second, the home groomer does not need transportation to work. Another factor affecting the female groomer may be small children whose care would require full-time help if she worked in a shop situation. Meals can be prepared between appointments or while waiting for a customer to pick up a dog.

It is less traumatic for certain dogs to be groomed in a home, especially dogs not conditioned to noise or commotion. Some dogs that are particularly pampered may be a nervous wreck if they have to spend extended time in a busy shop.

I have visited and photographed many fine home grooming facilities. The groomers have been well trained (training should be just as extensive as that of any shop groomer), and have a satisfied customer clientele. They also have a professional image, welcoming their customers in a pretty smock or tailored jacket.

The home groomer may have to contend with some problems that a shop groomer does not encounter. Customers who come to your home may expect extra privileges, such as bringing the dog very early in the morning or picking it up well after the supper hour. They may also bother you with calls for appointments at all hours. As mentioned earlier, the home groomer may have difficulty obtaining business insurance, with adequate liabil-

Figure 6. This fine example of a home grooming shop is part of Donna Foor's residence in Cary, Illinois. The area is well organized with cabinets and drawers for equipment, a hydraulic table, and a shop vac in the corner. (Photo - Val Penstone)

ity coverage for dogs serviced and for clients on your premises. Your home-owners policy will not cover a business set up. If you were sued for malpractice for any injury or death of a client's dog at your facility, you might find yourself in a very difficult position. Most of these claims are settled in favor of the plaintiff.

You may also run into difficulty with disgruntled neighbors, or another groomer may complain to local authorities of illegal operation of a business from your home. You need to be particularly careful not to disturb the neighbors. Noise, smelly messes or an undue amount of traffic, may cause neighbors to protest your business.

THE GROOMING SHOP

Let's look at the pluses for the groomer who owns a shop. Assuming that there is sufficient financial backing, the first plus is the pleasure of owning one's own small business. There is a certain amount of respect that goes with owning a shop in a business community. You will have greater visibility and will be able to take a more active part in community affairs. A well-planned shop will have room for expansion as the business grows, affording jobs for others in addition to yourself. You may want to branch out into the retail merchandising field to realize a greater profit margin on your investment. The one big plus for the shop owner is the saleability of the business. A home groomer might be able to sell the client listing to another groomer, but that would be a minor sale compared to that of an entire business.

A well-run grooming shop is a fine asset, particularly if there is a retail merchandising effort as well. If proper records have been kept and monthly profit and loss statements indicate that the business is growing and doing well, the groomer should be able to sell the business, if necessary, for a sum equal to or one-and-one-half times the yearly gross.

A seemingly minor consideration is the fact that you can go home from the place of business at the end of the day knowing you won't have to take any further calls. Cleaning up will not be as great a problem because your facilities will be designed for easy clean-up.

COOPERATION OF HOME AND SHOP GROOMERS

Shop groomers and home groomers can coexist if the home groomer is aware of one problem, PRICING! When the home groomer's services are priced far below the average prices of the local shops, there will be trouble between the two factions. If the low priced home groomer later decides to open a shop, the new pricing schedule will have to be considerably higher, and the customers who have been coming to the home will complain like crazy, and go elsewhere! Shops realize they cannot compete with the home groomer in the area of pricing because of the higher cost of overhead. But, if there is a shop groomer and a home groomer with the same abilities, pricing should not be that far apart, so that interaction and mutual learning benefits are possible.

In the long run, the grooming shop owner has a greater profit because of the ability to schedule more dogs and the possible sale of retail merchandise.

The well-skilled home groomer can be a help to the shop professional. There are a number of good home groomers in the area around my former shop. There were times when we had dogs that we felt would do much better in a home groomer environment, and because of close equality in pricing, we felt we could recommend certain home groomers to customers who preferred extra preferential treatment. We found that we did not lose any clientele because of this policy, but rather these customers compensated us for our recommendation by purchasing more of our retail items and recommending our shop to their friends. Recommending

a home groomer worked well for some older dogs that had to be done on a "straight through" basis, which might not always be possible in a shop situation. This built up a trust relationship with our clients that we would always do what was best for their pet. As a consequence, they would send other clients to our shop for "individualized" attention.

The professionals in our field are well aware that there are problems as well as benefits associated with some home groomers. The in-home grooming facilities may be far from ideal. Basements are not always kept clean and may harbor mold, mildew and other bacterial problems. These could cause allergic reactions in dogs or cats sensitive to pollen or mold spores. Bacteria are easily transmitted in unclean areas, in either the shop or the home. In traveling around the country and stopping to check on local shops, I have found some *filthy* grooming areas in shops as well! We ALL need to clean up our act. Hopefully, the time will come when legislation will require the inspection of ALL grooming facilities. Careless groomers who do not care about unclean equipment, or have bad habits that may cause disease or injury to a pet, must be eliminated from the profession.

MOBILE GROOMERS

In recent years, mobile grooming vans have made their appearance in large metropolitan and suburban areas. Some are an extension service offered by a large, busy shop. Others are operated by independent individuals who own their own van and service a wide area.

The grooming vans are purchased stripped down from the dealer and then outfitted by either the purchaser or someone who specializes in this type of installation.

Water for bathing the pet in the mobile setup is handled in one of two ways. One method is to use the water available from the pet owner's home, then completing the drying and finishing in the van. More preferably, the mobile van is completely self-sufficient with its own water supply, bathing tub, grooming table, dryers, and cages. The more completely outfitted the van is, the higher the purchase cost and cost of operation.

Mobile groomers do quite well in areas populated by retired pet owners who may not wish to drive to a shop. Another lucrative market is the affluent pet owner too busy to take the pet to the shop.

There are some excellent mobile grooming services around the country, but just as you find in the stationary shop, there are some that are pretty bad. The complaint most frequently heard from those who use a mobile grooming service is that the pet's coat is not properly dematted and bathed. Still, the mobile groomer has found a distinct place in our profession, offering a service for those who cannot or will not take their dog or cat to a local shop.

CERTIFICATION

Certification of groomer abilities, discussed later in the book, is awakening a new pride. At some time in the future, legislation may require groomers to prove their abilities in much the same way as barbers and beauticians. Perhaps a "grandfather's clause" will help those groomers who already have certificates attesting to their ability.

Figure 7. The shop owner or manager would be wise to remember senior citizens when looking to expand their staff. They often enjoy working with animals and welcome part-time employment for such jobs as brushing, bathing, and fluff-drying. (Photo - courtesy *Hinsdale Doings* newspaper)

3
Purchasing Equipment

The most important expenditure you have in setting up your shop is the purchase of proper equipment. Some groomers make the mistake of believing a salesman who touts some ''fantastic bargain,'' and purchase equipment that quickly breaks down, or for some other reason proves to be a bad deal. Take the time to research what equipment you need and then make the best choice for each item.

Assuming a shop has two working groomers, a skilled finishing groomer (usually the shop owner), and an assistant who would bathe, dry, and perhaps accept and discharge dogs, the following equipment will be essential to the operation.

Grooming Tables

There is a choice of styles and sizes to suit each groomer's fancy. Hydraulic tables on tip-proof pedestals are now made with rectangular, oval or round tops. When examining a table, lean on it to check for stability. Some of the tables do not stand securely if a large dog moves around.

Some hydraulic tables are electrically operated, while others are raised and lowered using a foot pedal. These revolve 360 degrees and can be adjusted for height in small increments to suit the comfort of the groomer. Most groomers find that a hydraulic table greatly reduces fatigue. A hydraulic table makes it easier to sit while performing certain functions in the grooming process. When the groomer uses a table that can be turned for easy access to the dog and can be raised or lowered by the touch of a toe, there is greater con-

trol. After years of standing and bending at a stationary table, a groomer often experiences spinal problems from the stress placed on the neck, shoulder, and lower back. Prices for hydraulic tables vary greatly from one manufacturer to the next depending on extra features offered. One new table has a surface lighted from beneath, thereby eliminating shadows under the dog. The lowest priced tables are around $450 and others sell for as high as $1,000 or more.

Stationary tables are available with adjustable legs, and this is a feature that should not be overlooked. If you have many different groomers working for you, tables with adjustable legs would be a good choice. If one groomer functions only as a

Figure 1. Each grooming station should be set up with the comfort of the groomer in mind. A stool with good back support, and hydraulic table will prevent unnecessary fatigue. Note groomer's uniform of hard finish fabric.

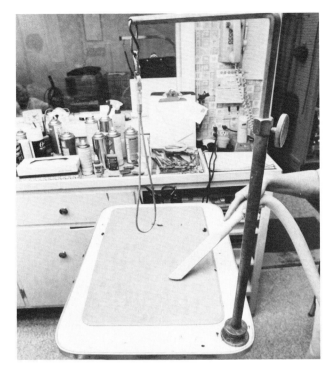

Figure 2. At this grooming station the telephone is within easy reach, appointment book directly below. Note a bin with raised edges to keep scissors and clipper blades or other tools from falling off the counter, hooks along edge of cabinet for clippers, shelves for reference material, a shop vac for quick hair clean up, and a removeable mat on formica top grooming table.

bather-dryer, a non-adjustable, stationary table should be satisfactory.

Grooming Post

A dog can be restrained on the grooming table in various ways. Some groomers use a restraint fastened to the ceiling to allow the dog more freedom on the table and to avoid the inconvenience of a stationary post. The most common method of control is a grooming post and noose, permanently fastened to the grooming table. There are also movable posts that can be clamped in any position on the table. Both types of posts are adjustable for height. It is advisable to get a sturdy post that will not bend or break when used with a large, strong dog.

Stools

Each groomer should be provided with a stool, preferably with a back rest. These are bar-stool height and are somewhat adjustable.

Dryers

Standing dryers are needed for finish drying, or for fluff drying certain breeds. The optional use

of cage dryers will depend upon what breeds you decide to groom at your shop. Certain short-haired breeds can be dried satisfactorily in a cage provided the cage dryer has a thermostat setting for very low heat. This type of dryer should never be used on dogs with heart, lung or other functional disorders. Also, cage dryers should only be used on cages that are open to sufficient air circulation, so there is less problem created by heat build-up. The Rapid-Electric Company[1] and others manufacture a multi-

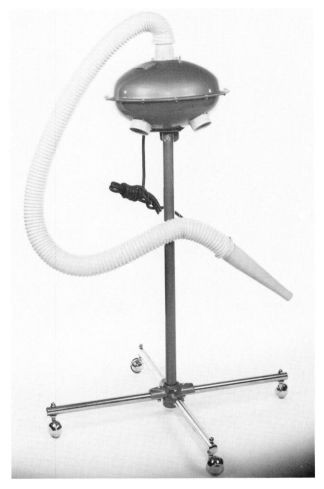

Figure 3. The high velocity *Speedy Drying Saucer*® manufactured by Rapid Electric Co. This dryer works well for removing excess water from the heavier-coated dogs, particularly large breeds. Water can be blown out of the coat while the dog is still in the tub, thus hastening drying time. (Photo - Rapid Electric)

_____

[1]The specific products mentioned in this chapter are those I have tested, found effective, and used at my former shop and in the care of my own dogs. Such a large selection of fine products is available that it would be impossible to cover them all.

dry cage unit with temperature and air flow controls. Rapid Electric also manufactures a free floating dryer that can be wall mounted.

If you cannot afford both cage and standing dryers when you first begin business, Oster's Professional Products Division has a dryer designed to function in both capacities. It is versatile as a cage dryer by the design of its attaching hooks and can direct warm air either at the top or the bottom of the cage. It can also be used on its stand for table drying.

A standing dryer should have a long arm with an adjustable nozzle that can be rotated 360 degrees, can direct air flow in any direction needed, and is adjustable for height. Floor dryers should have adjustable stands with sturdy, well-balanced legs on casters that roll freely and are designed so that hair cannot easily jamb the casters. When you are busily fluff-drying a dog, it is frustrating if you are unable to move the dryer because the casters won't turn.

If you dry dogs with extremely heavy coats you may want to invest in a high velocity dryer that has a stronger air flow. In that case, you also need a gentler dryer that won't blow a small dog off the table or frighten it with excessive noise. Some small breeds are easily spooked by a heavy air flow. If you can only afford one type of standing dryer, purchase one with an average flow of air.

High velocity dryers such as *Rapid Electric Speedy Drying Saucer, Rea/Edemco Force*, and others function well to blow excess water from the dog's coat. As air flow is directed into the coat, the water beads are blown off the hair shaft to dry the coat without brushing, provided the coat was de-matted before bathing. On a large, heavy-coated dog, partial drying can also be done by using a high velocity dryer while the dog is still in the tub. This will remove most of the water from the coat by blowing it off into the tub, making complete drying much easier. However, high velocity dryers do have certain drawbacks. Most of these dryers are extremely noisy. This could cause a noise tolerance problem for both dogs and people. If you are exposed to a great deal of noise from high-velocity

Figure 4. Various grooming instruments are displayed on this grooming table. In the background, an Oster standing dryer with variable heat settings. Dryer nozzle is adjustable 360 degrees. Dryer arm is variable for height and swings in any direction. Standing dryer should have easy-roll casters for mobility. Force of air flow should be sufficient to penetrate and move the hair for easy fluff drying. Dryer should not be too noisy if used frequently for drying small, shy dogs.

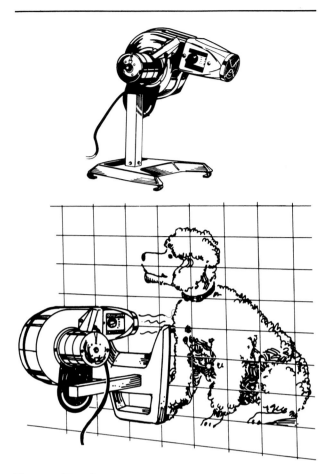

Figure 5. (Top) Stand dryer (Bottom) Cage dryer.

dryers, consider using ear plugs. Most of them are expensive, and you should check for UL approval.

Air flow and heat adjustments vary with each type and brand of dryer. Some have only low, medium, and high choices of heat selection, while others have heat ranges with many increments allowing the groomer to choose any desired heat between cool and hot. Some have thermostats that control overheating and automatically shut down the dryer if the motor becomes too hot. This can happen if the screen at the air intake becomes clogged with hair.

Companies that have been in the business of manufacturing dryers for a long time include such names as *General Cage, Groom-Rite, Oster, Rapid Electric, Rea/Edemco,* and *Safari.*

Bathing Tubs

The most popular tubs are stainless steel, institutional type tubs, and the porcelain, cottage-size bathtubs. Both types should be installed in a frame raising the level of the tub to waist height so unnecessary bending is eliminated. They should be installed in an area free of clutter, so portable steps may be used for large, difficult to lift breeds. The space underneath the tub should be open or have access doors so plumbing can be easily reached to clean out traps. This area can serve as storage for disinfectants and cleaning supplies. The bottom of either type of tub should be provided with a non-slip bath mat. Some type of restraint should be built into the wall behind the tub to prevent the dog from escaping or from injuring itself should it attempt to jump from the tub.

Plumbing for the tub should include one of a variety of hose and nozzle sprays for wetting and rinsing the dog. Some types allow you to adjust both water temperature and force of water on a single control knob. This feature is helpful when working on nervous dogs. Consult your plumbing supply house for ideas.

If three sides of the tub are enclosed, it is easier to control the dog and also prevents water from splashing all over if a large dog decides to shake while being bathed. Some groomers have been able to utilize the new all-in-one tub units made of fiberglass. The tub and surrounding walls are bonded into one smooth unit, making them easier to clean.

Figure 6. A cottage size porcelain tub raised waist high, with storage beneath. Perforations in doors allow air to circulate thus preventing mildew and odor.

In any case, it is important to enclose the tub with a surface that is easy to disinfect and that does not easily mildew. Ceramic tiling makes a professional finish. Use a white or off-white that will not change color. Some colors are sensitive to spotting from bleach or other products.

Cages

The number of cages needed is proportionate to the number of groomers working in the shop. Usually, six cages per groomer are sufficient. There should be enough cages to allow most dogs to be brought in during the first hour the shop is open. A better traffic pattern is established when you don't have customers returning throughout the day to pick up their dogs to free up cages for other clients.

The prices of cages vary greatly and you have to determine what you can afford. Stackable wire cages are the least expensive. A piece of washable enameled plywood can be placed between the rows of cages to prevent male dogs from spraying into the surrounding areas. Cage sizes should be divided between toy sizes; those for medium-sized dogs such as Cockers and Mini Poodles; and a few large crates for Standard Poodles, Collies, Shepherds, and such. With business growth and increased cash flow, you can purchase stainless steel or fiberglass units of four, six or eight cages. These are easy to clean and disinfect, an important consideration when virus epidemics make the life of the groomer one constant round of cleaning and sterilizing.

Clippers

Based solely on personal preference and experience, I recommend the purchase of at least two *Oster A5* clippers for each groomer. You may want to experiment with other brands, but because the *Oster A5* offers the largest assortment of blade choices, you will find it an indispensable tool. The *Wahl* and *Andis* Companies also make professional animal clippers of various types.

A new high-speed clipper has the motor separated from the clipper itself. The blades are driven at very high speed and have a tendency to heat up rapidly. Another innovative new tool is a vacuum attached to the clipper itself that sucks up and disposes of clipped hair as it is being removed.

Blades - Based on the use of the *Oster A5* clipper, each groomer should have *two* complete sets of the following blades: the Oster #4, 4F, 5, 5F, 7, 7F, 8½, 9, 10, 15, and 30.

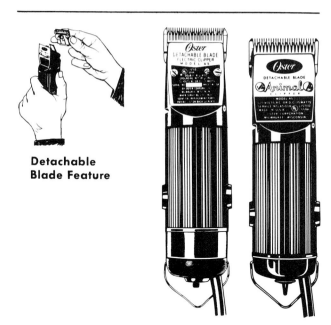

Detachable Blade Feature

Figure 7. These Oster A5® clippers feature detachable blades. Both are UL approved and the model on the left is also OSHA approved.

It is wise to purchase extra blades of the following: #4 to use for finishing, #7 and 7F for stripping and multi-purpose uses, #9 and 10 for general use such as underbelly cleaning and face and tail work on Poodles.

In addition, you will want some toe blades and pattern blades such as sizes $5/8''$, $7/8''$, and $8/8''$. These are narrower blades, easy to use for trimming feet and pattern work. They remove hair to the same depth as a #15 blade. Complete blade usage is explained in depth in chapters pertaining to grooming.

Figure 8. The narrow 5/8″ Oster snap-on blade makes it easier to remove hair around the toes and between the pads of a Toy Poodle foot. It is also used for pattern work on a small dog.

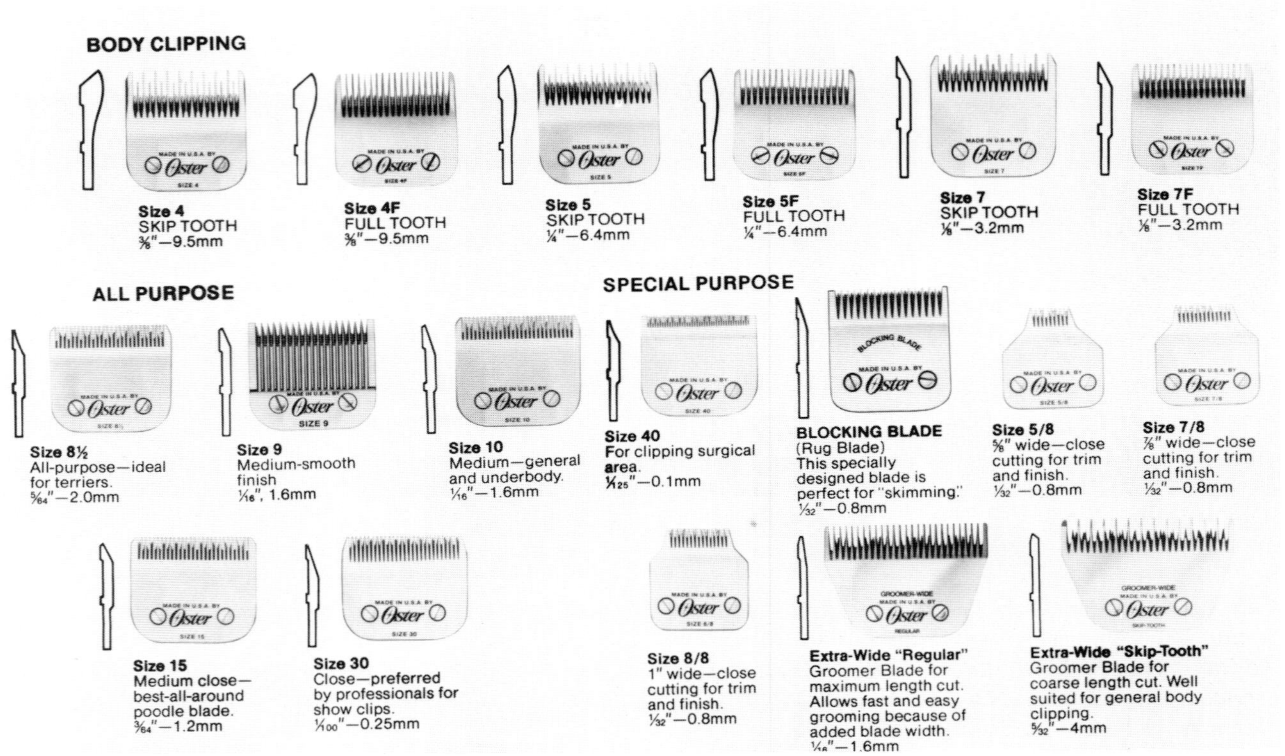
BODY CLIPPING
Size 4
SKIP TOOTH
⅜"—9.5mm
Size 4F
FULL TOOTH
⅜"—9.5mm
Size 5
SKIP TOOTH
¼"—6.4mm
Size 5F
FULL TOOTH
¼"—6.4mm
Size 7
SKIP TOOTH
⅛"—3.2mm
Size 7F
FULL TOOTH
⅛"—3.2mm
ALL PURPOSE
Size 8½
All-purpose—ideal for terriers.
5/64"—2.0mm
Size 9
Medium-smooth finish
1/16", 1.6mm
Size 10
Medium—general and underbody.
1/16"—1.6mm
SPECIAL PURPOSE
Size 40
For clipping surgical area.
1/25"—0.1mm
BLOCKING BLADE
(Rug Blade)
This specially designed blade is perfect for "skimming."
1/32"—0.8mm
Size 5/8
⅝" wide—close cutting for trim and finish.
1/32"—0.8mm
Size 7/8
⅞" wide—close cutting for trim and finish.
1/32"—0.8mm
Size 15
Medium close—best-all-around poodle blade.
3/64"—1.2mm
Size 30
Close—preferred by professionals for show clips.
1/100"—0.25mm
Size 8/8
1" wide—close cutting for trim and finish.
1/32"—0.8mm
Extra-Wide "Regular"
Groomer Blade for maximum length cut. Allows fast and easy grooming because of added blade width.
1/16"—1.6mm
Extra-Wide "Skip-Tooth"
Groomer Blade for coarse length cut. Well suited for general body clipping.
5/32"—4mm

Figure 9. Oster® professional blade sets for use with A2 and A5 clippers.

Clipper Supplies

Oster Blade Wash®, is a solution used in the care and maintenance of *Oster* blades. When new *Oster* blades are purchased, they must be immersed and run for approximately one minute in this solution to remove the preservative coating on the new blades. All *Oster* blades used in the shop should be run in this solution approximately once a week—more often if needed—for thorough cleansing and removal of hair or other debris. The blade is then wiped dry on a soft cloth or paper towel, re-oiled and sprayed with *Kool Lube®* lubricant for continued use.

Oster Kool-Lube® lubricant and other coolants are used to control heat build-up when a blade is run for a long time. They also help flush out hair or dirt, and keep the cutting surfaces clean. Lubricants can be sprayed on scissor blades and then wiped off to help prevent rusting and to keep the cutting edges clean.

Scissors

There are so many scissors available on the market today that it would take a separate chapter just to describe them all. Begin your collection of scissors with a blunt tip, short pair for working around the face and anal area and a short pair of sharp tipped scissors for fine work around toenails and for finishing small areas. You need at least two pairs of longer, well balanced finishing scissors. These could be either carbon steel, which hold a very sharp edge but are inclined to rust if not cared for properly, or a pair of stainless steel, ice-tempered shears with a serrated edge.

Many professional groomers are now using curved shears of various lengths for all contouring. You may have originally learned with straight shears, but with practice you will find curved scissors easy to use. When finishing large dogs, you

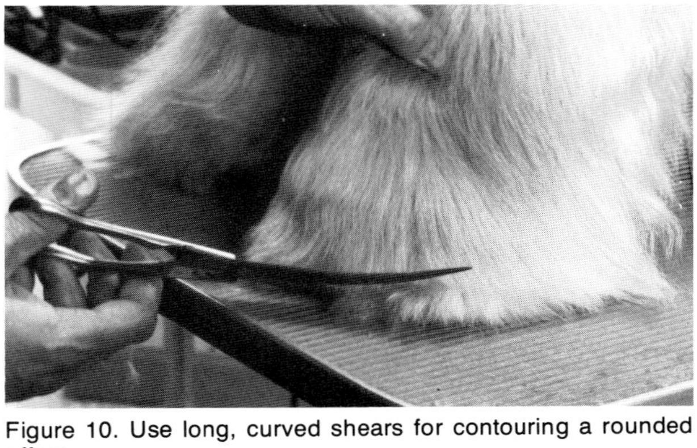

Figure 10. Use long, curved shears for contouring a rounded effect.

Figure 11. (Left to Right) Ten-inch shears speed the job of scissoring long, straight lines.　A short, blunt-tip scissor is used under eyes and around the anus...be sure to disinfect scissors after such useage.　Lightweight, well-balanced, stainless ice-tempered shears with serrated blades such as the Oster #928-36, has been the mainstay of my scissor collection.　Thinning shears blend and smooth.

will find the longer 10″ curved or straight shears save time. Scissors come with thin shanks or with heavier shanks for people with strong hands. A fine scissor that I have used for many years is the *Oster Model #928-36*. It is well balanced, stainless steel, ice-tempered, lightweight, and the blades have a serrated edge. For a groomer with problem hands, this is a wise choice. Two pairs of good thinning shears with different tooth configurations would round out your scissor collection.

Restraints

A haunch holder designed to restrain the dog on the table may be helpful to support dogs that have an inclination to be a "setter." The holder can be moved to any part of the grooming table, supporting the dog from underneath. A restraining strap keeps frisky dogs from stepping over the bar. Placing a towel over the bar provides additional padding for older dogs or those with abdominal tumors.

Muzzles should only be used as a last resort on dogs that are a problem. They are used more often by a groomer working alone who needs to shorten nails or de-mat a feisty dog. Muzzles come in a variety of sizes and are made of wire or leather. Some newer models feature adjustable velcro straps. Softer muzzles can be made using old nylon stockings or strips of material cut on the bias about 1½″ wide.

Figure 12. The Haunch Holder positioned at the tuck-up prevents the animal from sitting.

Figure 13. A mild restraining muzzle can be made of soft material. Place a strip of cloth across the bridge of the nose, pass the two ends under the chin and make the first tie. Next, bring the two ends around to the back of the neck, tying the ends securely. This will be effective for most small dogs but will not hold a large breed.

Mat Combs

There are many instruments designed for the de-matting process. In the past we used single edge, de-matting knives for opening stubborn mats. However, they were sometimes difficult to control, especially if the dog was inclined to be jumpy on the table. There are now many multi-blade de-matters that do not create a problem. They are constructed with a thumb rest for good control. They can be resharpened by removing the thumb screw and sharpening the individual blades. They are also useful tools for thinning coats. They can be adjusted for either left- or right-handed groomers. One of the newer combs on the market has a de-matting tooth at one end of the comb.

Figure 14. (Top) Using the Oster mat comb makes short work of mats. (Bottom) For best results with the *Speedcomb*™, insert the instrument diagonally at the base of the matted area. Keep the blade almost flat against the animal's body. Always direct sharp instruments away from the body to avoid raking the skin with the teeth. Comb out the coat with a series of rapid, downward movements. If the comb slips around in your hand, you are being too forceful. Work on slightly smaller areas using a short picking stroke. Always brace the loose skin with your free hand to minimize pet discomfort. (Bottom photo - Bill Lewis)

The *Speedcomb* is a special tool with teeth designed to work through a matted coat with much less effort than a regular wide-tooth comb. It does not remove excess hair when used properly.

It is recommended that a tangle removing liquid be used in conjunction with any de-matting tool. It cuts the mat removal time and makes the entire operation more comfortable for the animal.

Nail Trimmers

The manual guillotine-type nail trimmer is probably the best known type of nail groomer, and is widely used by professional groomers. There are many different brands on the market, so try various nail trimmers to find one you prefer.

Figure 15. The *Resco Nail Trimmer*® works on the guillotine principle. The hook at the end of the nail, up to the quick, protrudes through the slot at the end of the trimmer. Cut the nail on a slight angle toward the top of the foot.

Nail scissors are made in various sizes for dogs and cats. They work on the same principle as regular scissors.

Electric nail groomers require training for both dog and groomer to become accustomed to their proper use, but they do a beautiful job of smoothly sanding the nails.

Figure 16. The Miller-Forge® plier nail trimmer. Nail clippers must be operated with a quick closure action to make a clean cut. *Do not* squeeze gently and slowly as this causes pain.

Figure 17. The *Oster Nail Groomer®* has a motorized grinding wheel.

Nail File

A dog nail file is useful to shorten nails that only need to be taken back a little. Use them as a matter of course on nails that are split, or on nails of small dogs that are inclined to jump on their masters, where the rough nails may tear stockings or other materials.

Combs

Two types of combs are particularly useful: a stainless steel comb with both fine and medium spacing of the teeth, and the *Resco* comb with wider spacing and teeth of longer length. These combs will go through the coat easily. The longer teeth and wider spacing of the *Resco* comb make it a fine tool to use for lifting coat when doing finishing, and also for deep penetration of thick coats.

Figure 18. A deep tooth Resco comb is used on the furnishings of a Miniature Schnauzer.

Brushes

The groomer needs several types of brushes. The slicker brush is used for most general brush-out work. We found two types to be most effective, with the least danger of abrasion to the dog's skin. The *Lambert Kay Ever-Gentle®* brush does a fine

job for fluff-drying dogs with sensitive skins. A similar item is the *Warner's Dog Grooming Brush®*. Both are made with fine bent wire pins set in soft rubber padding for flexibility. Both of these brushes are gentle enough for careful use on properly textured show coats.

The *Universal* curved slicker brush comes in two sizes and does an excellent job of removing dead coat when "spring clean-up" time comes around. They work most effectively on the coats of Shelties, Collies, Cockers and breeds with dense double coats.

English pin brushes and natural bristle brushes have been the mainstay of show grooming. They are useful to the pet groomer for brush-drying long coated breeds such as the Maltese, Yorkie, Lhasa, and Shih Tzu in full coat. They would also be used for brush drying an Old English Sheepdog should one come in for grooming that doesn't need to be stripped. When examining a pin brush for possible purchase, be sure to feel the tips of the pins. They must be rounded and absolutely smooth so as to not tear coat or cause skin abrasions. The pins should be firmly set in a flexible rubber base.

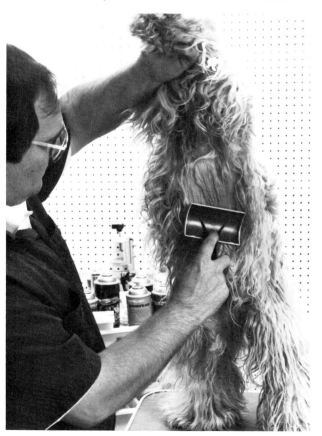

Figure 19. The Universal slicker brush removes leaves, stickers, mats and dead coat.

Figure 20. An English pin brush with smooth, rounded pins set in a rubber base is used to brush dry long-coated breeds. (Photo courtesy of *Groom & Board*)

Forceps

Straight or curved forceps are used to remove hair from the dog's ear canal. Great care must be used not to pinch the tender folds of the ear. If ear powder is used correctly, most hair comes out easily by a gentle pull with the fingers. If waxy matter in the ear makes the hair slippery, forceps help to get a better grip.

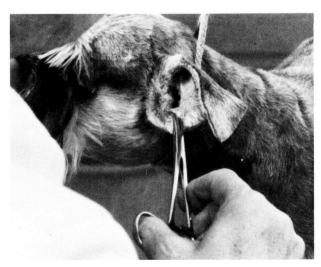

Figure 21. Forceps help remove hair lying along the bottom of the ear canal. Care must be taken to prevent pinching the sensitive ear membrane.

Shampoo

A number of shampoos are formulated with the proper pH balance to perform well on various types of coat. You will want shampoos for sensitive skin, shampoo to effectively remove parasites, and protein shampoo to keep the proper wirey texture for the coat of terrier breeds. This also works well for long-coated breeds where body and texture of coat are important factors. Conditioning shampoos are formulated to prevent tangles and to condition and shine the coat. They are especially nice for dry, brittle coats and for use on Lhasas, Maltese and Yorkies. They should not be used on the wire-coated terrier breeds because of their softening properties. There are also color enhancing shampoos available from a number of manufacturers.

For extremely sensitive skin and coats on white, silver, and apricot Poodles, or for the white-coated dogs of other breeds, one of the finest shampoos available is the *Gerard Pellham Code 7®* shampoo. The rinse formulated to use with this shampoo is *Final Touch®* .

Groomers should purchase small amounts of various types of shampoo for experimentation. Dilution and the condition of local tap water are important factors in the effectiveness of any shampoo.

Creme Rinses

Creme rinses are primarily used to condition coat and retard re-tangling. Certain shampoos are formulated with built-in conditioners and the use of additional creme rinses is unnecessary. However, with a standard shampoo it is usually wise to use a conditioning rinse on all long coated breeds. Creme rinses leave a pleasant fragrance on the coat, and by diluting it down quite a bit, can be used as a de-matting solution as well. Some rinses also build body for easier scissoring. It is wise to use a rinse that is formulated to work best with the shampoo you use, so check what each company has to offer and experiment with various rinses to find the best for the type of water in your area.

Medicated Products

Many dogs are plagued with problem skin. Dry, flaky skin is unpleasant to look at, and is usually associated with internal problems. It *is* possible to temporarily remove the dry, flaky look and create a shiny coat. One set of products that works well to accomplish this task is *Gerard Pellham's Liquid 8®*, *Code 7®* shampoo, and *Final Touch* rinse. This three-in-one treatment is effective, and particularly so on the backs of Schnauzers which are frequently plagued by scaly skin. Another method for controlling dry, flaky skin is the *Rich Health Hot Oil Treatment®*. Oster, Lambert Kay, Tomlyn, Best-In-Show, Ring 5 and many others manufacture medicated shampoos to treat a variety of problems.

Other medicated products that should be used on a regular basis include one of the available ear powders. An ear product that works almost instantly is *Holiday Ear Powder®*. It is effective for easy ear hair removal. No matter what ear preparation is used for hair removal, the ear *must* be washed with a special antiseptic ear solution afterward to prevent bacteria from entering the small abrasions where the hair follicle has been removed, and also to prevent ear powder build-up.

One of the finest ear washes on the market, in use for over 20 years, is *Gerard Pellham's Ear Gard®*. This product eliminates the itchy feeling which might cause the dog to scratch at its ears and face after hair has been removed from the ears. *Ear Gard®* will gently loosen ear wax, and the soil and wax can be wiped away from the outer ear canal with a tissue. This is one product that groomers ought to regularly sell to every customer for use at home. This is particularly true for those clients who own dogs with drop ears, where moisture and dirt builds up more readily. If used regularly from puppyhood this product practically eliminates the need for veterinarian attention to ear infections.

An ear wash should be used for cleaning the ears of *every* dog you groom. It is especially effective in cleansing the ear after the use of an ear powder for hair removal. The most important thing is to remove the powder so no build-up is allowed. Leftover powder might later fester and cause an ear infection. Other well known companies that supply ear medications include Rolf C. Hagen Corp., Hills/Pet Chemicals, Hilo Products, Lambert Kay, Rich Health and Tomlyn Products.

Keep preparations on hand to lessen the possibility of irritations generally blamed on "clipper burn." Irritations occasionally happen, even with the most careful clipping. This is particularly true for white Poodles. Aloe vera cremes are especially

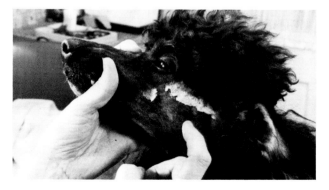

Figure 22. *Aloe Vera* based cream used after clipping will lessen the chance of abrasions or so-called "clipper burns." To be effective, it should contain at least 75% aloe.

healing. They can be obtained at shows or from your local drug or grocery store. Analyze the skin and if you think the dog has a problem, use a desensitizing product after clipping the face. A special spray for this purpose is available from Ring 5 products. Many products contain mild dosages of cortisone, and these are fine for controlling so-called "clipper burn."

Disinfectants

Each grooming station needs disinfectant spray to clean the top of the grooming table after each dog. Disinfectant should be used at the end of each day to wipe down cages in preparation for the following day's occupants. This becomes critical during virus epidemics.

Many effective commercial antibacterial disinfectants are available. A disinfectant cleaner can also be made with chlorine bleach and water diluted one part bleach to 30 parts of water. A hand pump spray bottle will easily dispenses this solution.

Alcohol is useful for wiping instruments such as the forceps after each use.

Eye Drops

Various solutions are available to clear the pet's eyes of matter or loose hair. These solutions are effective when cleaning the eyes of the Shih Tzu, Maltese, and Lhasa Apso. Dogs with bulging eyes benefit from having the area around the eye, and the eye itself gently cleaned with eye drops.

Flea and Tick Spray

In addition to using flea and tick shampoos and dip solutions, it is necessary to have an effective flea and tick spray on hand. If a dog comes in with parasites, you must control them immediately so they do not spread around the shop. Also, use the spray or a time release bomb for pest control during the months of peak exposure. Roaches and other insects that come into the shop on boxes of supplies must also be controlled.

Finishing and Conditioning Sprays

Gerard Pellham Groom and Set® is a non-lacquer, finishing spray, used on the coat just before finial clipping or scissoring. It sets up the coat and builds in extra body.

Gerard Pellham Whispering Mist® is one of the best conditioning sprays available. This spray is formulated for better management of dry, brittle

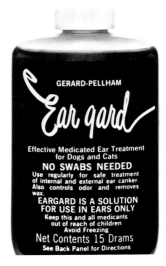

Figure 23. (Left to Right) *Ear Gard®* is one of the finest solutions for effective ear cleaning.   *Groom 'n Set®* spray will help limp, bodyless coat. It contains no laquer and leaves no sticky feeling.   *Whispering Mist*™ conditioning spray on the coat of a Yorkie, Maltese, Lhasa, or Shih Tzu, will prevent "fly-away" coat, has a healing effect on dry skin, and imparts a beautiful sheen on a short coat. (Photos - courtesy Gerard Pellham)

coats. It can be sprayed on a short coated dog, then wiped down with a chamois skin for a fine luster on the coat. It helps to nourish the skin on dogs that have been under stress. Other manufacturers provide conditioning sprays with various base formulas such as mink oil.

Cleaning Equipment

Clean-ups are easier with a commercial-type shop vac. Each groomer should clean the area around her station immediately after pre-work is completed and again after finishing the dog. This is accomplished most effectively with the shop vac. If a broom is used during the day, the vacuum should be used for clean-ups at the end of the day. A broom is not effective in the control of fleas and ticks.

You will also need a broom and dust pan, waste baskets, and trash containers for each grooming station. Plastic trash bags of a fairly heavy mil can be purchased from laundry supply houses. It is better to put the trash in a bag before putting it out in the trash bin. This cuts down on odor and insect problems, and does not attract wandering dogs.

Rubber Gloves - Wear protective gloves when handling pesticides or disinfectant solutions. Also wear them when handling a particularly dirty dog or one with an open sore that may need treatment. Use gloves when cleaning hardened stool from around the anus to prevent exposing yourself to parasite contamination.

OFFICE EQUIPMENT

Black Board

These boards can be purchased with either a black, green or white surface and are convenient for listing the dogs or cats for each day's schedule. The name of the dog plus the scheduled time for departure will immediately show which dog has to be finished first.

Client Appointment Cards and Cage Holders

Many groomers have file cases containing 3 × 5-inch file cards with the name and phone number of the client as well as the pet's name. There is also a larger card available to the groomer and kennel market. It measures 5 by 7 inches and has a much more detailed description for each pet. It contains space for listing medical problems, and more space for exact detailing of the type of trim desired. There is a space for the name of the client's veterinary clinic and the client's signature is required giving permission for veterinary treatment should it become necessary. On the reverse side is a time chart for functions performed, the date, and the charges for that visit. Or if the groomer wishes, charges can be noted by breed plus extra functions performed. The client fills out the card at the first visit and in the future all problems are noted and dated for easy reference.

Clipboard

Each groomer needs a handy clipboard on which to place the pet's grooming detail card. Also, whether the groomers are working on commission, or for hourly wages, it is important to have a detailed work sheet to note the time spent on each dog so proper charges can be made.

Work Sheets

Work sheets are a fairly new and innovative way to record exactly how much time is spent performing each function of the dog's grooming. This detailing makes it much easier for the shop owner to determine a fair price for the grooming, based on the amount of time spent on the pet.

Figure 24. Beautician's hair clips are useful in holding long-coated ears out of the way.

Appointment Book

In the past groomers have found the most effective appointment book currently available was one called *Week At A Glance®*. It can be found at most office supply stores. At this writing, an appointment book specially designed for the groomer is being prepared and should be available by the time this book is published.

First Aid Kit

Every grooming shop must have a kit or cabinet containing those things needed in the event of an emergency. The kit should be centrally located, and everyone working in the shop instructed in the use of its products. They should be taught how to administer emergency treatment to a pet, a groomer, or a client. The kit would contain the following basic items: gauze, adhesive tape, band-aids, antiseptic and antibacterial cream or ointment, a pressure bandage and some type of splint material. You may want to add some other general medications such as a headache remedy. Also, instant hot or cold packs that can be obtained from the pharmacy are useful in the event of injury or sprains. Sometimes they will give effective relief from tense, sore muscles in the neck and shoulders after a hectic day.

Fire Extinguishers

The cost of fire extinguishers is no longer prohibitive and one should be located where the greatest possibility of fire exists.

THE HOME GROOMER

The home groomer can begin business with a minimum of equipment. However, the quality of what you purchase for a home grooming business should be the same as that in a shop situation. If you are working alone you won't need the profusion of equipment needed in a large shop. You have probably already decided on the amount of business you can handle. The fact that you may or may not want to groom full-time at home should not affect the professionalism of your approach to the business.

Presently, it is not economically feasible to set up shops in all areas of rural America, but eventually the profession of pet grooming will demand the same standards throughout the country, whether you groom at home or in a shop. YOU MUST STILL CONSIDER YOURSELF A PROFESSIONAL. Your needs for home grooming are exactly the same, though on a lesser scale. Your most important tools will be clippers, blades and scissors.

THE COMMISSIONED GROOMER

The commissioned groomer hired to work in a shop, boarding kennel, or veterinary facility is responsible for bringing her own tools to work. In most instances, the grooming table, dryer, and shampoo are furnished by the owner of the facility. The groomer is required to provide clippers, blades, scissors, brushes, and all other equipment and sprays needed to complete the grooming. The assigned fee for the grooming is then split between the facility owner and the groomer on a pre-arranged basis. The percentage of the split can be anywhere from 60-40, 50-50, 40-60, or 30-70 for the groomer, depending on the ability of the individual and how much work that person can complete in a day's time.

For that reason, it is important that the commissioned groomer keep all equipment in good repair so that nothing conflicts with the ability to turn out as much work as possible. All equipment must be clearly marked as to ownership and kept in a small suitcase or tack box. Blades should be kept boxed to prevent breakage in transport.

When you apply for a job as a commissioned groomer, make sure that all agreements are spelled out *in writing* so that there is no opportunity for hard feelings and everyone knows what is expected. In most instances, the groomer working on a commission basis is responsible to report and pay her own income and witholding taxes.

If the shop owner supplies or cares for the greater part of the equipment you use, you have an obligation to maintain that equipment just as carefully as you would your own.

All professional groomers should attend conventions and seminars to see what new equipment is currently available. I can think of so many things I noticed first at a convention or seminar that have made my job easier during the past twenty years of grooming. I look forward to each convention and seminar as a time to listen and learn!

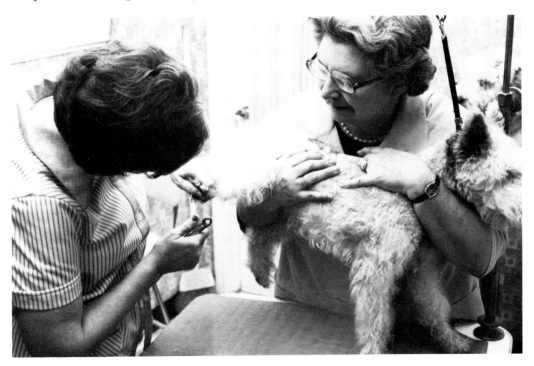

Figure 25. Professional groomers are acutely aware of the comfort of the pet they are grooming. In this photo groomer Anna Hanson supports the dog in her arms while the author clips the nails of a particularly nasty Terrier. Always cut the rear toenails first to get a feel for the dog's reaction to this procedure.

4
Pricing Your Grooming

A question often heard at grooming seminars or conventions is, "What do *you* charge for grooming?" This is also the question that groomers hear most often when the phone rings at the shop. The question usually entails a long explanation of how pricing is achieved—size of dog, breed, medications needed, etc. It is so much simpler to be able to quote one type of pricing that applies to every customer equally, and would cover almost every situation the groomer might encounter.

The government does not allow standardized pricing within any industry, so groomers are on their own to figure out what works best in an individual situation. The bottom line in figuring pricing is always cost of operation plus percentage for profit, divided by the number of hours the business is in operation. Unfortunately, many groomers have had no business training, and so, pretending to be a customer, they begin to call around to various shops in the area hoping to gain some insight into local prices and what they can charge to be competitive. It seems that groomers have a "holy fear" of charging more than anyone else in the area.

Asking price schedules from another shop is a totally unreliable way of pricing. Each shop is different, and expenses vary in every location. The groomer must determine the expenses and problems that are inherent for her particular business and location. Another difficulty that crops up when comparing the prices of other shops is that humans are not always totally honest. You may be given erroneous information that does you more harm than good. Pricing and income in any business is a very private matter. The entire grooming industry will be better off when each shop owner determines to make money, over and above all the expenses and business needs that must be covered.

The groomers who are well-trained and confident of their ability show a professional demeanor that inspires trust. If customers continue to return to your shop as repeat clients, your *only* real obstacle to success is how you price your grooming and merchandise. To succeed in any business you must know how to accurately determine expenses plus a reasonable percentage for profit. Throughout the grooming industry we find those who are satisfied to be "bargain basement" groomers. They are the ones who undercut everyone else in the area and advertise all sorts of grooming bargains in the local paper. Personally, I would rather be the best groomer in my location, with a thorough knowledge of my costs of operation, and charge accordingly.

It is understood that there will be great variances in the pricing of grooming around the country. A top quality shop in a high income, high rental area has higher operating costs, and thus has to charge higher rates to stay financially solvent. By the same token, a groomer in a small country town may charge only half as much because of lower operating costs. Either groomer may have the higher percentage of profitability, depending upon operating costs and pricing structure.

TRADITIONAL PRICING METHODS

Let us look at what has been common practice among most groomers in the past. After examining the various alternatives, you will have to decide what is best for you.

Prices at many shops are based on a set price per breed plus "tack-ons." The first fifteen minutes of de-matting, for instance, is included in the base price, and additional mat removal is charged in fifteen minute increments. Extra charges include such things as dips, medicated baths, special rinses, hot-oil treatments, nail polish or bows. Shops using this method may have additional expenses for printing charge sheets to verify each procedure and how much was added to the base price to compute the final charge for grooming.

Pricing is often subject to the whims of the shop owner, and not necessarily based on operating costs. As previously noted, some shop owners take an average of local charges and allow that to be a determining factor for their own shop. This is a very poor way to try to survive.

The usual method of indicating prices is to mount a board with various price quotations on it. There will be three quotes for Poodles—Toy, Miniature and Standard—followed by Terriers, Cockers, and on down the line. After the various breed prices are listed, itemize the extra charges for services such as de-matting, medicated baths, hot-oil treatments, bows and nail polish. A special customer charge sheet is used to explain the extras.

One area that is usually underpriced is the charge made for mat removal. This is the most difficult part of the grooming procedure and should be the most accurately priced. However, since many shops do not know how to figure cost of operation, charges for various steps in the grooming procedure may be too low. A shop may have difficulty in justifying grooming charges when pricing by the breed, with additional charges tacked on for various extra services. Men are especially suspicious of being overcharged. This is probably because businessmen have been educated to question pricing in all phases of business, whereas women have been conditioned to more readily accept charges. This, too, is changing as more women are entering the business arena and becoming aware of service pricing and the need for a shop to cover all expenses and turn a profit in order to stay in business. These customers appreciate a more businesslike approach to the grooming price problem.

HOURLY PRICING STRUCTURE

Early in my experience as a shop owner, my accountant and I, together with a management consultant, sat down and had a long discussion to resolve the problem of not enough income generated by the work being done. All the discussions seemed to come back to the same problem, how to increase the income from grooming and sales without drastic increases in the fixed price schedule with which the customers were familiar. (Also, I wasn't interested in booking a heavier load of dogs to groom.) The consultant was concerned that we were not taking into consideration the *entire* time that was being spent on each dog and therefore were not being compensated accordingly. He asked that we carefully record all time being spent on each dog serviced. By doing so we discovered we were only being compensated for approximately 60 percent of our grooming time. After the studies had been completed, we were able to book one or two more dogs per day by more efficient use of our time. We decided that the only way to deal with our pricing in the future would be to add up all our yearly costs of operation plus a percentage for profit, and divide this figure by the approximate number of working hours in the year. This figure could then be translated into an hourly rate that the shop would need to receive to stay in business. A new groomer's work sheet was designed, recording all time spent on the various grooming functions during the day. Based upon a predetermined hourly rate, we then knew how to charge each customer.

Then came the difficult part...how to inform loyal customers of the new pricing policy? It was no problem when new customers came to the shop for the first time; they were simply told that their grooming charge would be based upon the time actually spent on their dog, and that the time charge would include *all* phases of the grooming procedure. An approximate cost would be mentioned based on our knowledge of the usual charges for that type of dog. However, it was always stressed that they were *not* being given a definite price. Until we actually worked on the dog, we would not know how well he would cooperate. Coat condition was checked *before* the dog was put into the holding area to determine if matting would be a problem. On a badly matted dog, all mats or the stripped coat was saved to verify to the customer that greater time had been spent on the dog because of the coat condition. Dogs that were easy to do saved money for their owners. Frequent-

PLEASE PRINT ALL INFORMATION	DETAIL PET GROOMING DOCUMENT	DATE *01/10/00*

OWNER NAME *JOHN DOE*

PET NAME *JAQUE*

ADDRESS *100 PUPPY DOG LANE*

BIRTH *2/10/83* **TYPE OF PET** *POODLE - WHT.* **SIZE** *TOY*

CITY *ANYWHERE* **STATE** *WI* **ZIP CODE** *54519*

VETERINARIAN NAME *OWN VETERINARIAN*

HOME PHONE *UNLISTED* **BUSINESS PHONE**

VETERINARIAN PHONE

PET MEDICAL HISTORY

SEIZURES — SPECIFY _____

HEART DISEASE — SPECIFY _____

ALLERGIES — SPECIFY _____

BLIND ✓ SPECIFY *RIGHT EYE - HIT BY CAR*

DEAF — SPECIFY _____

OTHER ✓ SPECIFY *BAD STIFLE - LEFT REAR LEG*

In the event of an emergency, I do hereby authorize ____ *LOCAL VETERINARIAN* ____ to provide emergency treatment for my pet.

Signature *John Doe* Date *01/10/00*

FOR OFFICIAL USE ONLY

CUSTOMER NUMBER *100*

TYPE OF CUT *LAMB TRIM - #4F*

GROOMING COMMENTS & INSTRUCTIONS *DOG DIFFICULT FOR HEAD WORK*

USUALLY MATTED - WANTS DOG COMBED OUT - LEAVE MUSTACHE

SENSITIVE SKIN

© WALIN 1979

FOR OFFICIAL USE ONLY $15.00 PER HR.

GROOMING STATISTICAL HISTORY

BREED STANDARD TIME - 1½ Hr.

STRIP	PRE-GR	RGH CP	BATH	FINISH

BREED STANDARD DEVIATION

STRIP	PRE-GR	RGH CP	BATH	FINISH

DATE	STRP	PRE GR	RGH CP	BTH	FIN	AMOUNT	DATE	STRP	PRE GR	RGH CP	BTH	FIN	AMOUNT
01/10/00	1½ Hr.			30 m.	30 m.	$37.50							
2/28/00		15 m.	15 m.	20 m.	40 m.	22.50							
4/10/00		10 m	15 m	30 m rinse	40 m	23.75							
5/30/00		15	15	20	40	22.50							

© WALIN 1979

Figure 1. (Top) Front of the groomer's record card. (Bottom) Reverse side of record card. This dog was stripped at the first appointment. As noted on front, the dog is white and has sensitive skin requiring extra care in the stripping process. After the first visit the dog was groomed at regular intervals which resulted in a considerable decrease in the grooming charge. (By pricing the charges on an hourly basis, the groomer was adequately compensated for the extra work involved in the stripping process.)

ly their charges were less than they had been when they were charged by breed type alone.

All clients, whether new or old, were asked to fill out a newly designed client card. The front of the card asked all the usual questions for information about the owner, and also specific questions referring to the health status of the dog. Space was provided for grooming instructions, and for groomer comments concerning cooperation of the dog. The owner's signature was required, giving permission for immediate veterinarian attention should that ever become necessary. The owner's preference of veterinarian was used if within a three-mile radius. Otherwise, they would agree that their pet could be taken to a local veterinarian. The back of the card provided spaces for date of appointment, and for each groomer to record the time spent on each function such as comb-out, bath and dry. No extra charges were made, because anything extra that was done took time, and under the new system of pricing, TIME meant MONEY.

For longstanding clients whose dogs had a history of matted coats, there might be a considerable cost increase under the new system. In these cases, we took extra time to explain that charges in the past had not been enough to cover our costs. When you make drastic changes in pricing it *does* take time for the client to understand that service pricing must be done fairly, and that grooming is difficult work and must be accurately compensated. New charges were put into effect gradually. Clients were told they could keep costs down if they did more brushing and combing at home.

Temperament problems were harder to explain, so we questioned the clients to find out if they had problems grooming at home. Often they would finally admit that the dog was a real "pistol" when it came to combing or brushing, so they usually gave up and expected the groomer to perform miracles! We gently explained that *miracles do cost more.* If the owner indicated a willingness to learn better combing and brushing techniques, we invited them to attend free evening classes conducted at various times of the year to help owners of dogs with problem coats. If there was time, we showed them how to properly de-matt while they were there. All new puppies were given a free complimentary toenail clipping, ear check and cleaning if necessary, and owners were instructed on proper coat care.

One method of upgrading the professionalism of our industry would be to get rid of the misconception that all groomers in the same area must charge the same prices for their work, even though each shop may take a different approach to their clientele and their method of pricing. Cost of operations should be the prime consideration for grooming charges, but abilities and other factors influence how much of a profitability factor can be built into the pricing. These factors also determine what your salary as shop owner should be, and what salary or commission your groomers can expect to receive. We all expect to pay top prices when we purchase products from Neiman Marcus. We also expect more reasonable pricing of products at Sears or Montgomery Ward. The reason for the difference will be quality of goods and/or the part that competence and image play in cost of operation. These same factors will influence *your* cost of operation. If you go all out to create a boutique-type shop and hire or train the best professionals, you will have a higher cost factor to recoup.

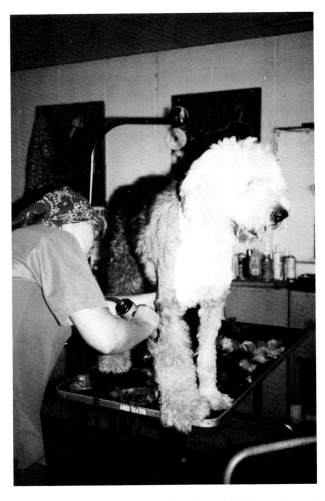

Figure 2. It isn't difficult to determine charges for the unpleasant task of stripping an Old English Sheepdog when pricing is figured on an hourly basis. (Photo - courtesy Canine Barber Shop, Milwaukee, WI)

The concept of pricing by the hour was covered in the January/February, 1981 issue of *Groom and Board Magazine* in an article by Clifford D. Walin:

A product's price can be directly influenced by a competitor's price only when both products are identical. These products are called perfect substitutes. However, in grooming, the finished product will always vary from person to person, depending on how the groomer visualizes the clip and his particular grooming skills. Thus, the groomings of two different professionals will never be perfect substitutes, which means price would be only one of many factors influencing the customer.

To illustrate the concepts of perfect and imperfect substitutes, consider the purchase of a pencil, and the cost of a woman's haircut.

An individual may need a pencil that meets the following requirements: No. 2 lead, can be sharpened, and has an eraser. Upon entering the store the person finds several brands of pencils, all of which meet the requirements. These are called perfect substitutes. Consequently, *price* becomes the determining factor in selecting which pencil to buy.

However, when a woman selects a beautician to do her hair, price plays only a small part in her decision. Generally, a woman will insist on having a particular operator. She will, at times, rearrange her schedule, endure numerous inconveniences, and pay whatever is asked (within reason) simply because she likes the look given her by that operator. Consequently, she will insist on having that operator, even though another beautician may be just as competent and cost less.

This example is not meant to imply that you can charge exorbitant prices for your grooming. Even though different groomings are imperfect substitutes, they *are* substitutes. At some point, either the grooming or the price will equally satisfy the customer's needs. Therefore, we need to determine the criteria used by the grooming customer in evaluating a groomers' value. Some factors include: your store's overall appearance, your ability and appearance, the concern you show for the pet, the general health care information provided by you, your relationship with local veterinarians, your store's location, parking, and your price.

Price is only one of the many factors used by a customer to evaluate the need for your product. Consequently, if you charge a fair price based on your operating expenses, and one that provides you a normal return on your investment of time and money, you need not worry about your competitors' rates.

When we switched to hourly pricing, we were able to lower the grooming charges for approximately ten percent of our customers with easy-to-do dogs. In some cases, we did get an argument from long-time clients with difficult dogs whose prices should have been increased long before to compensate for extra time involved. They had to come to terms with the concept that they had to pay for all work done, and if they couldn't be reasonable and pay us just prices, then we were better off without them as clients. Even though we lost approximately five percent of the old clientele who didn't like our price changes, we soon experienced a 20 percent increase in profitability. Consideration was given to senior citizens on fixed incomes. Any price increase for their dogs was minor or perhaps none at all if they were on time for appointments and kept them on a regular basis.

An interesting thing happened as we continued to grow and to use the hourly method of pricing. Clients that had left because of increased prices began to return, because they found that "cheaper" was not always better, and in many cases, not even close to the quality they were paying for at our shop.

Groomers must realize that they cannot afford to charge the same for a well behaved Toy Poodle that only takes an hour and a half to pre-work, bathe, blow-dry and finish as compared to one that may take two or three hours because it fights, bites, and is a matted mess. Groomers accept increased costs for everything they buy and services they receive because they are aware of the increased cost of operation for other businesses, yet they are often afraid of keeping prices current with the costs of overhead.

Benefits of Pricing on an Hourly Basis - One big plus for the owner is an immediate knowledge of how much actual time each groomer spends on her work. The groomer working on time charge work sheets has to keep a minute-by-minute record of the dogs she works on each day. It will be interesting for you to see how much actual "work time" is produced in the shop. If you find that the work sheets indicate less than six hours of actual work time for an eight-hour shift, you had better check to see how the extra time is being spent. Of course there are times when a groomer forgets to fill in a time sheet, and that has to be taken into consideration. It is amazing, though, how quickly groomers remember to fill out time sheets if it is made clear that compensation and raises in pay scale depend on good records, so that you, as the shop owner, can get a better overview of developing skill.

Another plus for keeping records for time charges is the ability to show the client accurate accountings of the time spent on various functions for each dog. If there are several groomers working in the same shop, it is necessary to compensate for a slower groomer's additional time. *We overcame that problem by simply having one of the experienced groomers do each new customer's dog to establish basic time segments for that dog's grooming.* If the dog came in basically in the same condition each time, the same charges were in effect. If, however, the dog was badly matted when coming home from the lake at the end of the summer, the only time segment that would need changing was the comb-out column.

When the grooming is completed, each time segment in the various columns is totaled. The total time multiplied by the charge per hour determines the price. A chart can be made and posted on the grooming room wall breaking down the charges into five-minute segments for those with mental blocks about math. Also, a small discount could be given as a bonus to those customers who keep regular five- or six-week appointments.

With this method of pricing, *it is never necessary to tack on charges for various extra services.* Coat conditioning treatments, left on for five, ten or fifteen minutes before bathing, are simply added to the pre-work time charges. Fluff drying automatically costs more than crate drying for the same reason. Simply, you charge for the groomer's time in the same way as the plumbing contractor charges for the man he sends to fix your kitchen sink. TIME IS MONEY and every extra function you perform is covered when using this method.

The greatest advantage is *profit* for the shop owner and groomer alike. Commissioned groomers make more as fairer prices are established for the work they do. They won't have to worry about their income for the day being less if they get stuck working on a badly matted dog. Groomers paid by hourly wages can be challenged to improve time and skills in order to move into higher hourly wages. But most important, the shop owner has an accurate picture of the worth of the business, due to more accurate cost-of-sales figures. These records, plus a monthly profit and loss statement, show you, and any potential buyer of your business, just what your growth pattern is, and your net worth and profitability percentage.

Now—doesn't it sound simpler to be able to say to a customer: "The charge for your Toy Poodle will be $26.25, based on a charge of $15.00 per hour because it took us an hour and forty-five minutes to complete all the work. We removed all her mats, bathed her in our finest shampoo, fluff-dried her and hand-scissored her coat. Doesn't she look beautiful?"

If she truly does look "beautiful," your customer should be pleased to hand over the $26.25!

5
Shop Policies

How does your shop function in the average course of the day? Is it quiet, harmonious, an organized place of business that runs like a well-oiled machine or, is it filled with strife, causing tension for everyone concerned? If you are a home groomer, is your day planned so you complete your dogs on time and still manage the rest of your life and activities efficiently? To insure efficient and harmonious operation, the shop owner must establish certain organizational rules. They should be fair, with equal distribution of the work load, so no one person is bogged down with all the responsibility.

THE NEW EMPLOYEE

Many shops hire and train their own groomers so there is less conflict over the way trims are to be executed. These groomers are usually placed in an apprentice situation and begin their instruction period learning the fine points of brush-out and bathing. As their skills grow, they master the grooming process in a step-by-step procedure. Sometimes, after six months or so, they are quite proficient at their task. Within a year, some become competent groomers. Then may come the shocker! The groomer walks in one day and announces that she is quitting your shop. To add insult to injury, this groomer then locates with another groomer in your area, or opens a shop in direct competition with you. How does this make you feel after you have spent many hours teaching this groomer all your skills? Not very good, I can guarantee you.

I hear stories relating this type of problem all the time.

There are various ways to solve the problem. Our lawyer suggested that we draw up an employee contractual agreement for all new employees to sign. It specified that if we hired someone on an apprenticeship basis, in return for skills taught or perfected on the job, the employee would agree not to work for any other shop in our immediate area, or open her own shop within a certain radius of our shop. In return the employee was given certain guarantees—primarily that a complete course of skills would be taught as per a pre-specified agreement and that wages would be increased in direct relation to abilities. A different agreement is needed when hiring skilled groomers. If you decide to pursue an employee contract, seek the advice of a competent attorney to draw up a legal document pertinent to your area and needs.

JOB DESCRIPTIONS

Each employee should be given a job description that spells out exactly what is expected. Doing this will avoid the old comeback, "You didn't tell me to do that!" when some duty is not taken care of as expected. The division of routine labor such as cleanups, garbage disposal, crate care, and the care of equipment can be spelled out for each person. If you own all the equipment and expect the groomer to clean it up at the end of the day, say so in the job description. There is a better taste in everyone's mouth if all employees share in the work load, so not just one or two people get stuck cleaning up all the time. Of course, if the shop is small the work load *does* fall on one or two people. However, the job description should designate who does what.

A shop runs at its best if there is only one boss, or perhaps the owner, plus a shop manager if it is a larger shop. There should be someone in charge at all times to accept responsibility for actions taken and to solve problems as they arise.

Harmony in the grooming shop is sometimes difficult to achieve. Groomers are artists, and artists do seem to have a different kind of temperament. Yet, if strife and dissension are allowed to continue in a close working relationship, they will undoubtedly tear the business apart. It is the owner's or manager's job to steer a middle of the road, balanced course. That job entails expressing pleasure with the employees' continued efforts to improve their skills. Keep lines of communication open, so if there is a problem, employees feel free to share their feelings.

Figure 1. Notice the professional apprearance of Anna Hanson, shop manager of The Velvet Bow in Hinsdale, IL. Dress codes at this shop require a professional uniform or a smock over slacks.

Once the employee is well established into the routine of the shop, there are some steps the manager or shop owner can take to help the employee feel like a valued person and part of the team that makes the shop successful. First, let the employee know how his work is progressing. Sometimes this can best be done by going to lunch with the employee on a periodic basis for an informal job evaluation. Explain what the job entails, and find out if the employee is experiencing any problems in reaching the goals that have been set

for each level of experience. It must be a two-way conversation. Without putting the employee down, conduct the conversation within the framework of how you feel the employee is doing her job. Emphasize the skills that are well done, and encourage those areas that need strengthening. A sound psychological approach avoids the "you do it this way, or else" theory in favor of working together to solve any problems.

Many shop owners are afraid of praising their employees for fear that they will ask for a raise, or of criticizing for fear they may quit and someone new will have to be trained. So they allow the employee to continue with less than the best effort, while they get ulcers stewing about how to tackle the problem. Don't be afraid to praise a groomer for a particular job well done, and thank her in front of the other groomers. This helps everyone to do their best job, so that they, too, earn your praise and pleasure. Just be sure that your praise is not always geared toward one person. If you try, you can always find something to praise in each person working for you, and that is a tremendous morale and ego booster. Everyone needs to feel good about himself. When you have to correct or criticize someone, do it in a private manner so as not to cause resentment. Criticism should be in the form of constructive suggestions rather than negative statements.

It is important to increase the loyalty of your employees to the business by letting them know that your are interested in their future plans for their career. Would they like to manage a shop someday? Perhaps the time might come when you would like to expand to the ownership of more than one grooming shop or merchandising effort. One of your employees might well be an important part of such a decision. You have the responsibility to groom them for that future position with you.

Ask your employees for suggestions to improve the functioning of the shop. If you have to put a new policy into effect that isn't too popular, explain your reasoning so that the employees will understand your side of the matter.

WAGES, SALARY OR COMMISSION?

The practice of paying for work done on a commission basis is very prevalent in our industry. There are many groomers working as independent jobbers, some working at more than one shop. Technically, groomers working on a commission basis are to provide all of their own equipment and

Figure 2. A view into the area where dogs are crated while awaiting grooming at The Velvet Bow.

are responsible for having everything they need to do the job correctly. An independent groomer's job is looked at in much the same way as that of a beautician. Most of them are merely renting a station in a particular shop, and giving a certain percentage of their earnings to the shop. For commissioned groomers, the rules need to be bent a little. It is impossible to carry around a big dryer, much less a tub. Provision for soaps, rinses and sprays may vary in each shop. The commissioned groomer should also feel responsible to complete trims in accordance with shop standards, not as an individual stylist. A commissioned groomer is responsible for making her own government reports and federal and state income tax payments. The shop owner must report social security withholding.

Commissions vary depending upon the skill of the groomer involved and the person supplying the equipment. The usual breakdown might be as follows: 40/60, 50/50, or 60/40. The first figure indicates the groomer's share, and the second figure the share that the shop would receive.

Some owners prefer to pay groomers on an hourly wage scale, beginning at minimum wage for the inexperienced apprentice and progressing upward to eight dollars or more per hour for a skilled, fast technician who does top work. This helps to eliminate the complaints that might originate from having a particularly difficult dog to groom. Wages vary depending upon your area of the country and have to be upgraded as minimum wage level is raised and to compensate for cost of living in-

creases. However, it is easy to see the relationship of low end wages for the apprentice to the higher wages of a skilled groomer. The big advantage of this method of compensation is that each level of competence can be paid a specific amount, as described in the employee contact. Thus, both the shop owner and the employee know exactly what to expect and this allows the worker to progress into higher pay scales by showing competence in each step of the learning process. If a skilled groomer is hired, the owner and groomer must negotiate an equitable wage. The wage scale and the job may be placed on a temporary basis, say for a month, to determine whether the groomer has the skills claimed. If it proves to be a negative experience, the job can be terminated at the end of the month, or perhaps sooner by mutual agreement.

Another big advantage of hourly wages is that the groomers cannot complain about not being able to complete enough dogs per day to make their day profitable. Difficult dogs or easy dogs, the groomer knows ahead of time that as long as she puts in the hours, the pay scale is established. Time and a half for overtime at busy times of the year may make the job more appealing. Or, if enough overtime hours are put in, perhaps the groomer can choose to take time off with pay at some slower time of the month.

The salaried groomer may also have some other pluses. If she works full-time, paid holidays and perhaps group health insurance may be offered by a larger shop. Tax deductions for the salaried employee are handled by the employer.

Figure 3. In the foreground is a sales receipt and cash drawer combination. Service work and merchandise sales are recorded in separately marked areas of the ticket so the owner can figure and report sales tax and verify income from the two different sources.

MANAGER RESPONSIBILITIES

Shop owners do not always think ahead to what might happen if they are unable to be in attendance at the shop for whatever the reason. Illness, family problems, or simply the need for some rest and rehabilitation can spell the need for a second-in-command to take over the responsibility. A shop owner should delegate authority to one employee to be second-in-command and take over in the owner's absence. The creation of a good manager takes time and effort. Sometimes it is difficult for the owner, because he may believe no one else is capable of running the store. The owner should set the standards for the manager to follow. The owner and manager have to work well together to develop understanding and communication skills.

A good manager gets along well with people, not only fellow groomers but also shop customers. Speech ability, mannerisms, personal habits, and appearance are of vital importance in the person who represents the shop's owner. A well trained manager can relieve the shop owner of much of the day to day tedium of decisions, especially on small matters. However, she needs to defer to the shop owner on major decisions, and only discusses the problem if she feels the owner is wrong. A good manager never makes the shop owner look bad in front of other employees or customers. She should keep the owner advised of any known problems or developing difficulties.

The shop owner has certain responsibilities to the manager. If the owner makes a policy decision that later proves to be unwise, blame must rest on the owner, not the manager. Promises made by the owner to the manager or to shop employees must be fulfilled or reasonable explanation given for the failure to do so. It is the owner's obligation to set an example of conduct and dress expected of those in the shop. The owner must make sure that verbal or written instructions are understood by manager and employee alike and must accept responsibility for the manager's decisions made in the owner's absence.

In training your manager, learn not to check every move she makes, as that puts the manager under too much pressure. Remember, the shop manager is in an administrative position, but she is still second-in-command and is probably feeling the stress of the extra responsibility. If you train your manager slowly and carefully, you may be able to take a vacation in Hawaii!

SOME GENERAL SHOP POLICIES

• Lunch breaks should be encouraged. Groomers should not groom with one hand and wolf down a sandwich with the other.

• Arrange the work load so each groomer can finish a specified number of dogs. Groomers on hourly wages should feel that they are getting a fair share of the work.

• Determine wages by the individual's ability, and review them on a six month basis until an acceptable rate is reached. After that, a performance review and pay raise once a year is sufficient.

• "No smoking" should be the rule in the grooming room, as people are working in close proximity. Some dogs, as well as people, may not tolerate smoke.

• Quiet music is known to help keep tensions low.

• A part-time helper in the late afternoon can be a big help. High school students can release dogs, wait on customers, and generally help with the end-of-the-day jobs. Since they are under different wage regulations, this can be an inexpensive source of help. Another possibility for a busy shop would be to hire a senior citizen for the brush-out and bathing process. Many men and woman in this age group are happy to work for minimum wage on a part-time basis for extra income.

• Set dress codes for your groomers. They should be encouraged to wear clean smocks or uniform tops and pants. This enhances their professional appearance when talking to clients, and is especially important if the grooming area is visible to the general public.

• Finally, under NO conditions should any animal brutality be allowed. There is NO need to hit a dog to make it behave. *Make it a shop policy that aggressive behavior by any groomer can be reason for instant dismissal, even if the dog bites first!*

6
Antiseptic Procedures
In The Shop

It's late Saturday afternoon. Perhaps you are talking to yourself: "Boy! This place is a mess! I better get it cleaned up again. Oh well, I could let it go until next week, and just come in early and get it washed up." If this happens at your shop, even occasionally, consider the problems caused by sloppy housekeeping.

When considering the importance of proper sanitary habits, divide the year into segments and think about the problems that occur seasonally. Groomers from year-round warm climates however, must be aware that many of these difficulties occur all year long.

The early months of the year, January through March, are often times when communities encourage clean- and paint-up projects. Similarly, this should be the time when shop owners take a good look around to assess the repairs and cleaning needed. Usually, shops experience a business lull in winter which makes it the ideal time to wash walls and ceilings and apply a fresh coat of paint or new washable wallpaper. Staying on top of maintenance and repairs makes general cleaning much easier.

In colder climates, January thru March are travel months for people seeking to escape the howling winter winds. As they travel to the sunny South with their pet, the animal may pick up some unwanted pests that return home with them. As a result the groomer may have customers complaining that their dog or cat is scratching from an unknown cause. You may be able to identify a flea allergy from either bites on the skin, small black-looking granules on the skin, or perhaps an active flea infestation. Carefully advise the owners that their pet has a problem, and suggest ways they can eradicate the infestation. The next time the dog or cat comes in, it may still have the problem. What area did they neglect to deflea? Probably the carpeting in the car is infested from the trip and the owners don't even realize it.

Normally, the groomer doesn't expect to see fleas except during warm, summer weather, but with increasing numbers of people traveling from one part of the country to another in all seasons, flea and tick problems can be encountered at any time. For example, I remember how upset I was when I found my first case of fleas in early February. They were the jumping, scooting kind that seem to spread all over. We swept, vacuumed, sprayed and set off pesticide bombs. Finally, the shop was rid of them, but not without a lot of effort. From that day on, vacuuming and spraying became part of the *daily* routine. Nooks and crannies were cleaned thoroughly to eliminate hiding places where fleas and ticks could propagate and spread. Heaven forbid that a customer should say that their pet picked up fleas from the shop. Groomers must always be concerned with the control of these pests.

It cannot be overemphasized that shop cleanliness is an *ongoing daily project,* and cannot be done in a slipshod fashion without encouraging various problems. May, June, July and August are the months to expect the greatest flea and tick problems. At that time of year, dogs and cats spend more time outside, playing or lying on the grass. Pets in the southern states may be spending more time in air-conditioned houses, but their problem with fleas is constant because in warm climates these pests are more resistant to various pesticides. In the summer months be doubly careful, not only in caring for the shop premises, but also with the instructions and advice you give the owners of the flea-infested dogs and cats. Groomers must know which products are most effective in flea and tick control, and either sell them at the shop or refer owners to a retailer or veterinarian who can supply them.

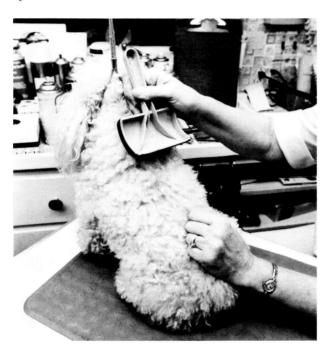

Figure 1. A tight, matted coat such as is shown on this Poodle, might harbor a flea infestation. It is important to check the dog for parasites and spray to control them as each dog comes in.

September and October are months of carry-over flea activity. Flea and tick populations begin to wane as cold weather arrives in the northern states, but many people will still be battling to eradicate these pests. The grooming shop may have the same problem if good housekeeping is not practiced all year-round.

In addition to parasites, poor sanitation causes other concerns. One problem is bacteria and viruses present on all surfaces. Another is dirt, secretion, or skin problems that plague dogs and cats that come for grooming.

In a home, if someone has a serious virus, the doctor gives precautionary directions to prevent the spread of infection. Likewise, precautions must be used to combat bacteria, viruses and the spread of infection within the confines of the shop. But, from observing the cleanliness of shops visited, I feel that many groomers are very remiss. Of course, hair falls to the floor during grooming, just as there is hair on the barbershop floor or around the beautician's station. However, every time I have had my hair cut, the beautician has swept the floor around her station immediately afterward. It would help a great deal to apply the same principle to dog grooming stations. Don't allow hair to accumulate all day just to let everyone know how busy you have been! It would go a long way toward shop professionalism if the area were vacuumed after each grooming. Of course, a thorough vacuuming of the entire shop at the end of each day is a necessity.

Are unpleasant odors present in the shop? This is a problem in pet shops that have grooming facilities because of the kenneling of various types of pets. However, the grooming area can still have minimal odor. No matter where the shop is located, if dirt and debris are kept to a minimum and bacteria controlled, foul odors need not be a problem. Commercial air cleaners effectively control odor for any pet or grooming shop.

To help eliminate odors, loose hair or any other matter must be removed from crates as each dog leaves. Keep holding crates as immaculate as possible. Bagging all loose hair and garbage at the end of the day also helps to eliminate smell. Try to arrange for in-shop garbage pick-up. This helps control the problem of stray dogs being attracted to the smell of the hair from various dogs groomed. Also, complaints from neighboring businesses can be kept to a minimum by careful housekeeping of outside premises.

Thoroughly scrub the grooming room floor at least once a week, more often if necessary. If you have a large, busy shop and groom many of the larger breeds that must be walked to and from the tub area, you may find it easier to hire a cleaning service to come in and do the floors on a regular basis.

During any outbreak of contagious virus (such as parvovirus), there is greater obligation to the client to follow a strict cleaning regimen and to insist that all dogs accepted for grooming have up-to-date inoculations. During times of viral outbreaks in your area, scrub every cage and tabletop following each grooming, using a solution of one part chlorine bleach to 30 parts water. (The use of gloves is recommended at all times when handling strong antiseptic solutions.)

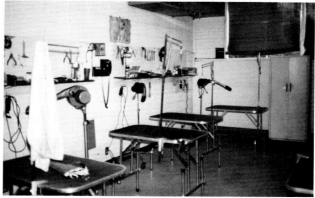

Figure 2. These photos are of the Ker-Mor's K-9 Barber Shop in Wisconsin. This shop, owned by Nancy Kiersey, is a fine example of a clean, well organized, odor-free establishment that handles upwards of 25 dogs per day. (Photo - D. Walin)

Not surprisingly, veterinarians more readily recommend a shop where correct antiseptic procedures are being practiced. Therefore it is important to establish a good rapport with a locally respected veterinarian. He or she can be of invaluable help if there is ever a crisis with a dog in the shop.

EQUIPMENT CARE

Next, take a critical look at the tops of your grooming tables. How frequently are they scrubbed or sprayed with an antiseptic solution? I hope your answer is "After *every* dog".

One of the best materials to use for the top of grooming tables is a formica-type material. Many veterinarians use this material because it is so easy to clean. However, it is much too slippery for the stability of the animal when grooming, so it should be covered with a removable mat. Both surfaces can be sprayed or washed with an antiseptic, helping

Figure 3. A formica top hydraulic grooming table with a removable rubber mat can be easily scrubbed and sprayed with antiseptic between dogs to help prevent the spread of infection.

to prevent the possible transmission of problems from one pet to another. The mat is easy to remove to the tub for scrubbing after each dog.

At a seminar in a large midwestern city one summer, a groomer passed my seat on her way to the podium to give a grooming demonstration. I noticed a very peculiar odor. I thought to myself, "She really needs some deodorant." However, on her way out, I saw the top of the grooming table she was carrying and realized where the odor was coming from. Every rib of the matting on the table was filthy with accumulated matter. That would be a health hazard for any pet. There is no excuse for accumulated dirt when it is so simple to take a small bristle brush and soap and water to wash away any debris.

The next check point should be clipper blades and scissors. Dirt and matter can build up quickly between the teeth of the blades. A stiff pastry brush or toothbrush does an excellent job of brushing away hair or dirt from between the teeth of the blade. Matter between the cutting edges of the blade can be removed by sliding the cutting edges apart and using a small brush to clean. If the blade has been used on a pet with a particularly dirty coat or one with skin lesions, the blade should be immersed or sprayed with an antiseptic solution while running, wiped dry and re-lubricated before further use. (Clippers should be held in such a way that only the blade is in solution. Certain solutions might be injurious to the plastic body of the clipper.) One benefit of keeping the clipper blades clean is longer blade life. Blades that are kept cleaned and lubricated retain a sharper cutting edge.

If the dog or cat being worked on has a heavy vaginal secretion, or accumulated matter around the vulva, remove the blade from the clipper and wash it in hot soapy water, spray with an antiseptic, dry, and relubricate. The same course of action applies if working on a male dog with pus around the penis, or if the penis looks swollen or irritated. When proper antiseptic procedures are practiced you are protecting other dogs, and yourself as well. A good product to use when an antiseptic spray is needed is *Oster Antiseptic Spray®. Another is Gerard Pellham's Aktinol®, a concentrated hospital-type antiseptic.*

Combs and brushes must be antiseptically treated in the same way as other tools. It is easy to forget that these constantly used implements must be kept clean. Soap and water plus a spray of antiseptic solution is sufficient. Scissors should be cleaned often, especially after they have been used to cut into a dirty coat, remove hair around the anus, or to remove drainage from under the eyes. Spray scissor blades with antiseptic and wipe clean. Add a drop of oil at the hinge and they are again ready for use.

Your ear hair pullers or forceps must also be kept clean. When visiting a shop a number of years ago, I watched a groomer clear a badly infected, smelly ear with ear powder and ear wash. There was a lot of matter in the ear that clung to the forceps as the groomer removed the ear hair. The forceps were laid aside on the table near the groomer, and I was horrified to see the same dirty forceps picked up again to be used on another dog without any attempt at cleaning the instrument before re-use. Can you imagine the amount of infection that would be spread if a doctor or a veterinarian were to be so careless! Disinfect forceps after *every* use. Do not merely wipe it off with a tissue. Wash the forceps in hot, soapy water, spray with antiseptic and dry. *No* accumulated matter should be left on this instrument. Unless forceps are

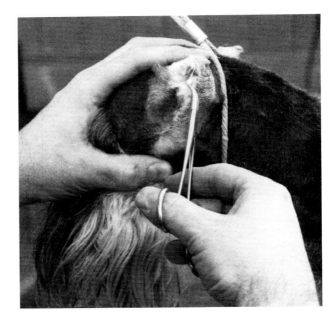

Figure 4. Forceps must be cleaned after each useage to prevent spread of infection from one ear to the other.

cleaned after each use in the ear, infection may be passed from an infected ear to a healthy one.

Included in this same category should be the groomer's hands which need to be thoroughly cleansed during certain procedures, and after each pet is worked on. For instance, after cleaning a dirty, smelly ear, wash hands thoroughly before cleaning the other ear or starting another grooming function. Bacteria and infection can be transmitted so easily.

I believe we are rapidly approaching the time when inspections and licensing will be required for all shops. The more cleanliness and proper antiseptic procedures become routine in grooming shops, the less problems there will be when the time comes for passing licensing inspections.

7
The Groomer As Veterinary Assistant

In many instances, groomers are the first to notice physical abnormalities in the dogs they groom. This is especially true with dogs seen on a regular basis. The groomer, therefore, has an obligation to notify the customer of any potential difficulty or abnormality discovered.

Veterinarians are often willing to speak at grooming seminars and conventions to assist groomers in recognizing symptoms of various problems. While many difficulties cannot be determined without extensive testing that only the veterinarian is capable of performing, groomers have an obligation to learn as much as they can about the signs of canine debilitating problems. Treatment or advice must be given with caution, however, for when litigation has been brought by the pet owner against the groomer many court decisions have been in favor of the pet owner. Groomers should record, for their own protection, any deviation from normal that they detect when a dog or cat is being groomed. When a pet is taken in for grooming, total responsibility for that animal rests with the groomer while it is in her possession. It is vitally important that the groomer know what to do in emergencies and maintain an excellent relationship with a reputable veterinarian. Although, in most instances, groomers should not dispense medical treatment or advice, their role is to advise the owner if the pet needs medical attention.

Naturally, groomers are interested in making the greatest possible profit from their chosen profession, but very little extra time is needed to check for the more obvious medical problems. As various functions of grooming are performed, it would be almost impossible to miss the more obvious visible symptoms. Most grooming customers are grateful to be notified of a potential problem that needs veterinary attention, although there will always be a few that consider any suggestions of medical needs for their pets as an invasion of privacy. By tactfully asking, "Have you noticed this problem that is causing 'Fido' some difficulty?" you are giving the client a chance to respond without embarrassment.

The reason many clients may not be aware of impending problems is that some owners, after the initial newness of having a pet has worn off, may only touch their pet briefly during the day. They put down a bowl of food, pat the dog on the head, and are on their merry way. As a result, a problem may become acute before the owner realizes anything is wrong. Some breeds are predisposed to certain medical problems. Groomers should be aware of these. All groomers ought to read books on general dog care in addition to periodicals that reference various canine medical problems. It is not necessary to go into all the medical details, but anything that instructs and increases knowledge will make the groomer more aware and conscientious, hence more capable. Professional groomers have an obligation to provide the best care possible for the pets serviced. As veterinarians realize that you care enough to spot medical problems in the pets you groom, they should willingly recommend your shop.

Advise your clients to take their pets for a complete annual physical when vaccination boosters are due. This should include examination of the

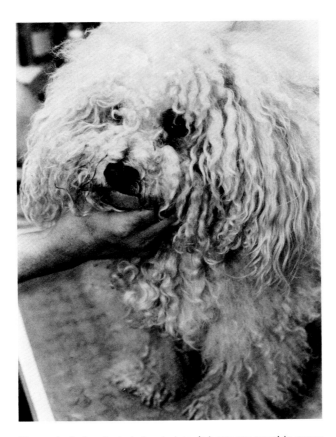

Figure 1. A dog that obviously hasn't been groomed in many months should be carefully checked for skin or parasite problems. (Photo - Groom & Board)

eyes, ears, mouth, heart, lungs, abdomen, vagina or penis, and skin condition. A stool sample should be checked for parasites and a urine specimen checked for blood or pus. This way, small problems may be detected before they become a major concern.

For proper recording and follow-up, use a professional client card to record any changes in behavior or body structure. The owner should then be notified, and the date of the notification indicated on the card. The next time the dog comes for grooming, it is easy to check to see if the problem has been corrected.

PROBLEMS OF THE YOUNG DOG

Such problems as progressive retinal atrophy, legg perthes disease, hip dysplasia, epilepsy, and patella luxation are seen with greater frequency in purebred puppies and young adults than in mixed breeds. Large breeds that grow quickly and often gain a lot of weight during their early months seem especially prone to hip dysplasia. Therefore, veter-

inarians recommend that large breed puppies be kept on the lean side to prevent any added stress that might interfere with proper bone development. One common problem in toy breeds is a luxating patella, more commonly called a slipped stifle. Many groomers must contend with this disorder when the dog's knee joints pop in and out as the groomer tries to comb or brush the rear leg.

While grooming, you might notice rib deformities from past injuries. Also check the chest cavity for a strong, regular heartbeat. Any vibration or abnormal heartbeat can be brought to a veterinarian's attention. The abdominal area can be checked for the following: a potbelly that might indicate parasites; hernias at the navel or in the inguinal area; whether or not both testicles have descended on the male puppy. The mammary glands of a bitch should be checked for the presence of any developing tumors.

In puppy bitches, vaginitis causes a discharge that might point to infection. If the puppy persistently dribbles urine in the cage or on your grooming table, it could mean that the urethra does not correctly connect to the bladder. In addition, ascending bacterial infections that are transmitted up the vagina into the urethra can cause kidney damage.

Check the dog's teeth at each visit. If puppy teeth are present at six or seven months of age, call this to the attention of the owner, recommending that they be removed before they cause any misalignment of the permanent teeth. Do the puppy's eyes appear to be symmetrical? Inverted or entropion eyelids cause scarring and tearing.

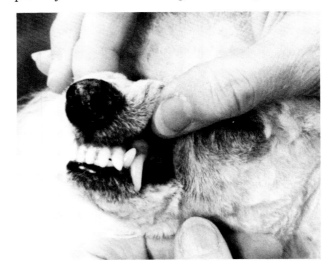

Figure 2. Check teeth at each grooming appointment. In puppies, check at six and seven months for retained puppy teeth. Check for tartar accumulation and gum line infection.

Many other physical problems can be seen externally. An open fontanel, or open skull may signify a hydrocephalic puppy. A domed skull and a nervous, agitated puppy may indicate pressure within the brain.

Another useful observation is to determine whether or not the dog's growth pattern seems normal. For example, does the dog appear unusually small or stunted? Is its coat dull, dry and brittle, or has the owner noted any changes in eating habits or behavior? All of these symptoms could indicate a heart problem, a parasite infestation, or a nutritional deficiency. Hair growth and condition is an excellent barometer of a dog's general health. A dull, lifeless coat may indicate a chronic or serious problem or simply incorrect shampooing and rinsing techniques.

PROBLEMS OF THE OLDER DOG

Often the groomer sees a potbellied older dog. Before making any assumptions, ask the owner if the dog is on a medication that includes cortisone. Cortisone, when administered over a period of time, can produce an enlargement of the abdomen caused by a thinning and weakening of the muscle wall. A bloated appearance may also be the result of a heart problem, which often causes fluid retention.

Figure 3. The use of *Eargard*™ from Gerard Pellham, will lessen the possibility of irritation to the ear associated with plucking the ear hair. Used on all dog's ears on a regular basis, it will help control the return of chronic ear problems.

Excessive thirst may signify a potentially serious ailment. For instance, dogs with chronic kidney disease drink more water. However, half of the kidney function will be destroyed before

changes are noted in the drinking habits. Excessive thirst may also indicate diabetes. If the owners of a dog mention that their pet is always thirsty, suggest that the dog receive immediate medical attention.

Many times a grooming client has asked, "My dog is acting 'funny'. Do you think I should take him to the vet?" Response should always be, "If your dog is acting in a way that is not normal for him, yes, you should have a veterinarian check him."

Groomers *cannot* diagnose any medical problem, and *definitely cannot* recommend specific medical treatment. However, when a dog is in the shop and suffers an epileptic seizure, heat stroke, or heart attack, the groomer must take emergency measures.

PROBLEMS OF THE HEAD AREA

Ear Problems

Breeds with drop ears such as the Poodle, Cocker, or Afghan need specific and regular ear care to prevent infection. The owners of these and other drop-ear breeds must be advised to check ears frequently to see if the ear tissue is light pink in color and appears normal. There are some excellent ear washes on the market such as *Ear Gard*, which should be used on a regular weekly basis.

Young puppies coming in for their first grooming often have infected ears. Infections of the ears and eyes are common in puppies that were whelped and raised in unclean quarters. Also if a bitch has an ear infection when she whelps, the puppies may pick it up from her. Sometimes an irritation occurs if the dog scratches the ear after grooming. Removing hair from the ear may cause itching unless a soothing ear lotion is used afterward. There is still controversy in various parts of the country as to whether or not the groomer is qualified and should remove ear hair during the grooming procedure. Ask area veterinarians for their opinion and note it on your client cards. Make it a point to call each veterinarian listed among your clients, then proceed according to their recommendation for that individual dog. In that way, you can avoid judgmental errors. Most veterinarians welcome the dog whose ears have been cleaned, saving them time and making the ear easier to examine.

Obviously, if the ear cavity is reddened, granular in appearance, or has a foul odor, you should refer the problem to a veterinarian. Cut away as much hair as possible from the front of the ear opening to make examination easier. If any dark reddish-brown secretion is removed from the ear, put some of it into an envelope to aid the veterinarian in diagnosing the problem. He or she may be unable to find visible mites because they are buried in the ear wax and debris. The customer should be advised to be faithful with prescribed home treatment because long-term preventive care is necessary to avoid return of the problem.

Some breeds, such as the Schnauzer, have a thick hair coating in the ear. Use an antiseptic, depilatory type of powder to lessen the discomfort when the ear hair is removed. After removing the hair, use an ear wash to remove all remaining powder so it doesn't build up or cause itching. However, some dogs are so sensitive to having their ear tended to that they will scratch as a matter of course. In a normal ear, use aloe cream or an anti-itch cream containing a small amount of cortisone on a cotton swab to gently wipe the outer channels of the ear to help relieve the itching.

Teeth and Gums

Accumulated tarter on the teeth is another trouble spot for dogs. Dogs fed on soft diets have this problem more than those fed hard bones and dry kibble. If allowed to accumulate, the tartar pushes down the gum line, causing infection. Groomers have all worked with dogs whose breath could knock them out. The teeth may be at fault, but more often then not, infection is the cause of fetid breath. Commonly, owners complain that their animal has an odor problem, but they don't know the source.

Sometimes the dog has an extremely sensitive muzzle. It may squirm or pull away from any attempt to hold the muzzle. Upon examination, swollen, reddened tissue is found that may or may not give off a putrid-smelling discharge. This problem is common in older dogs where an accumulation of tartar has caused a receding gum line. Whatever the cause of any problems in the mouth, again recommend immediate veterinary attention. The average dog needs to begin regular cleaning of the teeth when it is two years old. An annual cleaning thereafter is usually enough to keep the problem under control.

Personally, I feel that cleaning teeth is not part of the groomer's responsibility. Most dogs strenuously object to having work done in their mouth without anesthesia. Also, if any instrument used to clean the teeth were to slip and injure the dog, there would be serious trouble. Furthermore, the danger of being bitten is a serious consideration. Whatever the cause of any problems in the mouth, again recommend immediate veterinary attention.

Eye Problems

It is important to advise customers that their dog's eyes need regular care. This is especially necessary for the breeds with large, protruding eyes such as the Lhasa and Shih Tzu. In addition, certain types of eyes are predisposed to injury, foreign bodies in the eye, and other ailments. Entropion eyelids, for example, will cause scratching and scarring of the eye tissue. With so many environmental irritants in this age of pollution, it is sometimes difficult for even the professional to determine the cause of an eye problem.

Various types of synthetic fabrics are irritating to the eyes and skin. Poodles that have freshly clipped faces are prone to scratch their faces on furniture fabric or carpeting, which causes both skin and eye irritations. Irritants also include tall grasses, sap, leaf molds in autumn, and a myriad other sources. Advise clients to keep their dogs away from weedy areas where seeds can come in contact with the eyes or become entangled in the coat. Remind clients that if they allow their dogs to ride in the car with their heads out the window, both ear and eye problems may result.

If the dog being groomed has a heavy mat of secreted drainage below the eye, soak the area with

Figure 4. Hand-scissor accumulated matter from under the eyes using a small, blunt-pointed scissor. If a great amount of matter is present or dried into a mat, soak first with warm water. *Do not take a clipper and try to get under the matter; you may accidently remove skin that is already raw from the debris.*

warm water to loosen the secretion before trying to remove it. The area beneath the drainage may be raw and sore, so it is *not* advisable to take the clipper to remove the matted area as the skin might be removed at the same time. It is better to carefully hand-scissor the area beneath the eye with a blunt-tipped scissor to avoid any further abrasions to an already raw area.

Progressive Retinal Atrophy (PRA) - Progressive retinal atrophy (PRA) is an insidious disease. The dog loses sight very gradually, so that it becomes conditioned to its surroundings. The first indication of PRA may be the dog's reluctance to go outside at night. The dog's owner may casually tell you that his dog doesn't seem to see well at night. If blindness seems apparent by a lack of response to objects in front of the dog, or if the dog seems startled by your sudden approach, notify the owner that a problem may exist. The onset of this disease is not as physically noticeable as cataracts, since there is no change in the eye color or clarity. PRA can usually be indentified by any competent veterinarian, but the final determination for this problem rests in the hands of a certified veterinary ophthalmologist.

SKIN AND COAT PROBLEMS

Skin problems are a constant source of aggravation for both groomer and dog. It is difficult to turn out a perfectly groomed dog if skin and coat irritations exist. Hormonal imbalance can cause hair loss or a change in coat texture. Some dogs are allergic to various chemicals in shampoo. Even certain types of diets can cause extreme allergies that manifest themselves in skin irritations that are annoying to the dog and may cause chewing and scratching of the coat.

Hopefully, neither the groomer nor the dog owner is using a harsh detergent shampoo. I once visited a kennel where the dogs were bathed with liquid dish detergent. How badly those animals must have scratched their itching and dried out skin when they got home! Light colored skin and coats, such as those found on white, apricot, or silver Poodles are usually very sensitive to harsh shampoos. Also breeds like the Bichon, Maltese, and Yorkies must be bathed in gentle, well-balanced, non-tearing shampoos.

Any type of external parasite will leave evidence on the skin and coat. Those most frequently found by the groomer include fleas, ticks, mites,

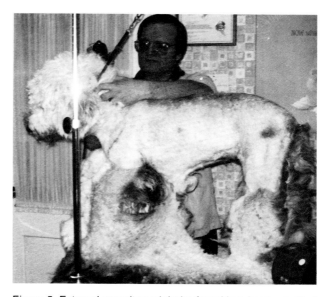

Figure 5. External parasites might be found in a heavy, matted coat such as the one being stripped from this Old English Sheepdog. Notice the dark spot over the hip area. The re-growth of hair comes in dark wherever an irritation is present, particularly in silver, brown, and apricot coats. (Photo - D. Walin)

and lice. Less frequently, maggots may be found under a very matted coat, especially if there is an open lesion under the mats. This is more common in dogs brought in from farm areas. Flea and tick infestations can be treated by the groomer using shampoo and externally applied medicines. More serious skin problems should be treated by a veterinarian.

Schnauzers often have a toxicity to the sap of evergreens. Their owners should be advised not to exercise their animals in areas where they come in contact with evergreen boughs. If lesions develop on the inner groin area from a toxicity to evergreen resins, it is important to keep the area very clean. Aloe cream is sometimes effective in healing the area. Veterinarians differ as to recommended treatment. Some prefer salves and creams while others will prescribe cortisone shots to stop itching and prevent the dog from licking the area. Cleanliness is of prime importance no matter what other curative agent is used.

COUGHING

Every groomer, at some time or another, has the problem of what to do about a dog with a persistent cough. There is no way to know if the dog is harboring a tracheobronchitis virus (canine cough), has a heart problem, or a bad throat. If heart disease has been noted on the client card, then that is the probable cause. If not, try to protect other customer's dogs by segregating the suspect dog and advising his owner of the problem. For precaution, question every client to see if their dog has had current booster shots containing parainfluenza vaccine. Wise groomers will not accept dogs that have not been immunized against all common diseases including parainfluenza and canine cough.

INTERNAL PARASITES

There are numerous parasites that can infest a dog causing many ill effects. Usually they cannot be identified without microscopic aid. However, if the groomer finds small, rice-shaped objects clinging to the hair around the anus, it is probably a tape worm segment. Carefully cut away the hair containing these small grains, put it in an envelope for the owner and advise him to take the dog to a veterinarian for positive identification and treatment.

Roundworms are very common in puppies. Some puppies are born with roundworms, having had them passed from the bitch into the unborn fetus. These worms may be passed periodically in the stool. They look like long, thin spaghetti, one to three inches in length and coiled like a spring. Afflicted puppies may be potbellied, have diarrhea, and eat excessively.

Other internal parasites include hookworm, whipworm, and heartworm. These parasites are identified by stool specimen or blood sample examination. All of these internal parasites are very debilitating to the young puppy causing listlessness, tearing eyes, dry, dull-looking coat, and runny noses. Notify the puppy's owner of any of these symptoms and encourage professional help before the problem becomes acute. Do not advise pet owners to try over-the-counter medications to treat their dogs, and if you suspect a worm problem, advise professional veterinary treatment for positive identification and correction.

ANAL GLANDS

The anal glands are located internally just inside the anal opening. They secrete a foul-smelling liquid that apparently lubricates anus. Occasionally, when chronic infection is present, the veterinarian recommends their complete removal. The groomer must learn to recognize the difference between a normal and impacted gland.

If swelling and redness is evident, the gland should be treated professionally to avoid the danger of internal damage. When the anal gland becomes clogged and impacted, the dog usually drags his hindquarters across the floor to try to relieve the intense pressure. He may also bite and lick at the base of the tail. Since this behavior is also indicative of worm infestation, the owner may not be at all aware of the anal gland problem. On occasion, the groomer may even find a perforated gland under a badly matted coat. The odor from this is so foul that it is impossible to imagine the owner did not notice.

Grooming too close to the anal opening or accidentally nicking the area may cause the dog to drag his hindquarters on a rug or other rough surface to relieve the itching, resulting in irritation and possible infection of the anal gland.

At many seminars I have attended, a veterinarian is present to speak about groomer's problems. There is often controversy concerning whether or not a groomer should express anal glands.

Most veterinarians agree that a groomer may express a normal anal gland. However, they also stress that it is vitally important to learn the correct way to perform this procedure.

Figure 6. When cleaning the anal glands, place the dog in a tub. Cover the anal opening with tissue to prevent the secretion from spraying on your skin or clothes.

How frequently these glands need to be emptied, will vary with each dog. Some have to be emptied on a monthly basis, while other dogs that exercise regularly outdoors may never have a problem. Impacted glands are more common in the toy breeds because many of them are fed a softer diet with less bulk which forms a softer stool.

It is best to clean the anal gland before bathing. Place a folded facial tissue over the anus, and place your thumb and forefinger just below and to either side of the anal opening. You should be able to feel the swelling of the glands under your fingers. Press gently together in an upward and outward motion until you feel the gland releasing. If it does not release easily, or feels very enlarged, advise the owner to have a veterinarian perform this procedure. After expressing the anal gland, wash and rinse the area carefully using a mild shampoo to remove all traces of secretion and foul odor.

BLADDER OR KIDNEY MALFUNCTION

Eventually every groomer encounters the dog that dribbles urine during the entire time it is in the shop. Sometimes this occurs in an excessively nervous dog. Occasionally, the groomer finds bladder problems in a submissive dog. Upon being touched, picked up, or greeted by a human, the submissive dog will dribble a little urine. However, there may be more serious reasons. If there is a constant presence of urine on the dog's coat, and perhaps a strong urine smell, an acute or chronic problem may be present.

Other symptoms of bladder or kidney difficulty are the following:

   a. Excessive thirst;
   b. Voiding more than usual amounts of urine;
   c. Night voiding when the dog has been completely housebroken under normal conditions;
   d. Painful urination;
   e. Blood present in the urine;
   f. Loss of weight.

Many diseases also affect kidney function. Some of them are canine leptospirosis, distemper, infectious hepatitis, pyometra, heartworm, bacterial infections, or drug reactions. It is interesting to note that more male dogs than females are afflicted with kidney ailments. Severe attacks may bring on listlessness, pain in the kidney region, dehydration, vomiting, diarrhea, and either increased urine or the loss of urine output. Changes in the condition of the skin and coat may be evident. If a dog being groomed exhibits any of the above symptoms, question the owner as to whether abnormal behavior has been noticed at home. Alert the owner to the possibility of an existing problem and the need for veterinary attention.

HEAT STRESS

Heat stress can become a problem in the grooming shop when there is inadequate ventilation combined with stress and excitement. Some breeds are predisposed to nervousness making them particularly prone to the problem of heat exhaustion. Dogs with heart and lung problems should also be watched for signs of heat stress.

Generally, heat stroke is associated with the dog that is left locked in a closed car on a hot day, but this is not the way groomers encounter the problem. Instead, an overweight, older dog, a heavy-coated large breed, or for that matter, any dog that is confined in a hot, humid enclosure where temperature and ventilation are not monitored, is the prime victim of grooming shop heat stroke. The potential for heat stroke exists for any dog that is crate dried without being constantly monitored, or if cage dryers are used at temperatures higher than the dog can safely tolerate. Summer months, with additional humidity problems, bring a higher incidence of heat stroke.

The outcome and severity of a case of heat stroke is directly related to how high the body temperature rises, and the length of time before the elevated temperature is lowered. It is important to have a rectal thermometer handy to take the temperature of any dog suspected of having a problem. The first symptoms are excessive panting or noisy breathing and an elevated rectal temperature. (Normal rectal temperature is 101.2 ° F. to 102.5 ° F. Some dogs show slight elevations simply from the stress of grooming.) A dog afflicted by heat stroke will have a temperature of 105 ° F. or higher, and may have a rapid heartbeat, salivate profusely, vomit, or show general weakness. As the heat stroke progresses, the dog may tremble or convulse; coma follows as shock sets in. Membranes of the mouth may turn grayish. Left untreated, the animal may suffer respiratory arrest and death.

If noticed and treated immediately, the outcome should be favorable. Mild cases can be treated by moving the dog to a cooler area or wrapping him with towels soaked in cold water. In more severe cases, a cold water bath followed by immediate veterinary attention is a simple and effective way to treat the symptoms. First, place towels in the bottom of the bathing tub and soak them with cold water. Lay the dog in the tub, and supporting the head, cover his body with cold water. Take the rectal temperature repeatedly, and when the temperature comes down to 103 ° F. to 103.5 ° F., discontinue the cold bath. Immediately transport the dog

Figure 7. Crate drying must be carefully monitored to prevent heat stress. A multi-unit dryer with temperature and air flow controls is shown here. The holding crates are fiberglass which does not heat up as quickly as those made of metal. This set up was easily visible to the groomers as they worked. (Photo - D. Walin)

to the veterinarian and notify the owner. The veterinarian usually begins intravenous fluid treatment to repair the electrolyte imbalance that has occurred. Drugs will be administered to treat any damage to the brain, kidneys, and other internal organs. Never try to treat this severe problem without medical assistance, and never return the dog to its owners without advising them of what has happened. If the dog goes into shock after leaving the shop, the owner may be able to prove legal responsibility involving the groomer or shop.

BONE ABNORMALITIES

Legg-Calve'-Perthes Disease (Hip Necrosis)

This problem is not common, but may be suspected from observing a limp in a puppy, particularly a toy breed under the age of one year. The puppy may begin to limp slightly and not want to bear full weight on one of its rear legs. If you feel the thigh muscles of both rear legs at the same time, one leg may seem thinner than the other. If you do find any difference in the muscle mass, show the owner and advise him to see a veterinarian immediately. If no muscle atrophy is present, advise the owner to watch the limp, and if the problem persists for more than a few days, to see a veterinarian for diagnosis.

Hip Dysplasia

Hip dysplasia is another crippling problem. Although primarily a problem for the larger breeds,

it is occasionally found in small breeds. Symptoms are similar to that of legg perthes disease except that the symptoms of limping and pain do not show up until later in life. Some veterinarians recommend keeping large breed dogs on the lean side, and stress correctly balanced diets to minimize the problems of poor bone structure.

Patella Luxation (Slipped Stifle)

Slipped stifles are common in the toy breeds. This is relatively easy to recognize since it is difficult to groom a leg when the knee joint pops in and out. A slipped stifle is obviously painful to the dog, and may happen very quickly if a small dog jumps from a chair or table to the floor. In most cases, if treated early enough, it is correctable by orthopedic surgery, where muscle tissue is used to hold the knee joint in position. If the condition is allowed to persist without treatment the dog may become permanently crippled and carry the leg to avoid pain.

EPILEPSY

A dog that suffers an epileptic seizure should be sent home without further grooming and be seen by a veterinarian as quickly as possible. If for some reason the owner cannot be contacted the dog should be kept warm and quiet with no further disturbance until the owner can be located.

A grand mal seizure can be scary. The dog loses consciousness, and usually defecates and urinates. It may fall into a comatose state for quite some time, and should be kept warm and quiet. As the seizure begins, the dog may thrash and roll around, so it is advisable to pad the crate with towels, or if the dog is small, roll it into a couple of towels.

A petite mal seizure will not have such drastic manifestations. There may be only trembling of the limbs. However, if the dog is suspected of having had an epileptic seizure, find out from the owner if there has been any problem at home. Note the finding on the client card so that the dog can be groomed quickly and sent home on a 'first out'' basis the next time it comes for grooming.

Epileptic seizures can usually be controlled with medication given on a regular basis. If they occur only when the dog is under particular stress, be sure the owner medicates the dog before bringing him for grooming.

CANINE BRUCELLOSIS

Of more recent concern to the professional groomer are facts brought to light by research on canine brucellosis, a serious venereal disease that causes abortion, stillbirths, or the sterility of the dog. This organism *can* be transmitted from dog to human during the handling of an infected animal, or dog to dog during breeding, or orally if a dog comes in contact with fluid from the vagina or penis of an infected animal. As yet, there is no known cure in the dog, but the infection can be treated in humans. Prior to 1966, little was known about this organism. Lately, it has been increasingly found in packs of wild dogs, large kennels, and boarding facilities.

Because of the rising incidence of this disease, the groomer must stress the necessity of keeping grooming tools clean, and using stricter antiseptic procedures to prevent the passing of infection from one dog to another.

The following are some of the facts to be aware of concerning canine brucellosis:

a. The organism which produces *Brucella Canis* has been isolated from the vaginal discharge, urine, and milk of the affected female dog.

b. The urine, seminal fluid and prepuce of the male dog have also been found to carry the organism.

c. Heavy vaginal discharge, especially from a bitch that has recently had a litter that was aborted before full term, could indicate the presence of *Brucella Canis.*

d. In a male dog, enlarged testicles, testicular atrophy, or a heavy discharge may be indicative of infection by *B. Canis.*

e. Any male dog or bitch that shows localized or generalized lymph gland involvement may be infected.

The owner of a dog showing any of the above symptoms should be advised to immediately have a veterinarian examine the animal. If brucellosis is found, anyone who has handled the animal should be notified to watch for symptoms indicating possible infection. These symptoms may be attributed to flu or mononucleosis, unless Brucella Canis is also suspected, as the symptoms for all three are strikingly similar. The veterinarian has the responsibility to advise the owner that his dog is a public health risk. This news is understandably traumatic for the owner of a valuable breeding animal, or a family whose pet must be destroyed.

ALLERGIES

Professional groomers should do everything within their power to eliminate any source of irritant that could cause allergic reactions in the animals serviced. For example, groomers should not wear excessive perfume and make-up, or highly perfumed hair spray. Both dogs and groomers may react to inhalant sprays. Pollens, dust, mold spores and various types of danders also provoke an allergic reaction in a susceptible individual.

Dogs tend to develop skin problems when they are allergic and bothered by inhalants. The problem may show up in various ways as generalized itchiness or on specific areas such as the feet, eyes, nose, and ears. Some dogs sneeze and wheeze. My two Poodles sneeze profusely if they come into the room when I am applying even a light amount of perfume or hair spray. Tobacco smoke is another considerable irritant to the dog, especially if a heart of lung problem exists. For this reason, smoking should not be allowed in the grooming area.

Dogs can be given allergy shots, or antihistamines for temporary relief. For more severe allergies, cortisones are frequently given. Groomers should be aware of this when working on a dog that has had cortisone injections over a period of time. The groomer should note the side effects. These include; increased appetite and weight gain, increased thirst and urination, a tendency to be less active, and suppression of hair growth.

Hopefully, the owner of an animal with an allergy will notify the groomer that a problem exists, but many times owners are not aware of the difficulty. The groomer may be the first to notice sore feet, runny noses, reddened ears or a host of other problems associated with inhalant allergies.

TUMORS

Tumors are known to exist in all animal species, and the dog is no exception. Since so many types of tumors exist, we will cover only those that are fairly obvious to the groomer.

A tumor is a disorderly, uncontrolled growth of cells which may be benign or malignant. This chaotic growth may occur anywhere and has many different appearances depending on the type of tissue in which it develops. The most common tumors are those of the skin. Fortunately, these are more often benign than malignant.

Growths are easily detected on short-coated breeds but long-coated dogs may hide various tumors under a profuse coat. Tumors frequently appear on the face, especially on the muzzle and eyelids. Wartlike growths, which are really small benign tumors from irritated skin glands, may become numerous as the dog ages. If they bleed, are repeatedly torn, cause the animal to scratch at the area, or begin to grow rapidly, they should be removed immediately and analyzed by a pathologist.

Warts and swellings anywhere on or under the skin should be noted on the client card, and the owner notified. Tumors may arise from the fat, muscles, vessels, and other tissues which lie just beneath the skin. They will appear as swellings which seem to be pushing up, though not injuring the skin overlying them. Although such growths may be benign, especially if they grow very slowly, many are malignant. Therefore, the veterinarian must be made aware of their presence to determine proper treatment.

The most common tumors in the bitch are mammary gland or breast tumors. They occur more frequently in dogs over the age of six. No particular breed is predisposed. Early spaying of the bitch decreases the likelihood of breast tumors. As with any other tumor, the best treatment of mammary cancer begins with early detection. Owners, handlers, and *groomers* should routinely run their fingers over each mammary gland, feeling carefully for any abnormal lumps within the glandular tissue itself. All such lumps should be brought to the immediate attention of the owner. Even though the mammary glands and tumors have been removed and so noted on the client card, continue checking the abdominal area for any additional tumors.

Oral tumors occur frequently enough to be of considerable concern to the groomer. Any time a dog objects to having his muzzle held, or displays unusual tenderness in the area, look for abnormalities in the mouth.

Bone tumors are malignant in the overwhelming majority of cases. They are most common in the large bones of the front and rear legs of the large and giant breeds. These tumors may occur in young dogs but are usually seen in dogs over the age of seven. The first symptom is usually lameness of one leg, with or without a swelling present. Owners will assume the dog has injured the leg in some way. Advise them that if the symptom has been present for more than two days, it should not be ignored. Early diagnosis is of utmost importance in fighting bone cancer.

SUMMARY

In concluding this discussion, let me reemphasize that *the groomer is often the first person to realize that a pet needs medical attention.* It is not the groomer's position to try to be the clinician, or to dispense medical treatment, but rather to help the owner in spotting a potential difficulty. Do not diagnose, but rather affirm or suggest that there is a problem that needs attention.

There may be financial reasons why certain problems have not been attended to, so a fine line of diplomacy must come into play. It is particularly hard for someone on a limited income to be faced with the possibility of extensive veterinary bills.

It is also important that you make it a point to visit with the veterinarians in your area. Make them aware that what they may call a "clipper burn" may be the result of the itching and scratching a dog may do after a fresh grooming on a coat that has been neglected for many months. Let them know that you do everything in your power to be gentle with the animals you service, that you notify your clients of any potential problem that requires veterinary help, and that you *will* follow veterinary instructions for the use or avoidance of specific medicinal products. Often, you can inform veterinarians of special breed requirements that significantly affect appearance. For example, it is impossible to make an attractive pompon on a Poodle's tail that has been docked so short that it destroys the *balanced* appearance necessary in the front and rear to execute an attractive trim.

When groomers help owners discover and battle any problem present in their dog, they prove that their concern and abilities extend to the total and complete health care that only *professionals* provide.

8
Groomer Health Problems

PHYSICAL STRESS

"Oh, my aching back!" How many times has that been the complaint of the groomer? What could be causing the back or leg pain? Many problems can be relieved by analyzing the working area. Is it free of the problems of clipper and dryer cords snaking across the floor? Is there danger of catching your foot in a loose cord and twisting your body into an unnatural position?

The position your body assumes while grooming can be another back killer. Every groomer should work in a position that keeps the body in the straightest line possible. Performing as many functions as possible from a sitting position will give the back and legs relief during the day. A comfortable grooming stool with leg and back support is just as vital to the groomer as a good secretary's chair is to the secretary. Also, try to move around as there is much less strain to back and leg muscles if you don't stand in one position for long periods of time.

I advocate using hydraulic tables if at all possible. Though your back may not feel any symptoms of strain during the first years of grooming, you may suffer additional pain and arthritic problems in later years from job-related abuse to your body. If you do injure your back, and the doctor orders you to bed don't take muscle relaxants to relieve pain and try to keep going. Follow the doctor's advice and go to bed, even if you are a groomer working alone whose sole income depends on daily grooming. Job insurance is worthwhile protection for just such a situation.

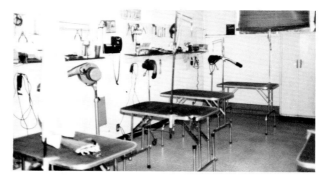

Figure 1. The clippers visible in this photo are hung on the wall at each grooming station. Dryers have their own plug-in. This avoids the clutter of electric cords on the floor that might cause injuries to the busy groomer. Photo taken at Ker-Mor K-9 Barber Shop, Milwaukee, Wisconsin. (Photo - D. Walin)

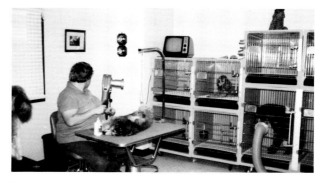

Figure 2. This photo shows many positive helps to promote the comfort of the groomer and the dog. Janice Skender, owner of Cedar Dale Kennels, is shown in the kennel grooming room. She is seated in a comfortable supportive chair while brushing her show Poodle puppy. The dog is positioned for Janice's comfort on a hydraulic table which can be raised or lowered for working ease. Notice the easy-to-clean vinyl flooring and the multi-unit fiberglass cages visible to the groomer at all times. (Photo - D. Walin)

When lifting, let your legs do the main work, not your back. Don't lift a heavy dog without help. Pet steps up to the table or tub will eliminate a lot of lifting. Adjustable tables can be lowered close to the floor so one end of the dog at a time can be maneuvered onto the table.

A cushioned pad on the floor around your grooming table is better than standing on bare cement or hard tile all day. Move around frequently to prevent the pooling of blood in your legs. Wearing support hose will relieve leg fatigue and help prevent edema in the lower extremities. Supportive shoes are an absolute necessity. Clogs can be dangerous and cause ankle injury if you turn quickly. *Under no circumstances should you groom in bare feet or sandals!* The danger of dropping scissors, clippers or some other sharp instrument into your foot far outweighs any possible comfort of standing barefoot. Give your feet quick relief by soaking them for a few minutes in warm water, then massaging them briefly.

Warm-up exercises before going to work help prevent muscle tension in the body. A warm bath at the end of the work day soothes aches and pains.

Your hands must also be protected from stress. The scissors you use should be properly proportioned to fit your hand. Seeing another groomer scissoring like mad with a particular type of scissor may lead you to buy the same instrument. That may be a mistake. If a scissor seems awkward or heavy in your hand, it is not for you. Heavier hands and longer fingers can easily manage longer scissors or those with thicker blades. Dainty, slim-fingered hands need lighter weight scissors to prevent fatigue. Groomers with arthritic hands need lightweight, easy action scissors.

Good lighting prevents headaches from eye tension. Light intensity in the grooming room should be as close to daylight as possible. Lighting should be placed in such a way that it prevents shadows under the dogs. A light-colored mat under the dog provides contrast and lessens eyestrain.

GENERAL HEALTH TIPS

There are ways to keep the body at optimum performance by some simple general health management. Medical science is continually putting new emphasis on holistic care of our bodies. Traditionally, doctors treated ailments after the fact. Now we are being encouraged to take preventive measures.

When our bodies are subjected to stress, as they are in grooming, we may experience symptoms that seem totally unrelated to our jobs. One of these may be gastrointestinal distress. We may not relate the fact that our stomach is upset to the fact that we had to face an unhappy client whose dog had to be stripped. Or we may have spent hours fighting it out with a dog that didn't want to be groomed.

How do we go about keeping our bodies at a high level of good health? Diet plays the greatest role in keeping body functions working well. A balanced diet of approximately two thousand calories per day works well for the average person. Seventy percent of those calories should come from the group of foods we know as complex carbohydrates; fruits, vegetables, nuts and grains. Proteins should comprise fifteen percent, coming from fish, poultry, lean meat, milk, eggs and cheese. Use unsaturated fats such as corn oil whenever possible. "Junk food" with wasted calories may fill us up temporarily, but not contain the building blocks to keep us going without breaking down tissue.

Supplementation of the diet is broadcast to us on every side. Because our profession is a "hurry-up, on the go" type of life style, most of us can benefit from the use of balanced supplements. The most important group of vitamins that keeps the groomer "sunny-side-up," are the B complex group. These vitamins have a calming effect when we are under stress. When purchasing this type of vitamin, look for one with a broad spectrum of the B's, especially B1, B6 and B12. Some of the complex B formulations are combined with vitamin C. There is still controversy as to the part vitamin C plays in preventing health problems, but I have found that taking increased dosages of vitamin C when I feel a cold coming on will usually prevent or lessen the symptoms. From 500 to 1,000 mg. per day is said to shorten recovery time from colds.

Vitamin E is especially important for women on the "pill." Estrogen therapy depletes this vitamin so supplementation is necessary. 400 I.U. per day will help this problem. According to some studies, this vitamin seems to help protect cells from the ageing process.

Calcium loss in women over forty depletes the bone structure of women at twice the rate of men. Milk and other dairy products are necessry to replenish calcium for bone regeneration. If you do not use dairy products to any great extent, you can replenish your body's needs with calcium tablets. Some also contain a balanced proportion of vitamin D and phosphorus.

Many people with chronic gastrointestinal problems have been helped by the introduction of the proper amount of fiber into their diets. Fiber is obtained from natural gains and such fruits and vegetables as apples, brussels sprouts, cabbage, lettuce, oranges and celery. A good book on nutrition can help you determine what changes you need to make in your diet.

DISEASES AND PARASITES TRANSMITTABLE TO MAN

Those who handle dogs day in and day out become so conditioned to this environment that they may not think about the possibility of contamination to themselves from the dogs and cats that are groomed. Both type of pets are host to numerous communicable diseases, parasites, or infections that can be transmitted to man. According to *Groomers Gazette*, Vol. 3, No. 2, 1976; the following are some of the problems that can be

Figure 3. Lighting in this grooming area is provided by ceiling fixtures tilted at an angle to provide an arc of light above the grooming tables. A total of three fixtures provide daylight-type lighting to prevent eyestrain. Pastel colored mats on each grooming table make it easier to see the dog's contours and are easy to clean between each grooming. Note supportive chair and hydraulic table that can be raised or lowered for working ease.

transmitted from dog to man: anthrax, amoebic dysentery, brucellosis, chicken pox, diphtheria, heartworm, hookworm, hemorrhagic septicemia, leptospirosis spirosis, mumps, measles, rabies, ringworm, Rocky Mountain spotted fever, roundworms, scarlet fever, strongylosis, salmonella, trichinosis, tapeworm and tuberculosis.

The first area of concern for a groomer should be the treatment of a bite. Bites are the avenue of entry for hemorrhagic septicemia, rabies or other infections, so the immediate treatment of the wound is important. Thoroughly wash the wound with plenty of soap and water for 15 to 20 minutes to lessen the risk of infection. Bleeding should not be stopped immediately since this washes out some of the bacteria. If the wound is serious, involving an artery or vein, pressure must be applied to stop bleeding and the patient transported to the hospital for further treatment.

Always wash your hands before picking up any food. If hands are contaminated in any way from an animal being worked on and you neglect to wash them thoroughly, you are creating an immediate path of entry for germs into your body. Parasites such as roundworm or hookworm can do damage in their larval state to the subcutaneous tissues of the body. Filariae can migrate to your eyes, brain or liver, creating serious damage before they die.

If you ever experience continuous symptoms of fever, chills, headache, and a general feeling of ill health, make your doctor aware that you *do* work with animals so that tests can be run to rule out any possible animal related sources. One disease in particular, canine brucellosis, has the same symptoms as mononucleosis, and might easily be misdiagnosed unless you tell your physician that you work with animals.

TOXOPLASMOSIS

I think a special word of caution about this problem is in order, and I would like to quote directly from a column written by Dr. James Corbin in the September, 1979 issue of *Pet Supplies and Marketing* magazine:

> *Question directed to Dr. Corbin -* "You reported in a previous column that pregnant women should not be permitted to work with cats or clean cages and litter pans since there is a possible contamination from cat feces. What and how?"

Dr. Corbin's answer - "Toxoplasmosis, technically *toxoplasma gondi*, is common throughout the world in almost all species of animals, including man, that have been tested. Many years ago an Englishman, Dr. Hutchison, made the discovery that toxoplasmosis could be transmitted to people by cats. Later it was shown that cats were the definitive host meaning that the coccidia harboring the *T. gondi*, although present in many animals, only complete their life cycle in the cat, thus the cat is the potent reservoir.

Cats shed the coccidial oocytes containing the parasite *T. gondi*. The oocysts are hardy and can survive for long periods of time in feces or under moist conditions. These oocysts can be transmitted by cockroaches and flies that might feed on cat feces and spread the oocytes from place to place.

Toxoplasmosis can cause abortions and neonatal deaths in some mammals including humans, therefore this problem should be avoided. Toxoplasmosis is also thought to be one of the causes of pneumonia under some circumstances. Detection can be made by several different tests. However, the Sabin-Fieldman dye test or the indirect fluorescent antibody test on serum is an acceptable test.

Should one of your employees become pregnant and claim an infection was obtained while working in your store, don't become too alarmed unless two serum samples have been taken two to four weeks apart and demonstrate a significant rise in antibody titer indicating a recent infection. After all, it is estimated one-third of all humans are infected with toxoplasmosis and swine and sheep are commonly infected in the U.S. Affected sheep often abort or if they deliver live lambs they may be weak and die within a few days. Abortions and deaths of young lambs may reach 50 percent in affected sheep flocks.

What you as a store owner can do:
1. Purchase clean, healthy cats, preferably from a single reliable supplier.
2. Constantly check kitten feces to be sure they are free of coccidia (your veterinarian can teach you this procedure in a few minutes); it will require an inexpensive microscope.
3. Treat infected kittens with a coccidiostat to help control coccidia.
4. *Don't permit pregnant personnel to clean litter pans.*
5. Use disposable paper or plastic litter containers if possible and keep them clean.
6. Since toxoplasmosis may be transferred by feeding raw or under-cooked pork or lamb to pets, be sure meat is well-cooked.
7. Warn your employees to exercise caution at home and wash cutting boards, knives, and utensils used to prepare meat prior to cooking. Some contamination of ground beef with pork can occur in meat processing."

From the above article we can glean certain facts. If the grooming shop does cat grooming, extra precautions will be necessary. Also, no pregnant groomer should be allowed to handle cats. Litter boxes must be kept clean, and disposable litter pans used if possible.

CHEMICAL CONTAMINATION

We receive repeated warnings about contamination from chemicals. Groomers handle various pesticides on an almost daily basis, and should receive proper instruction in their use as part of their basic training. Such products as lindane, rotenone, pyrethrum, malathion, butoxide and chlordane are present in flea and tick dips used for parasite control. Groomers should always use protective gloves when they handle these products. Aplastic anemia is thought to be the result of prolonged handling of these chemicals. Pesticides are relatively safe when used only on a periodic basis, but dangerous amounts of chemicals can be absorbed through the pores of the skin if they are handled frequently.

Adequate ventilation in the grooming room is a must. Continued exposure to poisonous fumes can be as dangerous as direct contact, and eventually could produce lung damage. Take the time to read the label of any product you use. Even sprays used to lubricate, or coat and finishing sprays could be harmful if used in an area without ventilation.

Grooming shops in areas around large metropolitan centers may have air pollution problems. Invest in a good air cleaner that helps make your working environment a healthier one. Many manufacturers have produced excellent air cleaners. Be sure the rate of air cleaned per hour is adequate for your needs.

GROOMER FATIGUE AND BURNOUT

Employee burnout in business has been the subject of many articles in recent months. Burnout is a very real problem for the harried, overworked groomer. However, there are definite ways to lessen the impact of stress to the groomer.

First, check your eating habits. If you eat a skimpy breakfast, or none at all, you experience a mid-morning drop in energy as a result of a drop in blood sugar levels. A breakfast low in sugar but high in complex carbohydrates and proteins gives the proper energy lift. Sweets provide false energy that soon lets you down and you feel worse than before.

Carrying extra poundage is tiring, so reducing your weight to its proper level brings greater stamina. Conditioning exercises such as jogging, swimming, riding a bike, or brisk walking help fight fatigue and increase your capacity for a greater work load. Taking time for a walk during the work day relieves tension and helps you work in a more relaxed manner. Don't allow work habits to interfere with proper exercise. You may want to try aerobics or enroll in a health club.

Be sure to sleep or rest the amount of time that suits your body's needs. Everyone is geared to a different inner "time clock." The amount of sleep or rest needed is highly individual so keep track of when you are sleepy and what time you wake up on your own. After a period of time you should find a pattern emerging, and then adjust your sleep needs accordingly. None of us reach our peaks of work capabilities at the same time. Some are "morning people." Others seem to swing into high gear as the sun goes down. Groomers have to challenge their energies to the "nine to five" group, no matter how we really feel inside.

Sometimes we get into our work problems to the extent that we can't seem to enjoy anything. We really need to stop and "smell the roses' occasionally in order to keep the proper perspective in our lives. There are ways to relieve the boredom and lessen the impact of stress in our everyday lives.

One great stride toward reaching the goal of enjoying our work, is to learn to ignore small difficulties. If we allow ourselves to dwell on certain problems of the past, it becomes harder to enjoy the pleasures of the present. Anger over problems that cannot be changed create tension and fatigue. Over the course of the day, our happiness factor is affected by the difficulty of matted dogs, impatient owners, ringing phones and dogs that are ready to bite if we make the wrong move. Our attitude toward the job of turning out the best looking grooming job we are capable of, affect our well-being to a very great extent. Mental attitude *can* make us or break us!

Psychological depression is one of the most difficult things to diagnose. Depression is even difficult to define. Are you unhappy with your job or the people you have to work with? Is your life filled with more problems than you have the strength to cope with? Emotional problems are the most common cause of prolonged fatigue. Not making enough money to take care of needs, having to care for small children as well as a job, problems in a marriage relationship, and a host of other anxieties may make you feel tired. This is your body's way of responding to emotional conflicts. When you bottle up these feelings, and do not bring them out into the open, you begin to show physical symptoms. You may experience sleep disturbances. You waken during the night with thousands of questions pouring through your mind. Then you get up in the morning feeling as though you have been run over by a train.

Vitamin therapy or tranquilizers may bring temporary relief, but unless you get the problem out into the open, you will probably experience prolonged fatigue.

There are some things that you can do for yourself to deal with fatigue and the "washed-out" feeling. First of all, check your eating habits. If you eat a skimpy breakfast, or none at all, you experience a mid-morning drop in energy as a result of a drop of blood sugar levels. You need a breakfast low in sugar but high in the complex carbohydrates and proteins. Sweets give a false lift in energy that soon lets you down and you feel worse than before.

Take a break between dogs sometime in both the morning and afternoon. You may say "I haven't got time," but a five minute walk morning and afternoon will refresh and relax you. Even walking in the rain can be fun if it isn't too cold. Forget you are an adult and splash in the puddles as you did when you were a child.

In a shop employing more than one groomer, get the group together on a regular basis to listen to one another for ideas to improve and make the operation of the shop more efficient. Would it help to schedule the more difficult dogs at the beginning of the week? Is each groomer satisfied with their abilities, or is there room for improvements? As work abilities improve, self-image increases.

If you feel too pushed in your daily routine, check if you have assumed too many jobs. Then free up some time for yourself. Some people are compulsive joiners and doers, volunteering too much of their time to projects that can easily be done by someone else. Choose an outside activity that pleases and relaxes you, perhaps an afternoon at the local library. Or try a new hobby not related to dogs. There are classes for every conceivable craft. Bring some new plants into the shop—a bowl of flowering bulbs is fun to watch. Or ask everyone in the shop to participate in a clean-up, fix-up party. Finish up with a pizza or carry out Chinese food.

One of the most helpful attitudes you can develop is that of closing the mental door to your work problems when you go home. The problems that plague you today will probably be there tomorrow, but you may be able to see them in a different light if you allow your mind a time of refreshment.

Another thing you can do to lift your spirits when you are in the middle of the doldrums is to plan new professional goals. Decide what semi-nars, conventions, workshops, or other types of professional enhancement you want to pursue, then budget for at least one. Would you like to be more visible in the industry? Then enroll in a public speaking course.

Remember, you can't possible do your best work when you are tired and frazzled. Your body must have some relief. If you learn to break up the monotony of what you are doing, and if your working conditions are the best you can possible make them, you will then be able to work in a different ''mental attitude.'' The quiet peace within yourself will be worth the effort.

9
Groomer-Client Relationships

UNDERSTANDING THE CLIENT

Each client's dog plays a particular role in the family circle. People purchase dogs for many reasons, and to some extent, that determines how each dog owner feels about the process of grooming. The elderly enjoy their dogs primarily for the companionship the dog brings into their lives. Perhaps the dog subconsciously replaces a child who no longer plays an active role in their lives. Usually, this age group is the most concerned about the appearance of the dog, and unless hampered by financial conditions, is willing to spend the money to keep up the dog's appearance. They enjoy small dogs that can share a lap or a bed, and so their pet must be kept clean and presentable. The younger family usually chooses a dog to be a playmate and companion for their children. It may be a dog adopted from the humane society, a present from parents, or perhaps a purebred purchased for the purpose of obedience or conformation work in the show ring. The country dog presents a different picture. Usually kenneled outdoors, the animal assumes a strictly utilitarian role such as warning of intruders or guarding livestock. His owners are mostly concerned about parasite control, and will occasionally bring the animal to the grooming shop for a bath and utility haircut.

Single people choose dogs akin to their own personalities. The shy, timid, fearful person generally brings a dog to be groomed that has all the same characteristics. Positive, happy surroundings and an extroverted personality in the owner usually produces a similar personality in the dog.

Groomers are in a position to be caring people. Be aware of the client's general appearance, mood and attitude when the dog is brought in for grooming. One facet of the man-dog relationship is the way the dog reflects stresses that are present within its family. For example, a dog may display symptoms of illness because its owner is ill. A beloved playmate leaving home for a distant school, job, or marriage produces stress for the dog. Home conditions may be affecting the dog's behavior. Listen carefully to comments made by the dog's owner when he brings the dog for grooming; they may help you understand the dog's erratic behavior.

Sometimes an owner's concern for their pet outweighs concerns for their own needs and they deprive themselves in order to properly care for him. If you suspect that might be the case, especially with senior citizens, you can make special grooming rates available in needy cases.

The most important link between the groomer and the client is communication. Be sure the client does not have unrealistic expectations of the services that can be performed. For instance, does the client understand that a groomer cannot fluff dry and hand-scissor a badly matted coat that should be stripped? Emphasize that the comfort of the dog is far more important than appearances. In reality, the dog does not know the difference unless the owner makes him feel ashamed by using a negative tone of voice when picking him up. Dogs have an uncanny ability to sense their owner's pleasure or

Figure 1. A client with a difficult dog stays to assist the groomer during the grooming process.

displeasure and react accordingly. If it has been necessary to strip a dog, it is important to talk to the customer before presenting the dog. Appeal to their concern that the dog not suffer torment as they would be the case if the groomer tried to remove the impacted mats. Reinforce the importance that the customer *not* ridicule the dog's appearance. This lessens the visual impact for the client when he first sees the dog after it has been stripped.

NOTIFYING A CLIENT OF AN INJURY

If the groomer inflicts a small nick or abrasion in the skin of the dog or cat during grooming, for whatever reason, it should be pointed out when the owner returns to pick up the pet. Offer any product or advice that will promote healing. It would be wise to also offer a ten percent discount for the grooming done that day.

If a more serious injury should occur, contact the owners immediately to notify them that the pet is being taken to the veterinarian for treatment. The name of your client's veterinarian should be on your pet grooming document in case you cannot contact the owner. If you have not been able to

reach the clients before they return for the dog, calmly explain the circumstances, and if appropriate, offer that your insurance will pay the cost of treatment.

One problem that all groomers face is how to deal with the owner of an aggressive dog. No owner wants to admit to owning a dog that is difficult to handle. However, the groomer has to be honest with the client. If the dog is too unruly, try to relieve the problem in a diplomatic manner so the customer is not offended. Perhaps the dog should be taken to a veterinarian to be tranquilized before coming to the grooming shop. In that case, request the owner to stay nearby to help, if necessary, during grooming.

HANDLING THE ANGRY CLIENT

Occasionally competent groomers encounter a client that is not satisfied with the type of grooming that has been done. This may happen if the groomer neglects to establish the condition of the coat and what grooming *can* be performed before the client leaves the shop. Sometimes, from lack of communication, the groomer will do a clip totally different than what the owner of the pet had in mind. A diplomatic, caring response would be to offer to do the grooming at the next scheduled appointment for a greatly reduced fee or at no charge. A request from the pet owner for a minor change in the grooming pattern should be done immediately if at all possible.

If the groomer remembers that a client probably retains only one-third of the information given, it will go a long way toward establishing good communication. Whenever a dog comes in for grooming, examine it immediately and write down on the client card any explicit directions given by the owner. If the condition of the dog makes it impossible to fulfill those directions, *be sure* the owner understands the alternatives. One time I accepted a badly matted Maltese for grooming. Knowing how tender their skin is for extensive brushing and de-matting, I said, "This dog is badly matted and I will have to *cut it down.*" After the owner left, I proceeded to strip off the matted coat. When the owner returned and saw the dog, she was in tears. She said, "But you told me you would only have to *cut it shorter.*" My choice of words *did not* communicate what I knew in my mind would have to be done. She was terribly upset when she left the shop. Ten minutes later I received a call from her very irate husband who could not stand the thought of having to walk a naked dog.

Another important role the groomer plays is that of a teacher—particularly to the owner of a new puppy. Take time to demonstrate proper care of coat, ears, and toenails. You then establish a link in what may become a long and satisfying relationship with a new client. This kind of caring attitude promotes goodwill and excellent word-of-mouth recommendations. Some clients will come with specific questions as to proper dog care. Others may be too embarrassed to ask questions for fear of appearing dumb. When answering questions or volunteering information about proper care, be sure the pet owner understands what is being said. Do not use groomer jargon. Use correct terminology that the dog owner can easily understand.

CLIENT EDUCATION

Every grooming shop should have some type of pamphlet explaining grooming procedures. It should discuss the need of regular grooming for the well-being of the animal. An explanation of how the determination is made to strip the dog should be included. Make sure the pamphlet stresses ''at

Figure 2. Finished, and ready to go home.

home'' care between grooming shop visits. The pamphlet can be helpful in establish payment policies and stressing that grooming is done on a cash basis.

Have a sign made to place on or near your check-out counter that states your payment policies. Do not accept charges unless the shop permits the use of specific credit cards. The average groomer does not have time to keep a double-entry bookkeeping system and send out billings. State clearly that an extra charge will be made for any bad checks.

Clients who do not pick up their dog before a specified time at the end of the day should be charged an extra fee based on the length of time you must wait for them. The average charge is $5.00 per half hour of extra waiting time. If the owner has notified you of an emergency that prevents his or her return on time, use your own judgement in deciding if the rule should be waived.

Owning a pet serves a highly personal need. The grooming shop can relate to that need by personalizing the walls of the shop with framed photos of some of the attractive dog clients. A bulletin board where owners contribute pictures of their dogs would also be nice. A notebook containing before and after pictures of grooming for various breeds can help show a client what to expect. This is particularly helpful when explaining the design grooming for mixed breeds.

CEMENTING GROOMER-CLIENT RELATIONSHIPS

When meeting a customer for the first time, your attitude can make or break a relationship. A friendly smile goes a long way. A person coming to the shop for the first time is going to be hesitant, and it is up to the groomer to put the client at ease. One of the poorest openers is ''What can I do for you?'' This tends to put a client on the defensive. The first impression your client receives of your professionalism is based on how you relate to your customer. Allowances must be made for ''people factors.''

Individualize and personalize the shop as much as possible. Make the client aware that their dog will receive the best of care. This may be difficult on a day when every dog tries to bite and ''Murphy's Law'' rears its ugly head at every turn.

There are times when a groomer can cement groomer-client relationships by being helpful in time of stress within the client's family. If there has been a death in the family, and the dog must be brought in for grooming on a last-minute basis, it would be a nice gesture to do the grooming on a "no-charge" basis. There are times when a family must have a dog groomed because of the arrival of unexpected guests. For a wedding, the family might enjoy having ribbons in the dog's hair that match the color scheme of the wedding party, especially if the dog is to be included in family pictures. Small dog owners appreciate seasonally colored bows fastened in the coat. Any unexpected nicety performed by the groomer cements the groomer-client bond.

Public relations play an important part in whether or not a shop is successful. Images must be positive and desirable. An interesting experiment can be conducted in the shop that will give you an idea of how the general public sees, or rather "hears" what is going on in the shop. Bring a tape recorder to the shop and turn it on during different periods of the day possibly without the knowledge of the others in the shop. Record how adept the groomers are in meeting the clients and accepting their dogs. Determine whether questions are answered correctly and to the customer's satisfaction. The general mood of the shop as the day progresses is recorded as clients bring in and pick up their dogs. This tape could be played back later as a learning experience for all employees.

The area outside the shop should be kept free of litter at all times. Make sure that all debris (loose papers, dried leaves, or any other mess) is removed from the entry area. Occasionally, a dog will defecate or urinate when leaving the shop. This must be cleaned up immediately, not only for appearance sake, but to eliminate possible contamination to another dog. Step outside occasionally during the day to be sure that there is no excrement or debris detracting from the shop's appearance.

TELEPHONE COMMUNICATION

A telephone call is often the first contact with a potential customer. Telephone manners, then, spell success or failure in convincing the dog owner at the other end of the line that *your* shop is best qualified to groom the dog. Always answer the phone by giving the name of the shop, followed by your name. This reassures the caller that he has reached the correct number. If the caller is a regular customer, he will then give his name and request an appointment.

If the caller replies, "I would like some information about your grooming procedure and prices," proceed as follows:
1. Ask "*Who's* calling, please?"
2. Ask what type of dog the caller owns.
3. Determine the *age* of the dog.
4. If the dog is a puppy, find out if this is to be its first grooming. If not, ask *how long* it has been since the dog was last groomed.
5. Try to find out the *general condition* of the dog, and if the owner has done any care at home. This question may produce any number of excuses for lack of grooming, some of which may be quite ingenious.
6. The next step is the *explanation of the pricing* policy. No matter if pricing is done by the breed with extra charges for various services, or is based on an hourly charge, make sure the caller understands that it is impossible to give a firm price commitment until he brings in the dog. This is particularly important for mixed breeds where each one is different.
7. The potential customer should be assured of a complete job, so mention *what the grooming procedure entails* such as bathing, fluff-drying, hand scissoring, nail trimming, ear cleaning and a general check for health problems.
8. At this time, confirm a *time of appointment* that is convenient for the customer.
9. Be sure the customer knows exactly where you are *located*.
10. Request the *customer's phone number and address*.
11. Suggest that the dog be brought to the shop for a *visit* to familiarize him with the sights and sounds of the shop.

Appointments are not always kept. Don't stew and fret. There may be a legitimate reason why the appointment was not kept, or the customer may have forgotten about it. Wait for an hour, then call. Be pleasant and don't sound upset. Check to see if there were problems in finding the shop. Tell the customer that the time slot is still open, if he brings the dog over immediately. If some emergency has come up just make a new appointment and indicate an apology for the inconvenience. Perhaps the dog was taken elsewhere for grooming and the owner was embarrassed to cancel the appointment with you. In any case, make sure the customer understands your willingness to be of help in the future.

When a new grooming salon opens in an area, or a home groomer begins to advertise extensively, there may be many calls requesting price quotations for grooming various breeds. Some calls come from comparison shoppers whose only concern is price. Other calls may be from groomers in the area checking prices. No matter who is calling, the name of the game is to stay cool and collected, answering questions with no indication of impatience. If, after giving requested information, the caller still won't commit to an appointment, don't be upset. Chances are the dog is in such bad shape the owner knows he will be in for a higher than normal charge and is calling around in hopes of finding a bargain.

Can you answer the phone with a smile in your voice when things aren't going too well? Perhaps you are in the middle of working on an obnoxious dog. Let the phone ring a couple of times while you think of a pleasant mental image, take a deep breath, and then answer. The smile in your voice establishes a positive link with your caller. An impatient answer may cause your customer to take his business elsewhere.

Telephone practice sessions can be of help to everyone in the shop. Various members of the grooming staff can pretend to be customers, while others answer, giving the correct information. It is usually best to have only one person in charge of answering the phone and giving out appointments. Speech and vocabulary should be taken into consideration when deciding who will be in charge of answering the phone.

Minor as it may seem, telephone location is very important. If your shop is large, extensions will be necessary. Also, it is more convenient if the phone is installed with a long enough cord so that it can comfortably reach the grooming table, making it easier to talk and work at the same time. A shoulder support on the receiver will free both hands for grooming.

Figure 3. A lot of T.L.C. while you are working with your dog may get you this kind of response when the job is completed.

10
Advertising

When you open a small business, one of the most important steps to take is the development of your own logo (identifying graphic) or logotype (type style uniquely designed for your business name). Just as a good logo is worth millions to a large company, your logo must be effective in your area even though it is on a smaller scale. It should make a statement about what you do. Stylized dogs, scissors, bathtubs, and clippers have all been successfully incorporated into interesting logos. Whatever the final design, it should be easily recognizable, yet unique to you. If you are artistically talented, you might like to

design your own logo, but it is usually advisable to enlist the services of a good graphic designer or commercial artist. This is a well-spent investment. The artist will develop your ideas into a workable symbol of identification.

The Velvet Bow logo was developed to create the impression of a "boutique-type" shop. I wanted the dog owner to be aware that fine grooming would make the dog look "elegant," hence, the mirror and fancy pillow. The various bottles and containers shown would emphasize that the dog would not only *look* pretty but would *smell* pretty too.

After you see what the artist has to offer, live with the design for a while. Ask friends and business acquaintances for their reaction. Is the logo easily identified with the grooming industry? If you don't feel good about it, go back to the artist for re-evaluation. Be *absolutely certain* you can live with this image for the duration of your business before you accept it.

Once you feel comfortable with the logo, use it on all business stationary and forms, Yellow Pages ads, advertisements, and your outdoor sign. If you sell retail merchandise and feel you can afford the extra expense, having your logo printed on your product bags sends your message out with everyone that leaves the shop.

ADVERTISING

Perhaps you are starting your business on a shoestring. How do you get your message out to

Figure 1. Logo for the Velvet Bow.

the general public? An inexpensive way to begin is to make some posters with your name, the name of the shop, your telephone number, and some sort of catchy phrase emphasizing the need for professional grooming. Deliver the posters to laundromats, supermarkets, shopping malls or any other place that offers a community bulletin board. Staple a number of small pieces of paper to the bottom of the poster with your phone number on them so potential customers can tear off the telephone number for future reference.

Creating steady income throughout the year is the prime reason for any type of advertising. Decide what percentage of your gross income is to be devoted to advertising and then determine where best to use your advertising dollar. The average output for advertising is ten percent of gross income. Most grooming businesses never reach this figure.

Research on the subject has determined that advertising in the Yellow Pages gives the groomer the greatest return for money spent. If you are the only groomer within a large area, you have it made as long as you do a good job. When advertising in a large metropolitan area, make sure your ad has something unique to catch the eye of the potential client; this is where an interesting logo plays such an important part. Also, advertise in a number of suburban telephone books if you are in an area where there are many suburbs close together. Think of your shop as being the center of a circle with a five-mile radius, and try to advertise in all phone

Figure 3. One would expect the very finest grooming available from the impression received when viewing the attractive exterior of The Cut Above located in Larchmont, New York. The shop is owned by Helen Trainer. (Photo courtesy of Val Penstone)

books within that area. You may think this is a large area to cover, but people are willing to travel great distances if they find a good groomer. If you have completed any phases of the Certification program, be sure to emphasize this in your ad. Extra services such as fluff-drying or hand-scissoring should also be given special mention.

Newspaper ads receive a more reasonable rate if you place them on a regular basis. Ads can be used effectively to coincide with certain holidays. However, most groomers are normally busy at that time anyway, and need to encourage off-period business. One way is to run a coupon discount for ''new customers only'' during a particular time segment. Be sure the ad specifies the time period; you don't need someone coming in for free grooming or a discount rate during the Christmas rush.

Television advertising is far too expensive for the average groomer. The only shops that would be able to take advantage of this media would be those located in large shopping malls that have joint advertising promotions. Radio is not a very effective tool because people seldom really *listen*. They are so conditioned to hearing piped-in music that spot commercials don't make much of an impact. However, if you are located in a rural area, you might consider sponsoring a local news broadcast. However, even that may be cost prohibitive. From all the various forms of advertising done at The Velvet Bow, the greatest response was always from the Yellow Pages and word-of-mouth recommendations.

Figure 2. Peter's Posh Pets, located in London, England, is owned by Peter Young, the 1984 Reserve Winner of the first International Grooming Contest. From the insignia on the window, one is made aware that Peter is familiar with correct Terrier grooming. (Photo courtesy of Val Penstone)

Figure 4. Cedar Dale Kennels is located on a major Midwestern highway outside of Lake Geneva, Wisconsin. This kennel and grooming facility is owned by Janice Skender. Janice began her grooming career when she lived with her parents in Westchester, Illinois. I saw her beautiful grooming on her Poodles at obedience classes, and asked her to work at The Velvet Bow. Her dream was always to have her own kennel, and now that dream has come true. Notice that her advertising sign is large, attractive, and easy to read. (Photo courtesy of Janice Skender)

PUBLICITY

Even small towns have a weekly newspaper. Any of the following newsworthy items should be submitted to the paper in the form of a news release: attending a seminar or groomers' convention; winning a placement in a grooming contest; completion of any part of the Professional Pet Groomers Certification Program; or the sponsorship of any type of local pet show. Submit a photo with the article when possible.

Take your business card to every veterinary office in the area. Invite the veterinarian to inspect your facility and make him aware that you groom to the correct breed profile.

Visit the local humane society. Offer to groom newly adopted dogs at a reduced fee, or groom for no fee to help the humane society place a particular dog. Some dogs cannot be placed until they have been cleaned up. Remember to use caution when handling a dog from this environment, as disease and parasites are frequent problems. The stress of being lost, abandoned, or put up for adoption is so traumatic that the animal may be especially difficult to groom and a prime candidate to be a fear biter. Make every effort to work quietly and make the dog feel at ease and loved. A kind word goes

a long way toward obtaining a positive response from the animal.

Visit local schools and offer your services for any animal related programs. If you feel particularly ambitious, organize a local pet show for the children of the community. Lower grade children are particularly delighted and attentive when allowed to watch the grooming procedure. Scout groups can earn points toward their animal care badges by participating in a grooming program sponsored by your shop.

You also want to promote yourself as a problem solver. Advertise your willingness to help with coat care problems by offering periodic classes in coat care.

The role of good public relations is to give the general public a favorable image of your shop. Let them know that your knowledge and grooming ability is an important link in the health care of their pet. We live in a competitive world. The name of your shop and the logo you develop must project an interesting and knowledgeable image. However, no matter how catchy the name or how elegant the image, unless you treat your clients fairly and their pets with utmost consideration, your advertising dollar *cannot* have its proper impact.

11
Retail Merchandising in the Grooming Shop

The American public spends billions of dollars annually for various pet supplies. Dollar estimates of spending for these products continue to rise at five to ten percent per year. Stop for a moment and think of all the places pet supplies are sold. Supermarkets, drug and variety stores, hardware and department stores, and mass merchandisers all have specialized departments to encourage the shopper to buy products for ''bowser'' or ''kitty,'' as well as for other types of pets. Centrally located pet shops do well even during periods of recession.

Should the groomer take the time and effort to cash in on this profit bonanza? *Yes,* because the pet groomer has a potential market at her fingertips. A captive audience visits the grooming shop twice for each appointment—once to bring the pet in for grooming, and again to pick it up. With a little effort the groomer can learn various product lines and select items that a pet owner needs or will buy as an impulse item.

The grooming shop that carries pet products is faced with two questions; what products to carry and how much space to allocate for that purpose. Large pet supply distributors have catalogs larger than a big city telephone book. How do you decide what items would be most likely to generate sales from your grooming customers? Another consideration is the potential for walk-in trade based on your location.

The May/June 1980 issue of *Groom & Board* magazine published the results of a survey that was randomly sent to groomers in all parts of the country. Some interesting facts were brought to light.

Eighty-two-and-one-half percent of those questioned carried products for resale. These sales represented twenty percent or better of the total income generated by the shop. This would lead us to conclude that *any* grooming shop that has the space, desire, and an active promotion of its pet supplies, could see a twenty percent increase in yearly income *without having to book extra grooming appointments.*

The approximate area devoted to sales averaged thirty percent of the total shop area. This included pegboard displays, glass counters, and various types of shelving. The best selling items and their percentage of gross sales were as follows:

Collars/Leads	22%
Combs/Brushes	9.5%
Shampoos	6.5%
Flea Spray	6%
Rawhide Chews	5%
Coats/Sweaters	5%
Toys	5%
Supplements/Vitamins	4%
Food	3.5%
Foggers	3%
Skin & Coat Conditioners	3%
Ear Medications	2%
Flea Powders	2%
Flea Shampoo	2%
Other	10.5%

Note that if all preparations for flea eradication had been placed in one category, the percentage of sales totals thirteen percent.

The groomers used an average of three or four distributors to obtain products, and thirty-five percent responded positively to having received merchandising assistance from their distributors. The average retail value of the merchandise inventory was $5,294.95. However, more than eight percent of the respondents *did not* know the value of their inventory. Mark-ups on merchandise varied from thirty-five percent for food to sixty-five percent or higher for impulse items such as collars, coats, sweaters and toys. Mark-ups depend upon the economic stability of the area, the appeal of the product, and its reception in the marketplace.

The average percentage of gross income budgeted for advertising was only five percent and the grooming industry spends sixty-seven percent of its advertising dollars for Yellow Pages advertising. That would mean that less than thirty-five percent of moneys set aside for advertising were spent on other media such as regular newspaper ads, direct mail, flyers, radio or other media.

WHAT PRODUCTS SHOULD YOU CARRY?

Assuming that there is limited space for retail inventory, what items will bring the groomer the best return for money invested? Combs and brushes are high on the list; also, various slicker and pin brushes for the long-coated breeds and curry combs for short hairs. Encourage the grooming client to use the proper tools for home care.

Collars, leads, and obedience choke chains are good items. These do not take a great deal of space when displayed on a peg board. If your location is in a high income area, include the fancier jeweled, studded, and design leather collars.

Rawhide chews and toys of soft latex and hard rubber sell especially well during the holidays. Display these items close to the checkout counter where they get peak exposure. Place large, glass fish bowls containing small chew items on the

Figure 1. A corner of the waiting room at Cedar Dale Kennels near Lake Geneva, Wisconsin. Notice the clever display of chew items and toys at the left. The rattan shelf unit holds sprays, conditioners, shampoos and vitamin supplements. The corner peg boards contain collars, leashes and a variety of other items. Although the area used is small, it is effectively managed by shop owner, Janice Skender, for good monetary return. (Photo - D. Walin)

counter for last minute impulse add-on sales. These also make inexpensive gifts for children to buy for their pets.

Flea and tick products have become items to sell year round. Educate customers to use various products to eradicate these pests in their homes, yards, and automobiles as well as on their pets. Caution customers to take a familiar brand of flea and tick repellent with them on vacation. There may be differences of opinion on using flea and tick collars, but remember that *over 50 million* are sold each year. These collars are also available with natural repellents for customers who prefer organic products.

Let your customers know that the brands of products *you* carry are often of better quality than those found in the supermarket. All flea and tick products *are not* the same. All groomers should spend time at pet industry trade shows and seminars talking to product representatives and listening to the discussions of various veterinarians in order to be educated about flea and tick related problems.

Coats and sweaters are seasonal items. Although your largest inventory of these items should be ready to sell from September through February, always have a few sweaters on hand for the owners of sick, old, or freshly stripped pets that may need extra warmth.

Depend on sales representatives to advise you when to purchase seasonal items. Remember, buying ahead for the coming season or holiday guarantees that you can get the best selection. When you are actually into a season, it can be difficult to get what you want.

If you decide to carry books, concentrate on those that describe the breeds that are groomed most often, and books on general care for various types of pets. You can always special order any other book that a customer may need from the book listings supplied by publishing houses. Obedience books, ranging from the novice through utility

Figure 2. Part of the merchandising area of The Velvet Bow. Products, grouped by type, are displayed on glass shelves. A raised, formica-covered platform below shows off various dog and cat beds. The glass shelves are attached directly to the wall by metal clips. They can be easily dismantled for scrubbing or painting. The length of this display wall is about ten feet.

training are also good sellers. In a small shop, book shelves may be arranged behind the checkout counter so that they are not soiled by general handling.

If the shop has adequate room, consider such items as dog and cat beds and cushions, and perhaps one or two items of cat furniture. These can range from inexpensive cushions to the plushy, velour-type.

If the shop has an adequate, dry, cool, storage area you will want to consider stocking dog food as a good source of sales. Canned foods are not profitable because supermarkets have a large variety at prices the average shop cannot duplicate, but specialty dry foods such as *Hills Science Diet®* or other high quality feeds do well when they become established as the food *you* recommend to your customers to keep their dogs in good condition.

Shampoos and coat conditioners appeal to owners of the small breeds. They may want to bathe their dogs at home between groomings, and if you educate them properly they learn to use the correct type of shampoo. Conditioners are an important add-on item to use at home for ease of brushing and to prevent retangling of the coat.

Dog and cat dishes sell well through most of the year and are especially good items for Christmas sales. Keep a supply of practical dishes of various sizes for cats and dogs, and for the holidays add some designer dishes. These are so attractive that the owner might purchase them on impulse as a Christmas present for their pet.

The home groomer may also want to offer certain products for sale, especially if there is no nearby pet shop. It may be profitable to carry a small supply of such things as collars, leashes, toys, and a few sweaters and coats. The inventory could be increased for the Christmas season, but kept at a minimum the rest of the year. Any item a customer might want can now be obtained by mail order, with quick delivery the norm for most of the country.

Shop owners and home groomers alike must obtain sales tax numbers and file proper returns. The thought of having to file these reports is one reason many grooming shops and home groomers are reluctant to offer products for sale, but I can't imagine anyone who would object to increasing gross sales by twenty percent or more. Start small! *Reinvest* money from product sales to enlarge your inventory to its fullest potential. Ask your accountant to teach you how to file the necessary reports. Sell down your inventory toward the end of the fiscal year to avoid paying tax on your inventory.

At some time in the future, you may find that sales have increased to the extent you can employ another person to do your ordering, product management, and selling. Wouldn't that be a worthwhile investment in the future of your business?

DISPLAYING MERCHANDISE

The method you use to display your merchandise may determine how quickly the products turn a profit for you. Peg board is the ideal display vehicle for such items as leads, collars, chains, and items that are blister packed. Rawhide chews, latex and hard rubber toys, combs and brushes as well as other items are packaged in this manner. Don't display items haphazardly. Organize them into groups of similar items.

Counters with glass tops and sides show jeweled collars with matching sweaters and coats to advantage. These displays are particularly effective if they have self-contained lighting. Also, higher priced items such as stainless steel combs and expensive brushes are less inclined to "walk off" if placed in a display case. Some product manufacturers supply free display units if you buy a certain quantity. Determine if you want to tie up that much cash flow just to get the display. When funds are limited, buy just enough to stock your shelves.

Shelving can be assembled from a variety of materials. Wood, metal, and glass all lend themselves to attractive displays, but glass shelving is the prettiest and most complementary to a boutique-type decor. The wall behind the glass can be painted a soft pastel color which is an excellent background to emphasize the packaging of most pet products. Since glass shelving is transparent, it gives the airy feeling of a larger shop. Metal shelf units are most often used for displaying product in grooming or pet shops. The shelves can be varied for products of different heights. They are not as pretty as glass shelves, but are more practical for displaying heavy items.

EFFECTIVE SALES TECHNIQUES

There are certain subtle ways your behavior can put a potential customer at ease. Begin your conversation with a general remark about the weather or the attractive appearance of the client, not with the overused and impersonal "May I help

Figure 3: This glass display case at The Velvet Bow contains jeweled and fancy leather collars, designer dog and cat dishes, and other fancy items. The pegboard wall behind the counter is used to display many different types of items. A trophy, won by the owner at a grooming contest, is prominently displayed.

you''. A *smile* will further put the customer at ease. To encourage further conversation, ask what type of pet the customer has. Listen for clues that indicate his or her needs or expectations. Only when the salesperson thoroughly understands a problem should she suggest a product to fulfill the need. This is the point at which a sale is made or lost. If you have the knowledge of products that would be satisfactory, and their correct usage, it indicates to the customer that you can be trusted as a source of educational helps. People do not read labeling thoroughly, so take the time to go over directions for product usage and offer information beyond that on the label. The customer may well return to you because you took the time to eliminate a potential problem by elaborating on the product's instructions.

The average customer is aware of only a few pet products. These are brought to their attention by large companies that can afford television, newspaper and magazine advertising. The products are usually found in supermarkets and chain stores. However, many of these products are *not* the best available. By attending trade shows, seminars, and grooming demonstrations, groomers can gain product information that can be effectively presented to their customers. Product literature from the manufacturer should be prominently displayed since these pamphlets help sell the product. Take the literature home and study it. Know what you are selling. Help the rest of your staff increase their knowledge by discussing a few new products with them each week. Everyone in the shop should be able to help when a customer is in doubt as to product choice.

A big ''no-no'' in product display is dusty merchandise. Another is empty spaces on the shelves. Grooming shop personnel have to do *more* housekeeping due to the problem of blowing hair. You might want to hire a student to come in after school to dust and clean as you are closing for the day. Emphasize the need to keep products neatly arranged and to spread the available products to fill empty spaces until the next shipment arrives. Check all new merchandise and return bent or broken items to the manufacturer or salesman. Continuing price changes require that you check old prices and update because you must pass on price increases to the customer or your profit margin will decrease.

Promoting merchandise to your customers is an attitude that should always be at ''ready-alert.'' Does the dog or cat you are working on need a new collar? Tell the customer. Is there a problem with fleas and ticks? Suggest a flea and tick eradication program. Does the pet's coat seem dry, brittle or dull looking? Suggest a conditioner to be applied or a supplement to add to the diet. When a customer brings a new puppy to the shop, be ready with a complete list of necessary products for the new pet. It should include such items as a collar, leash, I.D. tag, water and food dishes, a bed or crate, and various toys for chewing and play. If you sell dog food, give a sample of puppy diet. As a courtesy, check and clean ears, cut toenails if needed, and give a short check-up to see if everything looks normal. This free service may bring you a new customer who will support your shop for many years.

Don't try to be all things to all people. Concentrate on providing only quality products that quickly turn a profit. Offer better products and the expertise to sell them. Pet owners are loyal and will return over and over to those who offer expert service and in whom they have confidence.

CREATING INTEREST IN YOUR SHOP

How do you get your name and that of your shop before the general public without buying advertising space? The opening of a new shop is an ideal time to introduce yourself to the editor of the local newspaper. Make an appointment, dress professionally, bring a typed memo for the editor, and ask that a picture be taken when the shop is ready to have its opening. If you are purchasing a shop that has been in existence for some time, make a list of the services that the shop offers together with any future changes you plan to make. Comprise a list of personnel and include the job each performs. If there is a specialist in some department, be sure that person receives extra attention. If your groomers have attended well-known grooming schools, or have completed certification examinations, that information would also be of interest to the reader. Make a list of the various categories of products you offer to the public. Keep your editor informed about any legislation that pertains to pet owners.

The local Chamber of Commerce offers opportunities for members to serve on a committee and make business contacts. Service organizations are always happy to have volunteers, and if you are new in town, this is one of the best ways to become acquainted with your fellow business people. Chamber news about you will specify your business and bring you to the attention of the general public.

DOES YOUR SHOP APPEAL TO THE CUSTOMER?

As the door opens and a customer enters your shop, what impression would the customer's senses of sight, smell, touch, and hearing convey? Think about this for a moment. Have you ever gone into a business to look for an item you need, but after being in the store for a few minutes, you left because something about the place didn't create the mood to shop there? There are many factors that can create a negative climate for sales.

The first impression the customer receives is visual. Is the lighting correct to properly illuminate your product displays? What about organization?

Are similar products grouped together for easy identification? These factors can create an atmosphere for the customer to browse and think about product purchases. A bright, cheerful and nicely decorated shop establishes the first step to customer acceptance.

To be brutally frank, how does your shop smell? The time to note any offensive odors is when you first enter the shop in the morning. Sense of smell can be dulled if surrounded by odors for any length of time. Unfortunately, some of the nicest looking shops immediately assault the olfactory senses of someone coming in from the outside. Pet odors, stale tobacco, and odors from mold and mildew are particularly offensive. Perfume and slightly antiseptic odors can be expected in a grooming shop, just as certain smells are associated with barber and beauty shops. Other odors should not be tolerated.

Customers should not be assaulted by unpleasant noise. Of course there will be occasional barking in a grooming shop. However, loud, raucous music, foul language, or continually barking dogs must be controlled. This should be the norm for every grooming shop, whether products are offered for sale or not. You may not appreciate "canned" music, but it does create a quiet, gentle background of sound that doesn't offend the ears.

Do you enjoy going into a nice cool store when the temperature outside climbs into the uncomfortable range? What about cozy warmth when the freezing winds of winter assault the body? Climate control is important in the grooming shop, too. Select the correct temperature to keep dogs, groomers, and customers comfortable. Psychologically you are encouraging your customer to stay and shop when you offer comfortable surroundings.

Sometimes it is difficult to *honestly* evaluate your own shop. The realization of how quickly we can lose a customer's business because of negative impressions should prompt quick correction of any problem. Consider the things that can make *your* shop *tops* in its field.

12
Clipper Maintenance and Blade Care

BLADE CLEANING

"A question always heard at seminars is "Why do my clipper blades get dull so quickly? What can I do to get longer wear between sharpenings?" To maintain instrument quality of Oster clippers and blades, please follow the instructions as given.

Let's talk about new blades. Blades are costly, and to get long life and usage, you must follow certain steps. New blades must be attached to the clipper and operated in *Oster Blade Wash®* to remove the rust protective coating. This coating must be removed from the cutting surfaces or they will not clip through the coat.

Position the clipper and blade in a flat dish as shown in *Figure 1.* Fill the dish with just enough *Blade Wash®* to cover the blade. Turn on the clipper. As the blade begins to run in this solution, you will hear a change in the hum of the running blade. It begins at a low pitch, and as the coating is removed, the blade runs faster and the hum rises to a higher pitch. When there is no further change in the hum of the running blade, you are ready to proceed to the next step.

Remove the blade from the clipper and wipe the blade as dry as possible (*Fig. 2*). Use a lint-free cloth. It is important not to leave *Blade Wash®* on

Figure 1. Submerge and run the blade in *Oster Blade Wash*. Cover *only* the blade with the solution.

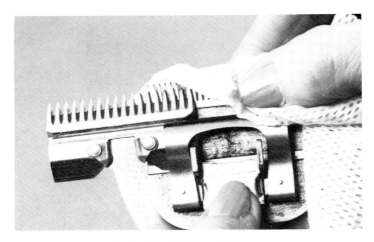

Figure 2. Wipe the blade with a lint-free cloth.

Figure 5. Place drop of oil where shown. *Do not* drop oil on teeth.

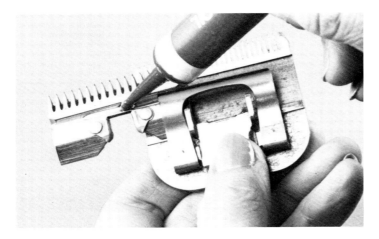

Figure 3. Place drop of oil on running rail as shown.

Figure 6. Use small, stiff brush to remove accumulated matter and hair from between the teeth of the blade.

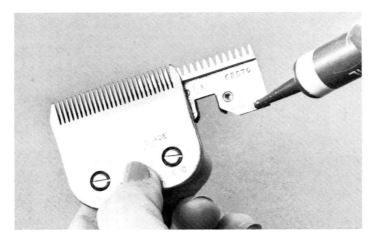

Figure 4. Place drop of oil as shown.

Figure 7. Separate the cutting edges of the blade as shown and brush away any loose matter. Hold the blade to the light to make sure that no small hairs are caught in the teeth.

Figure 8. *Oster Blade Wash, Kool Lube* lubricant, and *Spray Disinfectant* are formulated to be used together for the proper care of your Oster clippers and blades. Frequently spray *Kool Lube* through the teeth of the blades during grooming to lubricate, cool the blades, and remove loose hair particles. Remember to check blades frequently during grooming for heat build-up and spray entire blade with *Kool Lube* to avoid clipper burn.

the cutting surfaces. If you do so, hair will accumulate in the blade quicker and may cause the blade to run slower because of the build-up of hair between the cutting surfaces.

Next, carefully slide the cutting surfaces apart far enough to oil the running rails (*Figs. 3, 4 and 5*). Place a drop of oil on each running rail as indicated in these photos. More is not better. Do not drip oil indiscriminately onto the teeth of the blade. This may cause tiny pieces of hair to stick between the teeth, making the blades jam or pick at the coat.

Slide the cutting surfaces together, attach the blade on the clipper, turn on the clipper and as it is running, spray *Oster Kool-Lube®* through the blade teeth. This will give sufficient lubrication to the teeth. When you are working on a dirty, matted coat such as would be the case when you are stripping a dog, it is wise to stop periodically and run your clipper blade through the steps shown in *Figures 1 through 5* to prevent excessive wear to the blades.

At the end of each grooming day, or if your blades begin to pick during the course of a grooming, prepare your blades again. Use a small, stiff brush to remove loose hair or any accumulated

matter from between the teeth (*Figs. 6 & 7*). (Vegetable brushes and old toothbrushes work fine.) Hold the blade up to light and examine the spaces between the teeth. All hairs must be removed or the blade will continue to jam. (When examining blades from groomers who complain that their blades are dull and do not work, we frequently find matter and hair between the teeth of the blade.) Relubricate with oil (*Figs. 3, 4 & 5*). Spray with *Kool-Lube®* lubricant, wipe blade surfaces that touch the coat and try the blade. You may find you have saved yourself the cost of unnecessary sharpening. Cleaning your blades in this manner may also save your temper and your sanity when working on Bedlington Terriers and other extremely soft coats.

If you clip a dog that has questionable skin condition or after removing filthy coat during pre-work, coat from around the anus, vaginal area, or penis, always spray your blade with *Oster Spray Disinfectant®* before using the blade for any other purpose.

The three Oster products shown in *Figure 8* are formulated to be used together to protect, lubricate, and disinfect your blades.

Figure 9. Oil *Oster A5* clipper as shown. Oil only if motor develops a squeal. Do not over oil.

CLIPPER OILING

ALL MAINTENANCE IS DONE WITH THE CLIPPER UNPLUGGED.

Clippers come to you from the manufacturer properly greased and oiled. There is no need to oil or grease the clipper until it has been in use for quite some time. How soon you need to add oil or grease depends on the amount of use your clipper receives. If your clipper develops a squeal during use, inject a drop of oil in the oil cup. The *Oster A5®* clipper has one oiling cup (*Fig. 9*). Two places require oiling in the *Oster A2®* clipper. One is on the back of the head of the clipper (*Fig. 10*); the other one is at the bottom on the front of the clipper casing (*Fig. 11*). DO NOT OVER OIL. A tube of *Oster Lubricating Oil®* is included with your new clipper. Do not use any other type.

BRUSH REPLACEMENT

Clipper blades that run more slowly than usual may indicate worn carbon brushes. There is no way to determine exactly how long these brushes will last. Check the brushes at six month intervals to

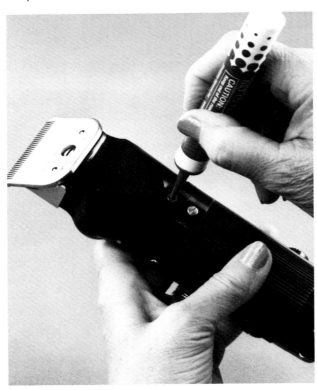

Figure 10. The *Oster A2* clipper is oiled in two places. The first place to oil is on the back of the removeable clipper head.

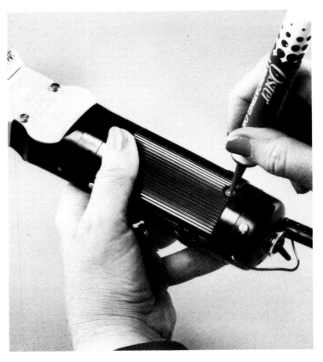

Figure 11. The second place to oil the A2 clipper is on the bottom of the front of the clipper casing. *CLIPPER MUST BE UNPLUGGED PRIOR TO REPLACING BRUSHES.*

insure proper length of brushes. The two brushes, located on either side of the clipper casing, must be replaced in pairs when they are worn down to the marking on the side of the carbon brush (about half way). A package with an extra set of carbon brush and spring assemblies is included with your new clipper. Unscrew the small button-like caps on both sides of the clipper casing (*Fig. 12*). CLIPPER MUST BE UNPLUGGED PRIOR TO CHANGING BRUSHES.

Use a forceps or tweezer to grasp and pull up the cap that can be seen after the cover screw has been removed (*Fig. 13*). When you remove the small cap, a spring will pop into view (*Fig. 14*). Grasp the spring gently and pull up removing the spring and carbon brush from its slot. Take note of the way the brush is seated so that if it is not worn down, it can be replaced in exactly the same position as before. If you accidentally reverse the brushes from their former position, the clipper may run hot until the brushes reseat themselves. When they are worn down to the marking on the brushes, both carbons must be replaced. Insert a new brush and spring assembly in each slot (*Fig. 15*). When you insert a new brush and spring assembly into its slot, make sure the curvature on the end of the

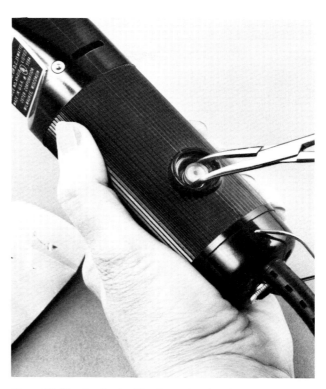

Figure 13. Step two in checking the carbon brushes. Use a forceps or tweezer to grasp and remove the plastic and metal cap that covers the spring and carbon brush assembly.

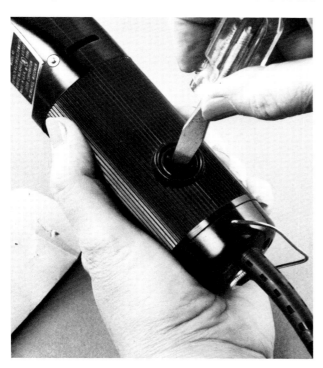

Figure 12. The first step to remove the carbon brushes for inspection and possible replacement, is to unscrew the caps on both sides of the clipper barrel. This view shows A5 clipper only.

Figure 14. Cap removed showing spring that holds the carbon brush in place.

carbon brush matches the curve of the armature that can be seen at the bottom of the slot.

END CAP MAINTENANCE

ALL MAINTENANCE IS DONE WITH THE CLIPPER UNPLUGGED.

Use a Phillips screwdriver to remove the two screws that attach the end cap to the clipper (Fig. 16). Vacuum the hair from the end cap and barrel of the clipper (Fig. 17) until they are completely cleaned out (Fig. 18). Realign the screw holes in the end cap and the clipper, reinsert screws and fasten end cap securely.

GREASING

As mentioned before, a new *Oster A5®* clipper is properly greased and oiled at the factory. You

Figure 15. New carbon brush and spring assembly ready to be replaced in clipper. Make sure that the curve of the carbon brush matches the curve of the armature that can be seen at the bottom of the slot in the clipper.

Figure 16. Occasionally, it is necessary to remove the end cap of the clipper to get rid of accumulated hair that may prevent the free flow of air through the clipper. Use a Phillips screwdriver to remove the two screws in the end cap. *CLIPPER MUST BE UNPLUGGED TO REMOVE END CAP.* This view shows the A5 clipper only.

Figure 17. Hair shown in the end cap and interior of the clipper. There is usually a great deal more hair than this caught in the various parts. A vacuum cleaner nozzle is the most effective method of removing this hair. Hair that does not come out easily may be removed using a tweezer or forceps being *careful* not to disturb wiring or parts.

need not do any additional greasing unless certain symptoms develop. The clipper that is in constant use should be checked periodically to make sure that the grease is still effective. To check the grease in the head of the clipper, begin by removing the face plate (*Fig. 19*).

In *Figure 20*, note the comparison of two clippers. The top clipper is new and shows the proper amount of grease which does not fill the entire cavity. In the bottom clipper you see the result of too much grease. If your clipper has been over-greased you must clean the parts and the cavity and then re-grease properly. Begin by lifting out the lever as shown in *Figure 21*. Gently insert a small screwdriver under the lever and lift it out. Next, in the same way, lift out the link (*Fig. 22*). Finally, lift out the gear (*Fig. 23*). Clean all old grease and dirt from the parts and the cavity as shown in *Figure 24*. Now you are ready to re-grease your clipper.

Figure 18. The end cap and interior of the clipper after all loose hair has been removed. End cap would then be reattached.

Figure 19. If your clipper seems to be running slowly, or is excessively hot, check for the proper amount of grease in the gear and link cavity. Unscrew the front plate of the clipper.

Figure 20. After removing the face plate of the clipper, the lever, link and gear should look clean with only a small amount of clean grease visible as shown in the top clipper. If you have overgreased your clipper in the past, it may look like the bottom clipper. If there is this much grease or any other accumulated matter in this cavity, you must clean and regrease your clipper or it cannot work efficiently.

A tube of *Oster Electric Clipper Grease*® is included with each new clipper and it will be sufficient to grease your clippers for a number of years. Insert the tip of the grease tube into the gear post as show in *Figure 25*. Squeeze in grease until it comes out through the two holes in the gear post. Do not squeeze grease into any other area of the cavity. Replace the gear on the gear post (*Fig. 26*). Also put a small amount of grease on the gear teeth as shown.

In *Figure 27* the link and then the lever have been set back into place. Another small dab of grease is placed where the link and the lever pass over one another. Replace the front plate and the

clipper is ready for use. Greasing the head of the A2 clipper is done in the same way with one exception: the link is removed before the lever. In all other respects the procedure is the same.

During the first few months of operation, your new clipper will run hotter than it will after all parts are worn and properly seated. This does not indicate that anything is wrong with the clipper. The ideal situation is to have two clippers available so that you can set one aside while it is cooling. If that is not possible, cover the air slots on the barrel of the clipper and turn it off. Spray with *Kool-Lube*® lubricant, wipe dry with a towel, and then continue clipping.

Figure 21. The first step in cleaning and re-greasing your clipper is to remove the lever as shown.

Figure 22. After you have removed the lever, remove the link as shown.

Figure 23. The last part you remove is the gear. Then you are ready to clean all parts, and the cavity, of old grease, dirt and hair.

Figure 24. This photo shows all the parts and the cavity well cleaned and ready for greasing.

Figure 25. Use the *Oster Electric Clipper Grease* furnished with your clipper and insert grease into the gear post only until grease comes out through the two holes in the gear post as shown.

Figure 26. Replace the gear. Place a small dab of grease on the gear teeth.

Figure 27. Replace link and lever. Ease the lever in carefully. Do not disturb the two small felt pads on either side of the lever. Place a small amount of grease where the link and lever cross one another. Replace the face plate, and your clipper is ready for use.

II
the
ART

13
The Art of Grooming

Every groomer should be familiar with the terminology that is used to describe certain parts of the dog as they pertain to grooming. These terms should become part of the groomer's vocabulary so her client can better understand the functions the groomer performs. These terms are also a part of artistic descriptions when teaching the principles of grooming. *Figure 1* shows the anatomy of the dog based on the structure of a Poodle and names the various parts of the dog as they are used in the grooming instructions in this book.

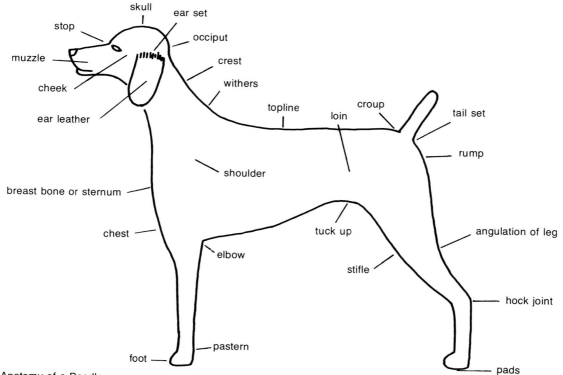

Figure 1. Anatomy of a Poodle.

THE PRINCIPLES OF ARTISTIC GROOMING

Every groomer assumes the role of a sculptor. As you pick up your scissors to finish a stylized pet trim, an elegant show trim, or to design an original style for a mixed breed, you are applying artistic principles. There are pleasing lines of sculpture that attract and hold attention; the same is true of well executed grooming. The eye is annoyed by grooming lines that are not in balance to one another.

Consider the definitions of the following artistic principles:

HARMONY
Harmony is achieved when all elements are working together in a pleasing manner. It refers to elements of likeness, but not necessarily sameness; the key is appropriateness and relativity. It relates proportionate arrangements of color, size and shape.

PROPORTION
Proportion requires all parts to be related to one another in size, length and bulk. Proportion creates areas that are similar, but not so alike as to be dull.

BALANCE
Balance is achieved by maintaining equal amounts of interest in either direction from the natural center of interest.

RHYTHM
Rhythm is created by the eye moving smoothly and easily, connecting points of interest without jerking from point to point.

EMPHASIS
Emphasis means attracting the eye to certain features and subordinating others.

Balance and proportion take an active role in the overall visual impact of grooming. As important as it is to relate the various parts or areas of grooming to one another, several other elements also need to be considered in order to establish a total, well-groomed look. The two halves of a dog—front and rear—are not identical, but should be visually balanced. This is called informal or asymmetrical balance (*Figs. 2 & 2A*). This is accomplished by shifting the points of interest that attract the eye. Grooming can make a dog look taller or longer in body simply by the placement of certain body and leg lines. For instance, the headpiece and the tail of the Poodle are the two points that must

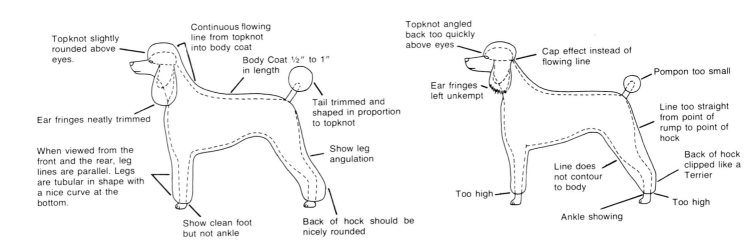

Topknot slightly rounded above eyes.

Continuous flowing line from topknot into body coat

Body Coat ½″ to 1″ in length

Ear fringes neatly trimmed

When viewed from the front and the rear, leg lines are parallel. Legs are tubular in shape with a nice curve at the bottom.

Tail trimmed and shaped in proportion to topknot

Show leg angulation

Show clean foot but not ankle

Back of hock should be nicely rounded

Topknot angled back too quickly above eyes

Cap effect instead of flowing line

Pompon too small

Ear fringes left unkempt

Line too straight from point of rump to point of hock

Line does not contour to body

Back of hock clipped like a Terrier

Too high

Ankle showing

Too high

Figure 2. Properly proportioned Lamb Trim.

Sketches by D. Walin

Figure 2A. Improperly proportioned Lamb Trim.

be balanced to one another so that the flow of the eye is not disturbed. Too large or too small a topknot, or too small or large a tail pompon will break the balanced look of the grooming for this breed (*Fig. 3*).

Each dog has its own proportions which must be taken into consideration. A balanced lamb trim (*Fig. 4*) has a rhythmic flow of lines that allows the eye to travel from one point of the dog to another.

A clip that may be beautifully balanced and proportioned for one dog may be totally inappropriate for another. The dog that appears long in body and short of leg must be visually shortened in body. The high-on-leg dog must be squared up by making the body appear longer.

The greatest and most admired professional dog handlers are those whose dogs appear in the ring groomed to absolute perfection with no unpleasant lines to spoil the picture presented to the judge's eye. If you ask professional handlers how they determine certain grooming lines they may only offer the explanation, "Because it *looks* right." Grooming teachers can instruct students to add or subtract length of hair in order to get a certain line, but the student will always have trouble if she does not have the ability to visualize where the line should actually be placed. Changing the length of hair by just a quarter of an inch can make a big difference in the final balanced look of a trim (*Fig. 5*). The ability to correctly place the line of a trim takes on ever greater importance in grooming competitions (*Fig. 6*). A judge may watch two groomers execute the same type of trim. Scissoring for both may be beautifully smooth. If there are no other determining factors such as hidden mats or abrasions, how does the judge make the final choice? In most cases, the overall balance and proportion of *that* particular trim in relation to *that* particular dog determines the final choice. (See

Figure 3. A well balanced topknot enhances the appearance of the head and the expression of the eyes. Good balance is achieved when the highest point of the topknot approximately equals the distance between the outer corners of the eyes. Measure the topknot from mid-point of the stop.

Figure 4. A well balanced lamb trim on a Toy Poodle. This Poodle had been shown in conformation as a puppy. She has nice body proportions and a good coat making it easy to produce a pretty trim. There is a pleasing flow of lines from one part of the body to another. (Photo - Groom & Board)

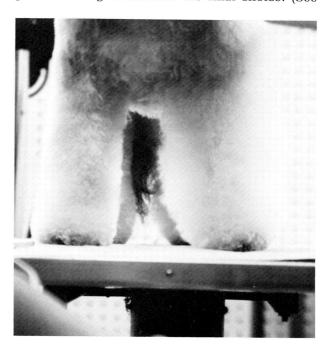

Figure 5. When first learning to scissor a correctly proportioned leg, blend down from the body coat in a smooth line over the elbow, then use that established point as a guide to finish the rest of the line to the foot. The dog shown is clipped in a Bichon-type trim so the feet are covered. Compare the look of the clipped and unclipped leg.

Figure 6. In competitive grooming, balance and proportion play a major role. Jaqui Bownam is shown winning a First Place in the Miniature Poodle class at the 1983 All-american Midwest Grooming Contest held annually in Chicago; judge—Lynette Wallace. The jacket trim on this black miniature is beautifully proportioned. (Photo - D. Walin)

Figs. 2 & 2A again for the comparison of a correctly and incorrectly balanced lamb trim.)

Every grooming shop should strive to hire groomers that can correctly scissor a balanced trim. If your shop instructs its groomers, then balance and proportion should be taught as a matter of course. In these days of intense competition it is not enough to know which end of the clipper does the cutting. Far too many shops use only clippers to do all body and leg work. Every groomer should also know the art of scissoring, the use of thinning shears, and how other grooming tools are used to complete a well-balanced trim.

Let's talk about how to balance a pet trim. A case in point would be an overweight, heavy boned, and long-bodied dog with a three month coat growth (*Fig. 7*). The owner is a busy man who travels a great deal. His home is in the woods, and the trim for his pet Poodle has to be short enough to make flea and tick care an easy task and allow the dog to play outdoors without picking up leaves and twigs in the coat. A "summer clip" was chosen as best suited to fill these needs. (This trim carries many different names depending on the part of the country where you work. It is most often referred to as a summer, Miami, Cavalier, or bikini clip.) The head of this particular dog appears in better balance after scissoring a round, full mustache to minimize the heavy cheekbones behind the eyes (*Fig. 8*). The length of mustache should balance the topknot to give a pleasing proportion to the entire

Figure 7. This silver Miniature Poodle presents a number of problems for the groomer. The coat is soft and tangles easily, so a utility-type clip is needed. Notice the length of body and the heavy boning requiring care in the placement of lines to achieve balance.

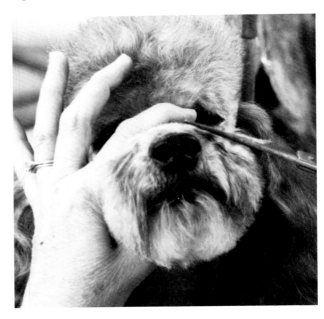

Figure 8. The round mustache shown here echoes the curve of the topknot. It helps to de-emphasize the heavy bones of the cheeks.

headpiece. The topline of the body was done with a #5 blade. The legs down to the bracelets, rears, chest area, and undercarriage of the dog were all done with a #7F blade to cut them as short as possible, yet leave a soft coating of hair on these parts (*Fig. 9*). The bracelets look large, but in actuality,

Figure 9. The finished trim of the Poodle shown in *Figure 7*. Larger-than-usual bracelets are left on the legs to help balance the heavy look of the body.

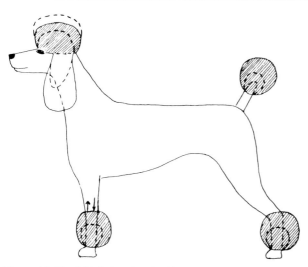

Figure 10. The bikini trim sketched here shows shaded areas to emphasize the points of balance in this trim. The placement of the scissored profile line will make a difference in the finished appearance. Notice the dotted lines within the shaded area of the bracelets. Numerous groomers are guilty of taking off too much coat on a bracelet and end up with something that looks like a large Ping-Pong ball on the bottom of the leg. The same is true of the tail. Also, notice the too short and too tall topknot as indicated by the dotted lines. Sketch by D. Walin.

the rear bracelets barely cover the hock bone. The dog is straight in stifle and long in the hock area. The front bracelets were left higher on the legs than usual to balance the rears and to bring into balance the four points of emphasis when looking at the entire dog—namely, the headpiece, tail pompon, and front and rear bracelets. By emphasizing these four points, the trim makes the dog appear squarer and less long-bodied and heavy boned (*Fig. 10*).

Scissoring a nicely balanced leg that gives proper appearance of support to the rest of the trim is as aesthetically pleasing to the eye, and is as *important* as properly proportioned legs on a table or chair. Look at the leg coat shown in *Figures 11 and 12*. The size of the leg is scissored in proportion to the amount of coat left on the body, and the leg lines are parallel when viewed from the front or rear of the dog. Faults such as cow hocks, barrel legs, and protruding elbows can be disguised by visualizing parallel lines and scissoring the legs accordingly. If shorter coat is left on the body, then

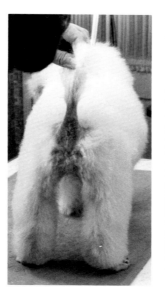

Figure 11 (Left). The rear leg lines shown here emphasize parallel lines, so the dog appears to be moving straight when gaiting away from the observer.

Figure 12 (Right). The lines of the front legs are also parallel lines. The outer leg line drops in a straight line from the broadest point of the body at the shoulder. If the dog is out at the elbows, leave more coat on the outside edges of the leg and scissor to blend with the body. If you have to leave more coat on the outside of the leg, scissor away more coat on the two inside lines to lessen the bulky look of the leg, although still disguising the out-at-the-elbow problem.

legs are also scissored shorter. *Figure 13* is a side profile view of the same dog shown in *Figure 12.*

Every groomer must know how to disguise various faults. Is the dog too tall, too short, cow hocked or out at the elbows? The breed profile must be kept in mind as the groomer works. Every dog is a "show dog" to its owner, and disguising faults is all in a day's work. When dealing with a pet quality purebred dog we almost always have a less-than-perfect animal to work on. *Figures 14 and 15* show the before and after views of a Miniature Poodle whose faults include a high ear set and a slightly overlong body. Head faults were minimized by blending the ear hair instead of defining the ear set where it joins the head. To give more height, the coat at the tuck-up and along the undercarriage was scissored very short, as was the hair on the chest and rump area. The topline of the dog was left longer to also create the appearance of more height. Longer hair was left on the front of the back legs and on the back of the front legs too shorten the body. The pompon on the tail was left as long as possible to give added height and to be in balance to the topknot, giving a squarer look to the whole dog. Sometimes Poodles leave grooming shops looking as though they are walking on stilts or have a body as long as a sausage. Distortions in pet grooming are also found in other breeds.

Lack of knowledge of how to hide faults and execute a trim closer to a correct breed profile may cause an awkward look to the finished trim. (Of course, we are not talking about the badly matted dog whose only salvation is a strip job.) A case in point is the grooming of pet Schnauzers. There are probably as many variations of clips for this breed as there are states in the union. Some are an awful nightmare. Skirting is left halfway up the rib cage, or legs are trimmed so every fault is glaringly obvious. Chests are often covered by a bushy bib of hair that is not at all correct for the breed whose breed profile calls for a cobby, square-looking dog.

Figure 14. A "before" shot of a Miniature Poodle bitch. She has a high ear set and is slightly long in body. (See Fig. 15 for the "after" look.)

At this point, let me define two terms that are frequently referred to in the balance of this book. *Breed Standard* refers to the correct structural requirements for each purebred as approved by their parent club and published by the American Kennel Club. It refers to such things as body structure, correct bite, coat texture, angulation of leg, or acceptable size. *Breed Profile* refers to the correct visual impression of what each pure bred dog should look like when properly groomed, and is based upon the finished profile of those conformation Champions that appear in the show ring as representatives of their individual breeds. The correct placement of topline, leg trim lines, tail set, and head piece should be similar whether done by a show groomer or a pet groomer; the only difference being the manner of execution. The only time this would not be completely true would be in the finishing of a Poodle over one year of age. The show trim for this Poodle must be either an English Saddle Trim, or a Continental Trim. The show Poodle under one year of age is finished in a puppy trim, which has become so stylized in the last few years as to be almost identical to a pet lamb trim.

Figure 13. The completed Dutch Trim on the Poodle shown in Figure 12.

The only difference is in the finishing of the neck coat and topknot.

Groomers should attend dog shows to establish in *their own minds* the correct breed profile for the purebred dogs they groom. It is also important to visit handler's working areas and quietly watch as the handlers set the correct pattern for their breed. Every groomer should own a copy of the American

Figure 15. In this "after" photo of the dog in Figure 14, the following procedures were taken to give better balance and proportion to this lamb trim: (a.) The topline was only evened off to leave as much height of back coat as possible. (b.) The hair on the back of the topknot and down into the neck area is left longer to shorten the appearance of the distance between the neck and the tail. (c.) The earset is blended into the topknot, not sharply defined, to lessen the look of the high ear set. (d.) More coat is left on the front of the tail pompon. (e.) Chest and rump area are trimmed shorter. (f.) The hair at the tuck-up is clipped as close as possible to give more emphasis to length of leg. (g.) Coat on the bottom of the leg is brought down almost onto the foot—again to give more length of leg. (h.) Coat on the front of the rear leg and back of the front leg is left longer to shorten the distance between the front and rear legs and "square-up" the dog.

Kennel Club's publication, "The Complete Dog Book" published by Howell Book House, containing all the breed standards for those breeds recognized by the American Kennel Club. The book is frequently updated when changes in the breed standard are made by the parent breed club. Each breed is illustrated by a picture of a fairly recent champion. If you study the picture and read the

standard, you should be able to come reasonably close to a correct profile. Your knowledge of the type of finishing that can be obtained using various grooming tools enables you to do a good job.

Let's consider the differences between show and pet grooming. The show groomer trims the coat of a show specimen with the sole purpose of obtaining ribbons and points to eventually capture a championship. The show groomer must know the standards of the breeds they work with in order to enhance the specimen and disguise minor faults. They must be aware of current trends and fads in show grooming. They work with coat that benefits from months of careful conditioning.

The pet groomer's first responsibility is to *please the customer*. This *may* mean grooming in some way other than the correct way for that breed. However, groomers now have grooming booklets, breed books, and other materials that can be used to present the correct profiles to their customers in hopes that they will be willing to allow correct grooming. The pet quality purebred usually has faults that must be disguised to the best of the groomer's ability. You may not need to know anything about show grooming, but watching those who prepare the dogs for the conformation ring is the best way I know of to learn what a good dog should look like, and to learn some of the tricks of the trade. However, the pet groomer must often work with coat that suffers from months of neglect, is short, broken, or tangled.

Show grooming produces uniformity within each breed and facilitates judging by making it easier to do comparisons. Show groomers know how to hide minor faults and accentuate good points in each dog. In this last respect, pet grooming and show grooming reach a common ground. The show groomer's proficiency will translate into more wins for the dogs she grooms. On the other hand, the more proficient a pet groomer becomes, the more customers she will have.

Your professionalism is enhanced when you know the histories of the breeds you groom, and can discuss them intelligently with the owners of these various breeds. The knowledge of the main characteristics emphasized in the Breed Standards helps you bring about a correct Breed Profile in your purebred pet grooming.

14
Basic Pre-Work for All Breeds

The grooming section of this book has included educational material as well as grooming instructions. Anyone who intends to make professional grooming a career—a veterinarian, or a pet owner who wishes to learn to groom his own pet—should be well-versed in the history, Breed Standard and correct breed profile for the dogs she grooms. It would create an encyclopedia of numerous volumes to give complete visualizations of the grooming instructions for all breeds, so this book concerns itself with those breeds most often groomed.

CURRENT GROWTH OF GROOMING

Professional pet grooming has grown tremendously in the United States, as well as in other metropolitan areas of the world. Show grooming for the conformation ring is still the usual realm of the professional handler and his assistants. However, many fine breeder/exhibitors are active in both show grooming and pet grooming. Some of them learned grooming by doing puppies and the pet quality offspring of their own litters, or by doing professional pet grooming to support their show hobby.

At this writing, there are over 25 thousand people active in full or part-time grooming. These are known as "professional pet groomers" because the trims they execute and the various styles used are unacceptable in the conformation show ring. Although some of these groomers have the capability to execute a correct show trim, their day-to-day grooming usually involves the pet dog. Although pet trims are not executed in the same manner as show trims, they should be properly done to a correct breed profile.

Interested groomers keep abreast of the changes in styling that have evolved over the years. In few other breeds is this as evident as it is in the Poodle. Ten years have brought visible changes of trims. Poodle trims are now stylized with crisp, pleasing, flow of lines for both the show and pet trims. Evidence of this evolution in the Poodle show ring is seen in *Figure 1*. In the top row, we see the Puppy, Continental and English Saddle clips as they were commonly done in the late 1960s and early 70s. In the bottom row we see the same three styles as they were shown in the Stud Issue of *The Poodle Review* magazine in 1983. Notice how much more precise and less bulky the lines of these clips have become.

The same evolution of line is true in other breeds. Clips are now neater and more precise as more groomers are trained to recognize correct technique and placement of lines. Few of the skilled groomers in the United States continue to use the old style Poodle trims that gave the legs the appearance of a "leg-of-mutton" sleeve. Straight lines pegged down to the ankle of the Poodle are now replaced with simple lines, showing angulation in the rear legs that give a more natural look. No matter what breed is being groomed, or what type of trim is being executed, lines are crisp, flowing, and in good proportion to one another.

New styles of clips are created for pet grooming in such contest classes as the "Creative Groom-

Figure 1. These photos compare grooming lines for the Puppy, Continental, and English Saddle clips for the show ring.
(Top row, left to right) Cliffspride Fancy That - 12 points - 1969 photo; Cliffspride foundation bitch, Ch. Suchan's Cinnamon Candy
- 1968 photo; Cliffspride Bit of Zodiac - 1971 photo. (Photos - D. Walin)
(Bottom row, left to right) Ch. Camelot Rocky Reflections - owned by Linda Kofmehl; Am. Can. Mex. Int. Ch. Evanz Chronicle - owned
by Marilyn P. Pauley; Am. Can. Mex. Int. 1978 World Ch. Evanz Evening Edition - owned by Marilyn Pauley. (Photos courtesy *The
Poodle Review* Magazine)

ing Class'' offered at major grooming competitions around the country. Most of these styles are used for exhibition purposes only as the average groomer would find them too intricate and time consuming to execute for the average pet. However, they would have some snob appeal for the pet owner who wants something different and is willing to pay the price.

STEPS TO GOOD GROOMING

A dog's good grooming behavior is a matter of *your* patience and persistence. It *cannot* be achieved by either physical or verbal abuse of the dog. The dog immediately picks up on your feelings about him, and reacts accordingly. What we do about the ones that bare their teeth and try to get as far away from us as possible is discussed in the chapter concerned with problem dogs.

One method of exerting control during grooming is using a table of proper size. Many groomers use tables that are larger than necessary. Terriers, Toy and Miniature Poodles, mixed breeds and all other dogs except the very large breeds, can be groomed on a small grooming surface.

While working as a full-time groomer, the top of my adjustable grooming table was 18 by 27 inches. It was custom-made because most tables available at that time had larger tops. I was able to groom most breeds, including Standard Poodles on this smaller surface and because the dogs had a minimal amount of room in which to move around, I found I could sit to do many of the grooming functions. Using a smaller grooming table also means not having to stretch as far to reach the area you are working on. The dog soon learns the limitations of the space he is standing on if he accidentally steps off the table with one foot. Dogs are very aware of their surroundings, and don't move around if there is no place to move to.

AT NO TIME SHOULD A DOG BE LEFT ALONE ON THE TABLE IN THE GROOMING ROOM. If you must leave the room to go to another part of the shop, the dog should be put back in its crate or holding area until you can begin grooming again. It would be tragic if a dog restrained in a grooming noose were to chew through the noose and escape. It would be even more tragic to find a dead dog hanging from the noose. These things *do* happen, so take heed.

BASIC PRE-WORK FOR ALL BREEDS

When a dog or cat is brought in for grooming, immediately analyze the condition of the coat. If you determine that stripping is necessary, it is easier to tell the customer while he/she is still in the shop. Sometimes the owners cannot be reached until they return for the dog, and a confrontation takes place over the naked pet. In most instances, you can feel for any suspicious lumps as you carry the pet back to the crating area. If you suspect that there is more to this problem than meets the eye, immediately place the dog on the grooming table and check more thoroughly for the degree of matting. Most Poodles with two or three months growth between groomings come into the shop looking like the Poodle in *Figure 2.*

Pay particular attention to the long-coated breeds between nine and fifteen months of age. This is the period when the coat is changing from the soft, puppy texture, to a more mature and denser coat. During these months, as the puppy coat dies off, it must be removed by daily brushing. If not brushed out, it remains in the coat, and as the puppy rolls about and plays, static cling causes these dead hairs to become entangled in the new coat growth. Before long, there is no remedy except to strip all the coat and allow it to regrow. More dogs are stripped during this time in their development because the owners are not aware of what is happening. Often they are not instructed in proper coat care when they acquire their puppy, and attempts at brushing are less than adequate. You, the professional, can instruct in proper grooming instrument usage for at-home care. We have all

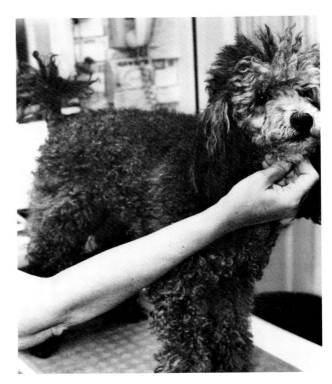

Figure 2.

heard the excuse, ''The dog cries when I try to brush him.'' Take a few minutes to brush with the owner present. Let him know that the dog is just pressing an advantage and that brushing must be done whether the dog cries or not. Patience and persistence is the name of the game. No dog is born with the knowledge that he is going to be groomed for the rest of his life.

BEFORE THE BATH

Preparations for grooming begin with the de-matting process. Lumpy, matted areas of the coat should be sprayed with a de-matting solution. Many companies manufacture products specifically formulated to neutralize the static of the coat and release the mats. If no such product is available, dilute a small amount of creme rinse in water in a pump spray bottle and use it to moisturize the coat.

The dog groomed at periods of six week intervals may need only a thorough brush through and comb out before the bath. However, the dog that receives no coat care at home probably has matting. If the coat is a solid felt mat, don't even try to save it. It is much too hard on the dog to subject it to hours of de-matting. Certain skin types are easily irritated, and brush burns could result.

If you feel the coat can be saved, saturate the matted areas with a dematting solution. Wait a few minutes to allow the solution to work, then begin working through one section of coat at a time with a de-matting tool or one end of a stainless steel comb (*Fig. 3*). Always begin working on the rear leg if you are unfamiliar with the dog's temperament. Begin at the bottom of the leg and work upward through a small area at a time. Insert the tool through the mat and work the mat open a little at a time. The tightness of the mat will determine how much of the mat can be opened with each

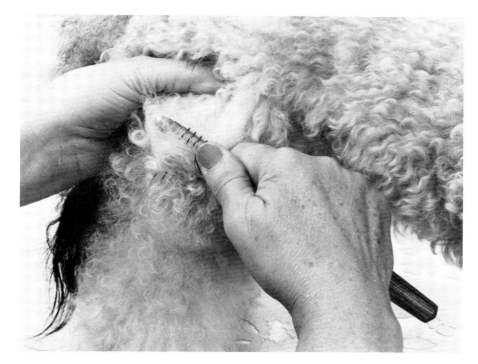

Figure 3.

stroke. Wherever you are cutting through with a de-matting instrument, use your other hand to brace the skin where you are pulling as this minimizes pain to the dog. De-mat all four legs, watching for the reaction of the dog. Be particularly careful when working on the front legs as you are working right under his mouth. If the dog shows any sign of aggression, such as showing his teeth or growling, use a soft muzzle to discourage this type of behavior (*Fig. 4*). Remember, the dog does not enjoy the de-matting part of the grooming procedure. Sometimes it helps an owner understand the importance of home care if he has to watch a dog, other than his own, being de-matted. Always work with the direction of the coat growth when de-matting, brushing, or combing to remove the mats. After the legs are completely de-matted, work through the body coat in the same way, beginning at the hindquarters and working up to the neck.

Figure 4.

After de-matting is completed, thoroughly brush the entire coat to remove the loosened mats. Again, begin with the bottom of the leg, and brush, working up the leg a small layer at a time (Fig. 5). Brush through all four legs, the entire body coat,

Figure 5.

Figure 6.

then the ears, topknot, tail and any whisker area on the muzzle. When you think the entire coat is well cleaned out, check one more time with a fine-tooth comb at the back of the hock, the underside of the tail, the "armpit" area where the front legs join the body, and finally, the underneath area of the ear set, ear fringes and tail; these are the areas where mats are most often missed. A word of caution: Use care when brushing the hock area. There is usually less coat growth over the hock bone, and a "brush burn" might result if the groomer is heavy-handed. Grooming assistants who do only brush outs and bathing are usually not as fussy about thoroughly cleaning out the coat until they have to begin finishing work. Only then do they realize how important this prework is.

Next, clip the groin area, and the inner flanks of the rear legs (Fig. 6). Learn to develop a light touch with the clipper by not putting any pressure against the skin, but rather by allowing the clipper blade to do the work. The groin area is usually clipped using an Oster #10 blade.

Many breeds such as the Poodle and the Schnauzer have a great deal of ear hair growth inside the ear that should be removed. Dust the hair in the ear canal with a *small* amount of depilatory ear powder, wait a few minutes, then gently pluck the hair out using your fingers (Fig. 7). Take care

Figure 7.

not to pinch the tender folds of cartilage within the ear if you must use a forceps to get all the hair out of the canal. After plucking, use one of the antiseptic and healing ear washes such as *Gerard Pellham's Ear Gard*™ to remove all traces of the ear powder.

Clean the area under the tail around the anus. Do not run the clipper directly over the anal opening as there is always the danger of nicking the tender folds of skin around the anus. It is better to use a small, blunt-pointed scissor to remove dry feces or any other matter that may be accumulated in this area (*Fig. 8*). If you do use a clipper blade to clean the area, clip from the side toward the anal opening rather than with an up or down motion (*Fig. 9*).

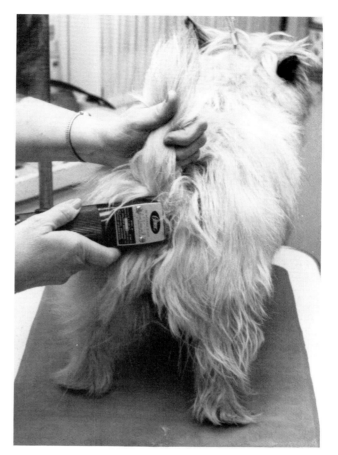

Figure 9.

NAIL AND FOOT CARE

The question of whether to cut the nails of the dog before or after the bath is a matter of choice. If a nail is accidentally cut too short before the bath, any blood that might stain the coat could be washed away during the bath. However, nails are easier to cut after the bath because the water tends to soften them. Whatever course you follow, keep some styptic powder close at hand to quickly stop the bleeding if you accidentally cut the quick of the nail.

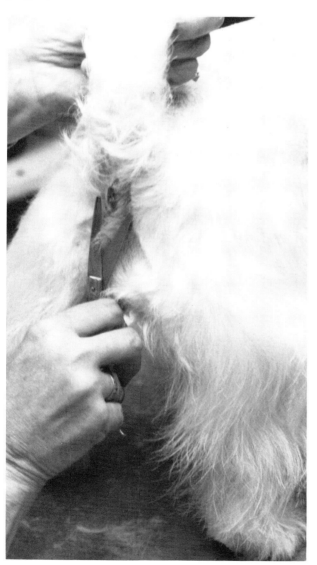

Figure 8.

The most commonly used nail cutting instrument is the guillotine clipper such as the one manufactured by Resco (Ch. 3, *Fig. 23*). Also popular is the scissor-plier type (*Fig. 10*). Another method of shortening and smoothing the nail in the same operation is to use an electric nail grinder (*Fig. 11*).

Check between the pads on the underside of the foot for gum, tar, or other debris embedded in the coat between the pads (*Fig. 12*). Both gum and tar can be loosened by using cooking oil or peanut butter. Other debris can be cut away with a blunt pointed scissor or the clipper blade. Mud should be soaked and sudsed off in the bath.

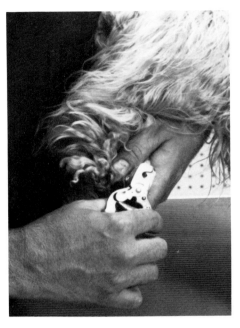

Figure 10.

Figure 11.

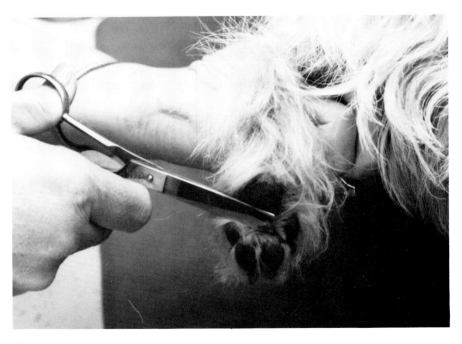

Figure 12.

THE BATH

Make sure the bath water is warm, not hot, to lessen the chance of irritating the skin. Use the proper type of correctly pH balanced shampoo for the coat you are working with. Most dog shampoos are tested for eye tolerance and are safe when used as directed. My only caution would be to not use a medicated shampoo on the head area if it can be avoided. Should the condition of the skin necessitate the use of a medicated shampoo, suds and rinse the head with a milder shampoo first and them continue to the body coat carefully following the instructions. Protein enhanced shampoos do a nice job of maintaining the texture of a terrior coat. The mildest of shampoos must be used on those dogs with sensitivities. These would include most white-coated dogs, plus silver, apricot and silver-beige Poodles, Maltese, and Yorkies. A fine formulation for this type of coat is *Gerard Pellham's Code 7™*.

As you begin the bathing process, wet down all the body and head using lukewarm water (*Fig. 13*). Keep the spray nozzle right on the coat to force the water all the way in to the skin. If the nozzle is held away from the body, the water bouncing off the coat can frighten a spooky dog. Also, water does not properly penetrate the coat when sprayed from more than an inch away from the coat. Next, apply the shampoo onto the body coat. Massage thoroughly with your finger tips to raise a good lather, and to stimulate the skin. (*Fig. 14*) Begin rinsing at the head using a softer force of water. Use one hand to hold the ears close to the head to avoid flushing dirty soap water into the ear. Cotton can be placed in the ears of dogs with heads so broad that holding the ears down with your fingers is difficult if not impossible. Also cover the eye area from the full force of the water. Bend the head down to prevent water from going in the nostrils or ears. Continue on to the neck and body, keeping the water nozzle against the coat to force out the shampoo. You must rinse until the coat no longer feels slippery, but rather feels "squeaky" clean. The only exception would be if you are using a shampoo with a built-in tangle preventing conditioner which gives the coat a silkier feel. Immediately after the bath, towel dry the ears to remove any remaining moisture.

Figure 13.

Figure 14.

AFTER THE BATH

While the dog is still in the tub, begin the drying process by squeezing off the excess water (*Fig. 15*). On a large, heavy-coated breed, you can save time by using one of the new high-velocity dryers,

finish is desired (*Figs. 17 & 18*). This type of drying is accomplished most efficiently by brushing only where the flow of air from the dryer is striking the coat. It is a waste of time to brush here and there with the dryer blowing in the general direction of the dog.

Figure 15.

and blowing off excess water while the dog is still in the tub. For smaller dogs, blot off excess water with towels. Wrap the dog in a towel and carry it to the table thereby avoiding water dripping on the floor from the wet dog. Many groomers now use the high velocity dryers to completely dry larger breeds. However, many smaller dogs are afraid of the louder noise of this type of dryer. I personally feel that any groomer wanting to do contest work can achieve a fluffier, more velvety finish if the coat has been brush dried working on one area of the coat at a time with a conventional dryer, and keeping the remainder of the coat covered with a towel until each area is thoroughly dried. When working on a long-coated breed such as the Maltese, Yorkie, Lhasa, or Shih Tzu, *blot* the water out of the coat with a towel rather than rub the coat vigorously (*Fig. 16*). Drying methods vary, depending on the breed and the type of coat. Fluff drying is the best method when a plush, clippered, or hand scissored

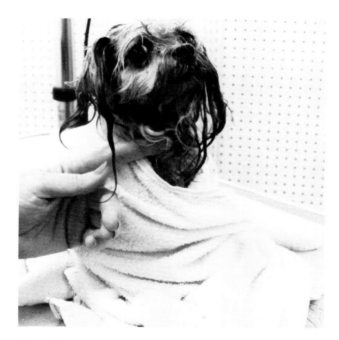

Figure 16.

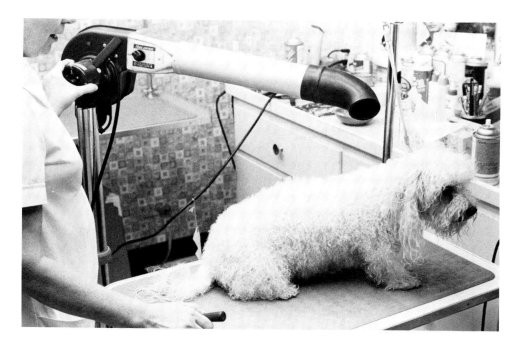

Figure 17.

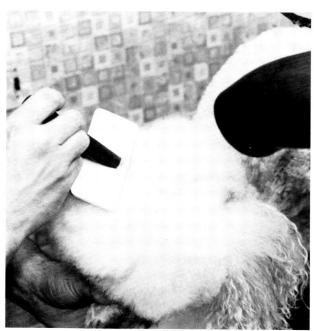

Figure 18.

In order to maintain the harsh texture of Westie, Cairn or Scottie coats, *do not* brush or comb the wet coat. Finger-drying the dog (*Fig. 19*) moves the coat around for faster drying and lets you check for dampness in the undercoat but does not break down the desired harsh texture. When these breeds are crate-dried, the surface may *feel* dry, but the undercoat may still be damp. Comb or brush only after this type of coat is completely dry.

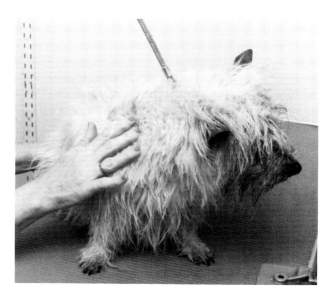

Figure 19.

15
Finishing the Poodle

Before describing the work necessary to finish the grooming of the Poodle, I would like to offer a brief history of the breed and discuss various parts of the Poodle Standard as they pertain to the grooming for a correct breed profile.

BRIEF HISTORY OF THE POODLE

The actual beginnings of the dog now known as the Poodle are obscure. A common error is reference to a "French Poodle." Cynologists believe the dog originated in Russia or Germany. The antiquity of the Poodle can be understood when we realize that its likeness was shown on early Greek and Roman coins and carved on Roman tombs as far back as 40 A.D. They were also depicted in many paintings during the Middle Ages. A later French painting shows women busily clipping dogs into patterns that somewhat resemble what is now know as a Continental clip. It is amazing to realize that they were doing all this fancy trimming with only a pair of scissors or a straight razor.

Ancestors of our modern day Poodle include the Water Dog or *Canis familiaris aquaticus*. In Germany, his name, *Pudel*, comes from the German word, *Pudelin*, meaning "*to splash in water*." The French name, *Caniche*, is derived from a word meaning "*duck dog*." The background probably includes other curly-coated hunting dogs. The Poodle was a favorite water dog used to retrieve fowl in most of Continental Europe. Shaving the hindquarters of the dog, leaving small areas of hair to cover and protect joints, helped the Poodle swim more efficiently when retrieving. A large mane of hair on the chest and forequarters gave protection from chills when the dog came out of the water and added buoyancy while swimming. This practice gave rise to the phrase "Lion Dog." The forelocks were tied up above the head to keep the long hair out of the eyes, aiding the Poodle in locating his quarry when retrieving in the water. (Today, groomers recognize that a proper Poodle coat is water resistant. If you run water over the top of a Poodle coat, you will find dry coat underneath the top layer.)

During the reign of Louis XVI, the profession of Poodle grooming took an artistic flair. As these dogs became pets of the court, they were decorated with intricate patterns; no design was considered too difficult and some patterns even included small pointed beards and pompadours to imitate the men and women of the court.

The present day Standard Poodle is about the same size as were the original Poodles. However, the size reduction that has given us the Miniature and Toy varieties is believed to have been achieved by introducing other breeds similar in structure and coat, though smaller in size. Some size reduction was achieved by breeding down from the runt of a litter. The white Toy Poodle may have both the Maltese and Bichon in their background. This could account for the difference in coat textures seen in this variety, particularly in white Toy Poodles. The Bichon has a coat either silky or harsh in texture depending on its background origin. All groomers are familiar with the soft silkiness of the

Maltese coat. When this silky factor is present in the Poodle coat, it makes the coat more difficult to groom. Its tendency is to lie flat rather than to stand erect. It does not have the density of the coarser coat, and does not lend itself well to a pattern trim.

The Poodle is no longer considered a retriever. The Miniature and Standard varieties are shown in the Non-Sporting classes at Conformation Shows. However, some devotees of the breed again encourage the use of the oversize Miniatures and the Standards for hunting fowl.

THE MODERN DAY POODLE

Today, the three varieties of the Poodle breed as they are known in the United States are as follows:

Standards - All Poodles measuring more than 15 inches at the withers.

Miniatures - All Poodles measuring more than 10 inches and no more than 15 inches at the withers.

Toys - All Poodles measuring 10 inches or less at the withers.

One problem that confronts the pet Poodle owner, breeder and groomer alike, is the fact that there are crossover sizes. In our pet grooming shops, we see a variety of size crossovers. Tiny two or three pound "tea cup" Poodles are only runts of the litters. Oversize Toys, dwarf Miniatures, oversize Miniatures, and all other size deviations present their own problems of grooming to minimize apparent faults.

The Standard calls the Poodle an active, intelligent dog, carrying himself proudly. Grooming must enhance this image, not make fun of it by improper proportions that call attention to the "not-so-perfect" dog. The Poodle should be squarely built, moving with sound, fluidlike movement. He should have an air of distinction and dignity. The proportions of pet grooming can help to "square up" the profile. If the work we do pleases the customer, he conveys this happy feeling to the dog, and the dog leaves the shop with its dignity intact, head held high, and tail wagging.

The head of the Poodle should be lean but not snippy. The Standard mentions a long lean head with no skulliness. Scissoring the topknot in close to the head behind the eyes helps to make the head appear leaner. Nothing distorts the look of the head as much as seeing a headpiece that looks too large in relation to the total dog. At no time should a

topknot flair out directly behind the eyes which then makes the Poodle appear heavy headed. Clipping an inverted "V" between the eyes elongates the look of the muzzle. The Standard also calls for a cleanshaven face. There are times when a small mustache, or a larger rounded beard hides such faults as overshot or undershot mouths, or snippy muzzles often found in our pet Poodles.

The neck is to be well proportioned, strong and long to carry the head high and with dignity. The pet groomer often works with short, fat necks and must understand how to deepen the shaved area on the front of the neck, or build more height at the topknot and back of the neck to compensate.

The tail should be set rather high and docked at sufficient length to give a balanced profile. The easiest explanation of "sufficient length" is that the height and size of the tail should nearly balance the height of the topknot. The overall balance between head and tail enhances the desired square look of the Poodle.

The front and rear legs should give the appearance of parallel lines when the Poodle is moving. When properly scissored the legs can appear to move correctly. To prevent the Poodle from appearing straight in stifle, angulation must be shown in the rear legs.

The foot of the Poodle is shaved, but care should be taken to leave the ankle covered. Years ago it was common practice to expose the ankle when clipping the foot. Today the leg hair is gently rounded off just above the foot. The Poodle foot should always be shaved when grooming unless the digits are swollen or the foot shows sensitivities or allergies. Accumulated hair between the toes of the foot can cause the foot to splay (spread out) over a period of time.

Clipping The Face

While viewing the illustrations of this book, pay particular attention to the way the clipper is held to complete various functions. At no time should you take a death grip on the clipper, or put excess pressure against the skin. Rather, the clipper is cradled gently in the fingers while the blade is guided to do its work. The blade should be checked frequently during clipping, and sprayed with a coolant to help prevent irritation to sensitive skin.

The right-handed groomer should place the Poodle facing the groomer and clip the face beginning just in front of the Poodle's left ear. Fold the ear back out of the way so you can better see the ear opening. Place the clipper blade flat against

Figure 1.

the head and clip in a straight line from the ear opening to the back corner of the eye. Do not clip above this line because you then remove coat that belongs in the topknot (*Fig. 1*).

As your clipper blade approaches the eye, continue clipping the lower eyelid (*Fig. 2*). The dog will naturally close its eye as the clipper blade approaches, so do not stretch the eyelid with your fingers as this might cause the clipper blade to cut too close and cause an abrasion in this tender area. *Never* clip any of the area above the Poodle eye

with a blade; always finish it with scissors. Occasionally, you have to contend with a Poodle owner who insists on whacking off the hair above the eyes right down to the hide. The result is quite hard to conceal when finishing. Try to convince the owner to leave well enough alone and bring the dog to you for any necessary repairs. A topknot trim between regular groomings would control the problem of hair falling down over the eyes.

Continue clipping forward along the muzzle to the nose. If a mustache is desired, clip only to the back corner of the mouth. Angle the back line of the mustache from the back corner of the mouth slightly forward toward the nose to keep the longer coat away from the eyes.

To do the other side of the head, reach your hand around the head from the back and grasp the muzzle from the other side (*Fig. 3*). Repeat the process.

When clipping a cleanshaven muzzle, be sure to clip along the flew in the bottom lip. As you are holding the head, raise the upper lip with a finger, and with the fingers that are under the chin, stretch the skin of the lower lip. This procedure makes it easier to remove the hair in the lip indentation (flew), or any accumulated matter that may be dried into the hair at that point (*Fig. 4*). If a mustache is left be sure to clean any accumulated food or matter from the hair in the flew.

Clip an inverted "V" shape at the stop between the eyes. This accentuates the length of the muzzle and gives a pleasing expression to the foreface (*Fig. 5*). A small clipper was used to do the muzzle of this Toy Poodle puppy. Notice how small the head is in relation to the hand holding it. The entire

Figure 2.

Figure 3.

Figure 5.

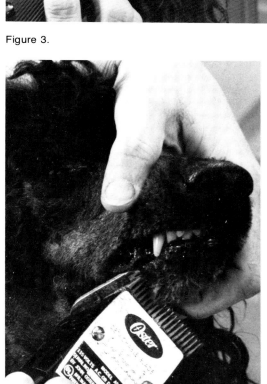

Figure 4.

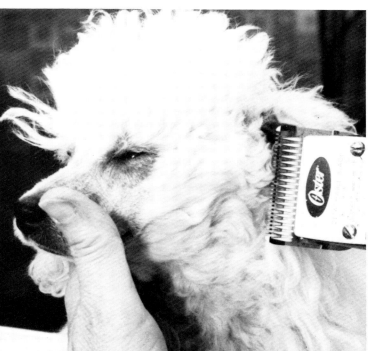

Figure 6.

muzzle and under eye area was done with a blade similar in cutting depth to the *Oster #15* blade. Another good blade to try on a small puppy's face would be the Oster $5/_8$ " blade which cuts to the same depth as a #15 blade. An Oster #9 blade was used to clip the cheek, underjaw, and front of neck working with the lay of the coat because of the puppy's sensitivity to clipping (*Fig.* 6).

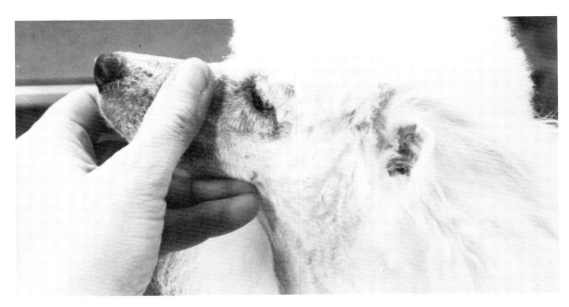

Figure 7.

Try using two different blades if the Poodle is prone to scratching the cheek area after clipping. Use a #10 or #15 blade for the muzzle and under eye area, then change to a #9 or #7F blade for the cheek, underjaw and neck area. Two blades were used to finish the face of the Poodle shown in *Figure 7.* A #15 blade was used on the muzzle, and a #7F against the grain of the coat on the cheeks and front of the neck. This changeover in blades does not show when the ears are hanging down to frame the face, and there is less danger that the dog will feel itchy after grooming if the coat is not clipped as close on the cheeks and front of the neck.

Figures 8, 9, and *10* show a tiny, three-pound Poodle with a short muzzle and an old-fashioned, round head. The dog is also sensitive, and only about ¾-inch on the top of the muzzle was done with a close blade. The rest of the face and neck were clipped with #9 blade, and a small-doughnut shaped mustache was left to de-emphasize the round head.

Use desensitizing cream or lotion on the face and neck of any Poodle that is suspected of scratching his face. Aloe products and cortisone creams applied frequently after grooming, can usually prevent this problem described by veterinarians as "clipper burn." The Poodle owner must be cautioned to watch the dog carefully at home for any scratching or rubbing of the head. If a Poodle or any other breed is allowed to rub his head on furniture fabrics or on synthetic carpeting, it won't take long to develop a serious abrasion. Keep after-clip lotions and creams on hand to sell to those customers whose dogs have shown sensitivities in the past.

Figure 8.

Figure 9.

Figure 10.

Figure 11.

Figure 12.

Clipping Poodle Feet - Learning to clip the feet of a Poodle scares more groomers than any other function they must learn. Poodle feet should be clipped in most instances. Exceptions would include feet where allergies have caused swelling or scaling. They should not be left in "teddy bear" style simply because the groomer may dislike doing feet, or is in a hurry. Hair allowed to grow between the toes encourages the foot to splay. Occasionally, you find a Poodle that objects so strenuously to having feet done that is isn't worth the hassle. At that point you have two choices—leave the feet in their natural condition and trim around them as best you can, or have someone else hold the dog. Occasionally, you may have to hand scissor the entire foot. A sling can be used effectively for this type of dog if it does not struggle too violently.

Learn how to press open the digits of the foot for easy access between the toes. *Figure 11* shows the placement of the thumb just at the base of the toes. The forefinger is underneath the foot between the pads. As you press these two fingers together, the toes will spread apart.

For a small foot such as the one seen in *Figures 12* and *13*, use either an Oster $5/8$" blade or some other small clipper. If you have a foot to clip with a heavy growth of hair, skim off the hair from the top of the foot so you can more easily see where the toes begin. It is not difficult to remove the coat on the outside edges of the foot. As you begin to work between the toes, use a scooping motion down the side of one toe and up the side of the next. Do not ride the edge of the blade along the side of the toe as it may catch the webbing between the toes in the teeth of the blade and clip into it. At first it may be difficult for you to clip a foot without making a small abrasion. Use powdered

Figure 13.

alum or Kwick-Stop on the nick. To neatly finish the appearance of the foot, use a small pointed scissor to clip off any remaining unsightly hairs around the nail or along the edges of the pads (Fig. 14).

An Oster ⁷⁄₈" blade works well to clip the foot of a Standard Poodle. Notice how this dog (Fig. 15) turns her face to the side, wrinkling her nose with an expression of disgust at having her feet clipped.

Figure 15.

Figure 14.

After completing the work on the top of the foot, bend the foot back and up, turning it in such a way that you are able to remove the coat between the pads on the bottom (Fig. 16). There is a natural indentation in the foot at the base of the large pad (see arrow). The Poodle foot should never be clipped higher than this point to avoid exposing the ankle, and giving the bottom of the clipped leg a "high water pants" look. Remove any straggly hairs below the indentation of the foot (Figs. 17 & 18).

The bottom of the leg coat can be rounded off by combing all the leg coat down, folding your hand around the coat with the thumb and forefinger closest to the foot, and sliding your hand down to a point directly above the foot. Take your scissors and cut the coat in an even line all the way around the leg at the point of indentation on the foot. Your scissors should be kept at a right angle to the leg. When you release your hand after scissoring, you should have a nicely rounded edge at the bottom of the leg coat.

Patience is the name of the game when learning to do feet. My first Poodle foot took me an entire evening to complete. Thank goodness the dog was patient. Persistence won out and I was soon doing feet with confidence. YOU CAN TOO!

Figure 16.

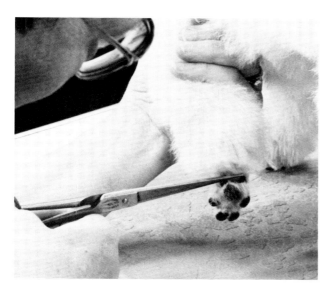

Figure 17.

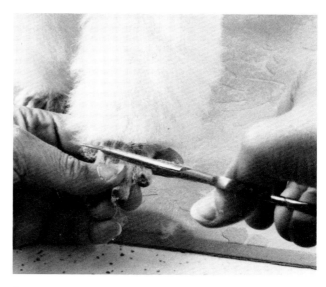

Figure 18.

Clipping a Cap Topknot

A cap or "V" topknot is used when finishing a number of different clips. A Sporting, Utility, Town & Country, Jacket, and Dutch Clip are all complemented by this type of topknot. The back of the cap topknot should end at the bottom of the occipital bone to be properly proportioned. If the cap is brought further down the back of the neck, it shortens the look of the neck. If you want to do a "V" shape on the back of the topknot, the top outside of the "V" must begin at the occipital bone at the back corner of the ear. Proportion the distance the "V" extends down the neck by the length of neck of each dog. A Poodle with a short, fat neck should not be finished using a "V" shaped topknot.

To begin the work on a cap topknot, your first step is to clip the back of the neck. Bring the head of the Poodle forward and bend it down. Use your fingers to determine the exact location of the bottom of the occiput. Place your clipper at that point and begin clipping the neck, working toward the body. For a Sporting or Utility clip, use a #9 or #10 blade (*Fig. 19*). For a pattern trim, clip the neck with a #15 or #30.

Clean the entire neck area to the point where the neck joins the body (line and arrow in *Fig. 19*) at which point blend off into the body coat. Do not clip below the actual neckline into the shoulder area or withers as that throws the rest of the pattern out of proportion. If you are in doubt where to stop, raise the head, and again use your fingers to determine the exact point of the base of the neck.

Sometimes it is difficult to see exactly where your clipper is going if the body and neck are covered with overgrown coat. Check frequently to be sure the shaved area of the neck ends exactly where the neck and body meet. Finish clipping the entire neck area, going around under the base of the ear. Check and remove any straggly hairs under the base of the ear.

After you have finished the neck work, the next step is to begin shaping the side of the topknot. Comb through the entire topknot again, carefully fluffing the coat forward above the eyes, outward above the cheekbones, straight up on top, and following the curve around the back of the cap. Repeat this fluffing frequently while scissoring the cap. *Never* use your fingers to pull stray wisps of hair into place. Always comb and fluff. This is true

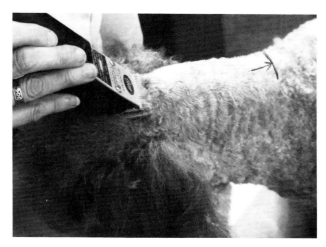

Figure 19.

Figure 20.

Figure 21.

Figure 22.

for all finish scissor work. The more you comb and fluff the coat, the easier it will be to achieve a final, smooth finish.

When you have completed fluffing the topknot, place your scissor against the planes of the cheek behind the back corner of the eye. Point the scissor upward as you lay it against this plane of the face. Notice that the scissor naturally slants slightly away from the head. It is not a great degree of slant, but rather a pleasant continuation of the planes of the face. Begin just behind the eye and scissor away any hair of the topknot that extends out beyond the cheekbones of the face, keeping the side of the topknot on a slight slant outward. (*Fig. 20* and Ch. 13, *Fig. 2*). Continue scissoring until you have shaped the entire side of the topknot from the back of the eye, over the ear, to a point at the back of the ear. A note of caution at this point. If the dog has a high ear set and you still want to use a cap topknot, scissor the side of the topknot only to the front of the ear. Then blend the coat at the top of the ear into the topknot (*Fig. 21*, where a Lamb trim topknot is pictured.) Repeat these steps to shape the other side of the topknot. Remember, *do not* extend the topknot down onto the cheek area as this distorts the leanness of head desirable for a correct Poodle profile. Turn the ear leather back

and trim off any loose hairs in front of the ear opening and along the line of the topknot to make sure there is a smooth junction where the topknot meets the cheekbone behind the eye (*Fig. 22*).

Do not scissor a vertical plane on the side of the topknot, or slant the side of the topknot inward.

Figure 23.

Figure 24.

You might end up with either a squared look or a "Denny Dimwit" look. A squared-off topknot does not have lines that are balanced and pleasing.

To finish the back of the cap, again bend the head forward and follow the line at the base of the occipital bone, scissoring a nice curve around the back of the head from the back point of one ear to the other (*Fig. 23*). When you have finished setting the bottom line of the back of the cap, raise the head, and looking at the back of the cap in profile, scissor a gently rounded cap. The shaded area on the back of the headpiece (*Fig. 24*) indicates the difference of line between a cap and a lamb trim topknot. Arrows in the same photo indicate the top of the ear set and the line of the bottom of the topknot from the back corner of the eye to the front of the ear set. When you have completed the back of the topknot, you should have a balanced, pleasantly rounded line of the cap (*Fig. 25*).

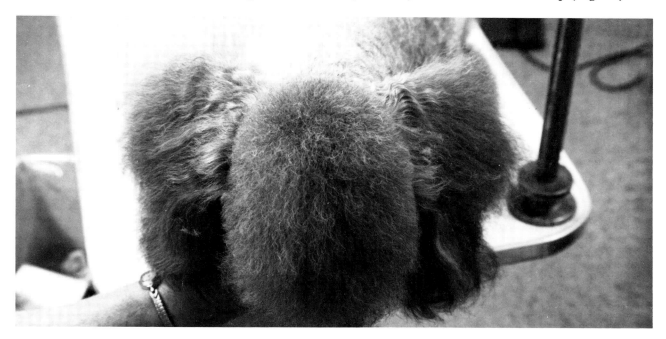

Figure 25.

To determine the height of the topknot, a pleasing proportion will be achieved if the distance from the center of the stop to the highest point of the topknot is only slightly more than the distance from the outer corner of one eye to the outer corner of the other (*Fig. 26*).

Figure 26.

After the height of the topknot has been established, scissor the rounding of the topknot sides, back, and front over the eyes (*Figs. 27 & 28*). It is easiest to achieve a nice line when scissoring if you view the line you are working on in profile. Be sure that the topknot directly above the eyes is rounded forward slightly and does not slant back

over the eyes steeply toward the top of the head. Repeatedly fluff the hair forward above the eyes to make sure that area is evenly scissored in a rounded contour. *Gerard Pellham's Groom'n Set*™ finishing spray holds the coat in position for easier scissoring. The finished cap is shown in (*Fig. 29*). Also notice the finish of the topknots in other Poodle head studies in this book.

When the topknot has been completed, comb through the ears. Spread the ear fringes on your hand and round them off slightly at the bottom to remove any straggly appearance. If all other lines of grooming are smooth and rounded, it is offensive to the eye to see an irregular line at the bottom of the ear fringe.

Scissoring Technique

No matter what position the hand must assume in grooming, the greatest flexibility and dexterity of hand movement controlling the scissors is achieved with the thumb positioned in one of the finger grips and the fourth finger of the same hand in the other grip with the little finger resting on the

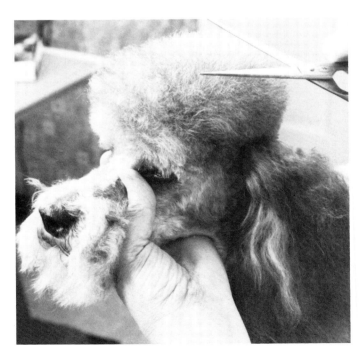

Figure 27.

Figure 28.

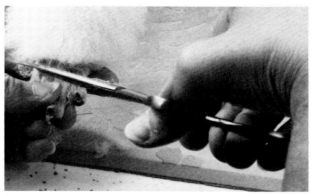

Figure 30.

Figure 29.

finger rest for directional control. Only the tip of the finger, up to the first joint, slips into the grip. If you are currently using another technique, begin practicing this scissoring method by positioning your fingers as shown (*Figs. 30-34*) and resting the scissor in your other hand. Open and close the scissors, moving only your thumb rather than your entire hand. Pretend you are scissoring a line in the air, again moving only the thumb. Practice these finger exercises until the motion of the thumb

Figure 31.

seems natural. Flex your hand at the wrist and practice opening the scissors using only the thumb motion until you can do it quickly and easily. You will feel awkward at first but when you conquer this technique, there will be less strain on your hand and wrist muscles. If you have slim fingers, purchase rubber finger grips to achieve a better fit.

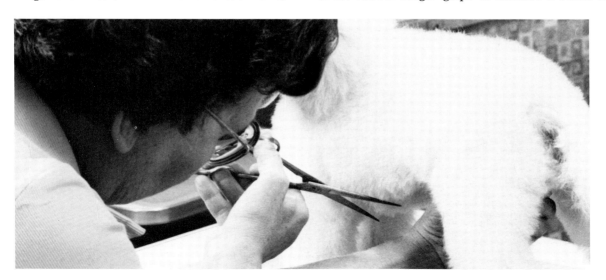

Figure 32.

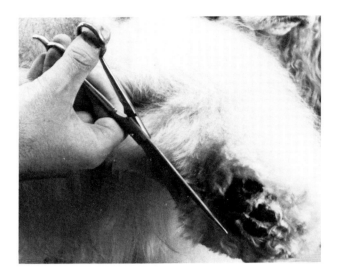

Figure 33.

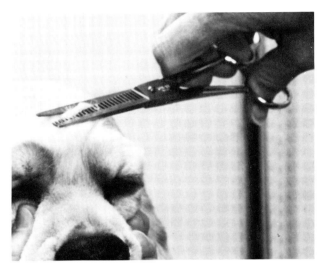

Figure 34.

When you examine scissors with the intent to buy, place your fingers in the position described above. Open the scissor with your thumb, slip the thumb out of the finger grip and see if the scissor closes almost all the way without any pressure from your fingers. Scissors must operate easily and smoothly to prevent the hand from cramping and aching.

Finishing the Tail

The balance and proportions of the tail of a Poodle can make or break the overall look. Sometimes it is necessary to finish a shorter tail than we would like because the tail has been docked too short to be in good proportion to the entire dog.

The clipped portion of the tail is usually ⅓ to ½ the entire distance from the base of the tail to the end of the pompon. Clip the shaved portion of the topside of the tail against the grain of the coat, and the underside in the direction of the coat growth. The underside of the tail is sensitive and could easily be irritated if you run the clipper blade against the lay of the coat. There is a cord of muscle on the underside of the tail, and if it is irritated, the dog might chew at the tail to relieve the irritation.

Comb out the entire tail. *Make sure all mats are removed.* Take the tail hair in your hand, slide your hand to the end of the tail grasping all the hair together, and twist the hair at the very end. Raise the tail erect and sight the length of the tail in relation to the topknot. Clip from the twisted end, any excess coat in order to balance nicely with the topknot. When you release the coat from your hand after clipping off the excess, you find a rounded top of the tail, and you can see if you need to repeat the process to remove more length of tail coat for proper proportions. The length of the tail must pleasingly balance the headpiece.

Use the comb to fluff out the tail again. Spray the tail coat with a light mist of finishing spray. Begin scissoring with curved scissors at the base of the tail pompon. (*Fig. 35*). Look at the tail in profile and scissor a circular line to the top of the tail (*Fig. 36*). Continue sighting and scissoring the profile line of the tail all around until it is completed (*Fig. 37*).

Figure 35.

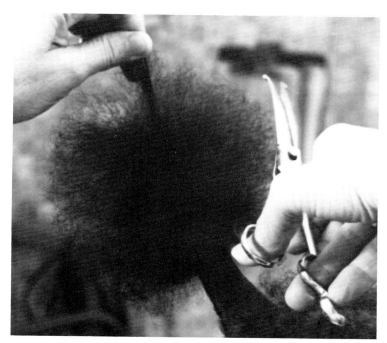

Figure 36.

Figure 37.

Some dogs do not allow you to hold their tails erect. They may have a low tail set which causes discomfort when the tail is forced erect, or there may be a disc problem along the spine which causes pain. If the dog shows agitation or immediately sits down when you handle the tail in this manner, have another person support the dog comfortably and bring the tail out only a little way from body. If you are working alone, improvise a sling for the rear of the body using a portable grooming post and noose. Other types of support for the dog that persists in sitting are shown in Chapter 3.

Setting a Bracelet Pattern (Miami, Clown, Summer, Cavalier, Bikini)

Determine the *exact* point at which the bracelet should start just covering the hock bone on the rear leg. Grasp the leg coat with one hand at that point, holding down the hair below it (*Fig. 38*). With your other hand, clip down to the point where you are holding the leg. Keeping your hand tight around the leg coat at that point prevents the dog from unexpectedly pulling up the leg causing you to clip off more than you should. Most groomer use an Oster #7, #7F, #5, #5F or an equivalent blade on the body work for this pattern. After you have clipped down to this point, reverse the direction of the blade and define this line around the leg by clipping upward for about one-half inch (*Fig. 39*). To do the front leg in a bracelet pattern, measure or sight across from the rear leg hock joint and make the top of the front bracelet exactly parallel to the rear bracelet.

Fluff out the bracelet with your comb and lightly spray with finishing spray. Scissor the pro-

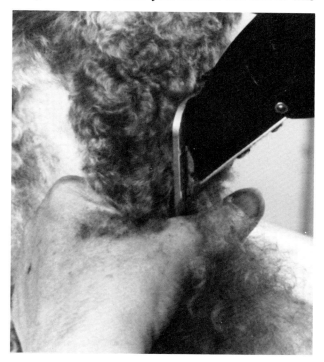

Figure 38.

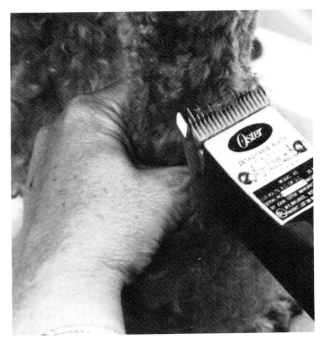

Figure 39.

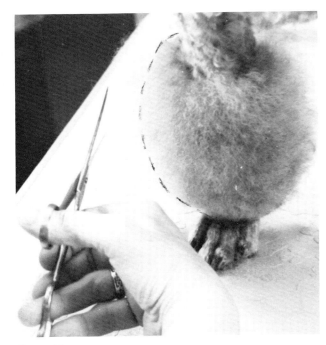

Figure 40.

Figure 41.

file lines (dotted line *Fig. 40*), to achieve a globular look. Remove any straggly hairs around the bottom of the bracelet and round it off at the foot (*Fig. 41*).

Finishing the Body of the Poodle

The blades used for finishing the body coat of the Poodle vary with the type of clip desired. For a Kennel trim, body work can be done with a #4, #4F, #5, #5F, #7 or #7F. Some Standard Poodles with a very tight, curly coat can have a bracelet trim done with a #9 blade, working with the lay of the coat.

When doing a Lamb trim or pattern clip, greater depth of coat is needed to give a nice contrast to the pattern lines, or to the look of a soft Lamb. The #4F blade leaves a smooth, velvety finish as shown in the Lamb trim in Chapter 13. For a pattern trim or longer Lamb trim use a clip-on attachment (*Fig. 42*).

In every trim where the hindquarters are covered with a pack of coat, the coat directly in front of the tail is scissored in a fan shape, angled toward the head (*Fig. 43*). Leaving any coat at the base of the tail takes away elegance from the tail set and gives the dog a longer bodied look.

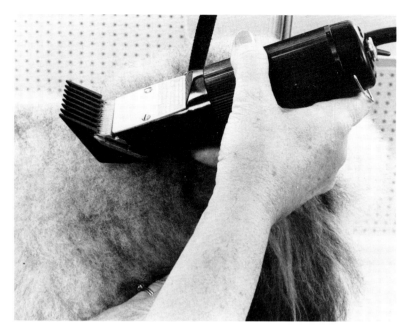

Figure 42.

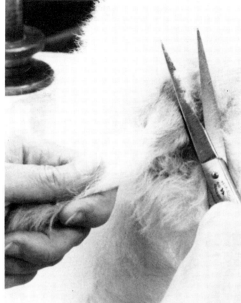

Figure 43.

Figure 44.

Clipping A Puppy

A puppy's first trim should be a light shaping of the coat to remove wispy ends. (*Fig. 44*). Also included would be a face, feet, and tail clipping. Nails should be trimmed and ears cleaned. Try to use the puppy trim until the dog is at least seven or eight months of age. When the puppy coat begins to blow, it may be necessary to do a shorter clip for easier home care. If it is the owner's first Poodle, he may not be prepared for the daily brushing necessary while the puppy coat is changing into adult coat. Remember to keep the puppy trim simple with flowing, rounded lines. Use a curved scissor on curved portions of the coat.

Always blend the body and leg coat to flow in smooth lines from one part of the dog to another. Your scissor strokes should follow the line of the coat growth (*Fig. 45*). Most puppy coats are not dense enough to support cross cutting against the lay of the coat; ridges may result. The finished puppy pictured in *Figure 46* was four and a half months old at the time of this first full haircut. It had its first face, feet and tail trim at six weeks.

Figure 45.

Figure 46.

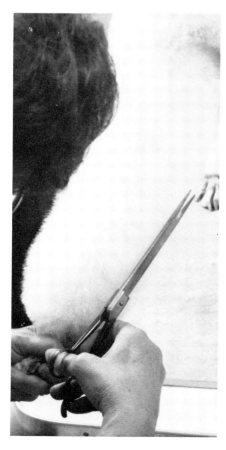

Figure 47.

Figure 48.

Figure 49.

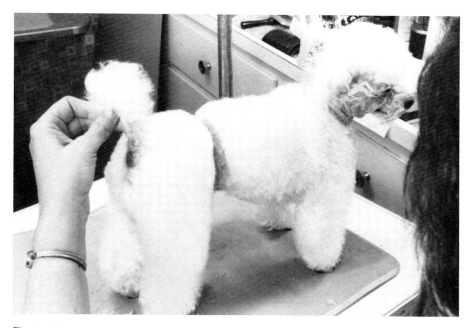

Figure 50.

Other Hints

Always use scissors that match the type of work you are doing (*Fig. 47*). Here the groomer is using a long pair of straights to finish the long lines of the leg work on the Standard Poodle shown in *Figure 48.* On this dog, the body work, rears, blending into the leg work, shoulders, chest, and underbelly work were finished using the Oster #4F blade. Dotted lines indicate the areas where scissor blend-ing was done at the point where the clipper work on the body was blended off.

Figures 49, 50, 51 show three stages of the grooming procedure for the tiny Toy Poodle shown earlier in this chapter. In *Figure 49,* the face, feet, tail, underbelly, and pattern set have been clipped. Then a complete brush-out, bath with a mild sham-poo, and fluff-dry was completed. *Figure 50* shows the plushness of the coat after fluff-drying. Some coat was removed from the body using a clip-on attachment over a #30 blade. The coat was again fluffed, a light finishing spray was misted over the coat, and the entire trim was scissor finished (*Fig. 51*). A small, red bow was tied into the back pack just above the tail.

Patterning

Patterned areas on a Poodle coat must have precise edges, and all clipped edges rounded smoothly with *no* tufts of hair left in the pattern stripe. The pattern clipped on the large Miniature Poodle shown in *Figure 52*, was done against the

very close pattern stripe is desired, clip the same stripe again, working *against* the grain of the coat with a #15 or #30 blade.

The side pattern stripe is placed no further back than the high point of the tuck-up. That placement is only correct for a Poodle with good proportions. For any Poodle whose body proportions do not give a square appearance, the side stripe would be placed slightly forward on the tuck-up area to pull the appearance of the longer body into better proportions. Before clipping any side pattern on the Poodle, use a comb to separate the coat at the point where you think the stripe should go and

Figure 51.

grain of the coat using a #15 blade. Another view of the pattern, shown after the bath and finishing is seen in *Figure 53*. The completed trim is shown in Chapter 13, *Figure 12*.

When doing the pattern stripe for a Dutch trim, use a blade whose width cuts a stripe complimentary to the size of the dog's body. After the neck and tail have been finished, begin at the center point where the neck and withers meet. Clip in a straight line to the top center of the tail set and checking frequently to keep the line straight. If a

check to see if the pattern placement looks correct. A single side stripe such as what would be used for a Dutch Pattern would not be placed forward of the last rib.

Learning to "see" the correct placement of body and leg lines in clipping the Poodle is perhaps the most difficult part of learning to groom. Some groomers who have a natural ability to artistically evaluate the dog they are working on will have less trouble with this art. For others, it will be an acquired art as they watch and practice.

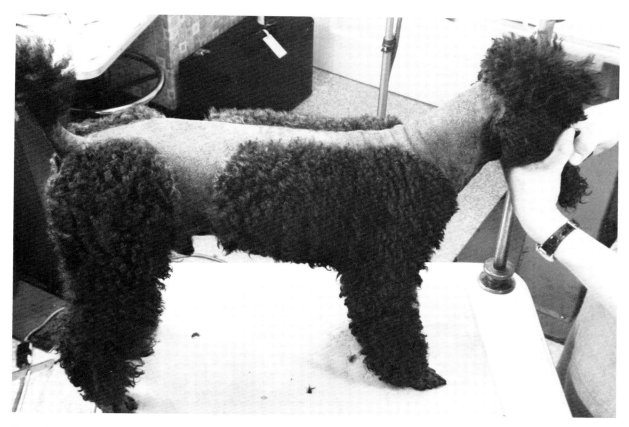

Figure 52.

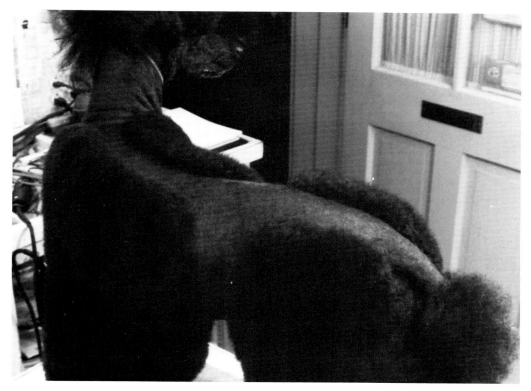

Figure 53.

16
Grooming the Miniature Schnauzer

In this chapter we will deal with two types of pet Schnauzer coats. One has a dense, soft coat, (*Fig. 1*), the other has the open, soft coat, more commonly seen by the pet groomer (*Fig. 1A*).

As has been the case with many breeds, the Miniature Schnauzer evolved by the process of breeding down from the smallest of the Standard Schnauzers. They came from the same original stock, but along the way may have had the Affenpincher introduced to reduce size while still retaining Terrier characteristics. The Miniature Schnauzer is shown in the Utility Group in Great Britain, but he competes in the United States in the Terrier Group. Whatever the country, his high-spirited and vigorous characteristics are encouraged in the show ring.

The Schnauzer breed originated in the southern part of Germany where the word "schnauzer" means snout. The Schnauzer was so named for its heavy beard which draws attention to the snout, or muzzle as it is more commonly called.

The original Standard Schnauzer was a combination of black Poodle, Wolf Spitz, and Wire Haired Pinscher. From this background, the Miniature Schnauzer inherited certain characteristics that are usually found in a larger breed. He is hardy and tough, and defends his own territory. He has a good sense of humor, and when kept properly conditioned, enjoys hiking and jogging.

Miniature Schnauzers may be shown in the conformation ring with either a cropped or uncropped ear. However, the uncropped ear is seldom seen in the Championship ring.

Ch. Kady - J. Editorial "Quincy." Bred and owned by Master Groomer, Paul Bryant. Agent, Carol Garmaker. (Photo - Booth)

After World War II, Miniature Schnauzer registrations began to increase rapidly in all parts of the world. The breed continues its popularity, and for those people interested in a smart, small dog, the Miniature Schnauzer is a satisfying choice. His size makes him a good choice for apartment dwellers or large home owners alike. If properly socialized when a puppy, he usually develops a pleasing personality that reacts well to proper obedience training. Schnauzers seem particularly happy when freshly groomed.

The Miniature Schnauzer matures early and reaches full maturity around a year of age. Gentle but firm training should begin early—eight weeks is not too young—to establish a pleasant temperament in the adult dog.

SCHNAUZER PUPPY GROOMING TIPS

Early training to accept brushing and combing may be a struggle but if the owner of a Schnauzer puppy quits brushing because the puppy whimpers, a habit may form that is difficult to break. Therefore, when the owner of a Schnauzer puppy calls to inquire about the correct age to start grooming, advise him to start "yesterday." If the puppy

Figure 1.

Figure 1A.

is mature enough to leave the litter, it is mature enough to be gently combed and brushed.

A modified professional grooming should be scheduled at no later than four months of age providing vaccinations are complete. Such grooming includes ear cleaning, nail clipping, combing and brushing, bathing, and fluff drying. This will acquaint the puppy with the grooming procedures that will be a part of his life. If any part of the grooming causes difficult behavior on the part of the puppy, the owner can be taught how to work with it at home. Frequent trips to the shop for some combing and brushing may eliminate problems at the next regular grooming.

The soft, cottony coat found in some Miniature Schnauzer strains requires extra care at home to prevent complete stripping of the coat, furnishings, and whiskers if matting occurs. When a dense coat must be stripped, it may not grow back with the same luxurious density.

GROOMING THE SCHNAUZER

Before the Bath

The average Schnauzer comes for grooming looking the worse for wear. Furnishings may contain such debris as evergreen twigs, weed seeds, or gum. Prepare the furnishings for de-matting by spraying them thoroughly with a tangle remover.

De-mat the furnishings as described in the pre-work section of Chapter 14. Pay particular attention to the armpit area, hocks, and action points at the top of the legs (*Fig. 2*). For badly matted whiskers encrusted with dried food or other debris, use the Oster Mat Comb (*Fig. 3*). Firmly grasp the whiskers on one side of the mouth and de-mat the other side. Schnauzers don't fool around when they bite, so use caution. After all mats in the whiskers have been opened, use a slicker brush to remove them (*Fig. 4*). Again, hold the whiskers on one side of the muzzle while you brush out the other. Finish cleaning out the beard by thoroughly combing through it to be sure all matting is removed down to the skin (*Fig. 5*).

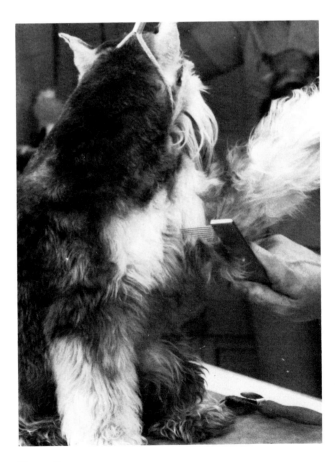

Figure 2.

Figure 3.

Figure 4.

In order to make drying after the bath easier, remove excess body coat prior to bathing (*Figs. 6 & 7*). To keep a coated look on this Schnauzer, Paul removes body coat with a #7F blade. Begin clipping at the base of the occipital bone, down the neck and body to the tail in one continuous stroke. Work

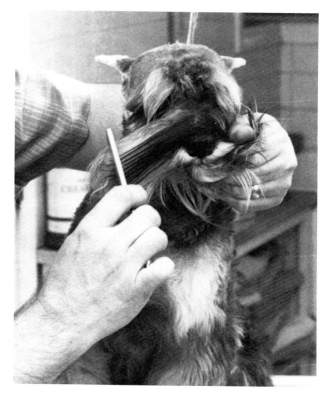

Figure 5.

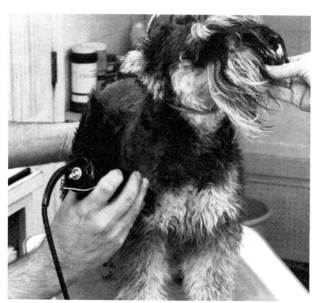

Figure 6.

Figure 7.

with the direction of the coat growth, blending leg and coat furnishings at the elbows, rib cage, and rear legs along the furnishing line indicated by the dotted line. (*Fig. 8*).

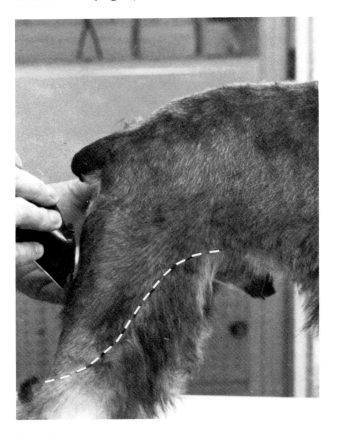

Figure 8.

The rear leg of the open-coated Schnauzer is shown in *Figure 9*. The arrow points to the angulation line just above the hock. The length of the rear leg is different on every Schnauzer and a determination must be made where to taper off the angulation line on the back leg. For the average leg, the point is midway between an imaginary extended line across the leg from the stifle joint and the hock joint as is being pointed out in this photo. For a short leg, the line would drop almost to the hock joint, and for a high-on-leg Schnauzer, would be a little higher up. The breed Standard calls for a square, cobby dog. When properly placed, the angulation line on the back leg creates this illusion.

After removing excess body coat, rough clip the head before bathing (*Fig. 10*). Begin clipping the head at the back of the eye socket where the eyebrows change color. Clip the entire skull, blending into the neck below the occiput. Place the clipper at the back corner of the eye and clip toward the ear. In this case, an Oster #9 blade is being used for the head work. Clip to the base of the ear. Take care not to nick the junction points of the head and the ear. Next, place the clipper at a point just behind the line of the mouth, and clip back and down toward the neck. There is a whisker nodule on the underside of the muzzle almost in line with the mouth opening. It usually has a stiff, dark hair growing from it. Place your clipper at that point, and clip with the grain of the coat down the front of the neck to the junction of the neck and the body. Leave the chest hair to be clipped and scissored after the bath. You will go over these areas when

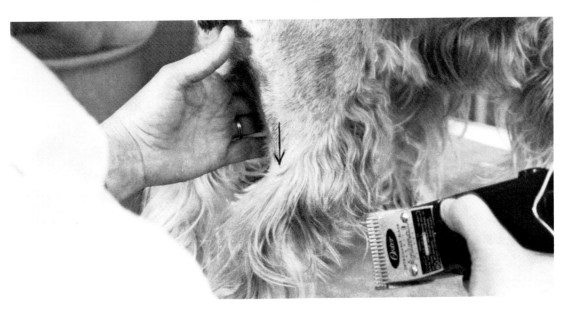

Figure 9.

finishing, so don't worry about smoothness of coat at this point.

Many groomers are more comfortable using an Oster #10 blade for the head and body work. With the availability of the #7F and the #9 blades, there is greater choice of coat finishes. For an older dog with a sparse body coat, use the #7F blade which gives a longer-coated look. The sketch (*Fig. 11*) shows the direction of the clipper stroke for body work. Follow the slant of the coat growth on the rib cage to avoid the ridges that may show in the coat if clipping lines are vertical. All body and rear leg work on the open-coated Schnauzer was done with the #9 blade, head coat with a #10, and blending lines with the #7F.

Figure 10.

Figure 11. Sketch by D. Walin

REAR
VIEW

Figure 12.

Remove inside ear hair. The ear can be clipped and finished before the bath. Begin at the base of the ear and clip toward the tip (*Figs. 12 & 13*) and from the center of the ear toward the outside edges. Always brace the ear between the thumb and fingers to give a firm surface while clipping. To trim the edge of the ear, brace the ear between your thumb and forefinger and place your scissors at a 45-degree angle to the edge of the ear (*Fig. 14*). Holding the scissor in this manner allows a close finish to the ear without nicking the ear leather as the scissor blade slides off the edge of the ear, taking off the coat and leaving a neat edge. When you scissor with the blades of the scissor at direct right angles to the edge of the ear, there is greater risk of nicking the ear. Ears bleed profusely when nicked!

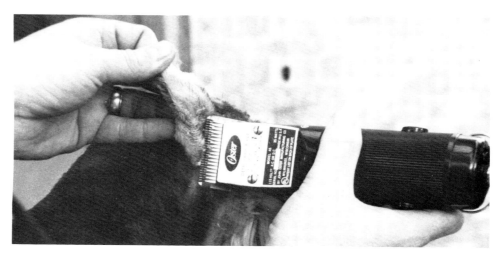

Figure 13.

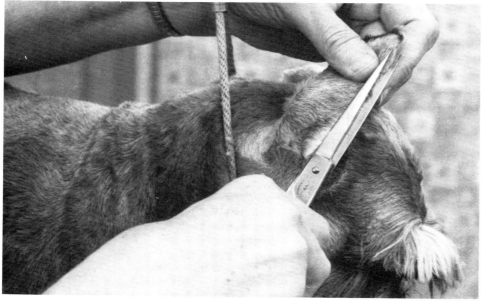

Figure 14.

Bathing and Drying

Brush off loose coat and bathe the Schnauzer. Suds the leg furnishings and whiskers twice; rinse until the water runs clear. A protein shampoo gives the furnishings more body for easier scissoring. Do not use a rinse that softens the coat. The best rinse I have found to set up coat for finish scissoring is *Final Touch*™ from Gerard Pellham. (As noted earlier, products mentioned are those I have used. Groomers should try samples of many kinds of products to find those that work best for them. The criteria for choosing a product is—it must work as advertised, and must not irritate the dog or the groomer's hands.)

A smooth finish on the body coat of the Schnauzer can be more easily accomplished if the body coat is back-brushed while drying (*Fig. 15*). Then apply a light coat of *Groom and Set*™ to give extra body and hold the coat which will allow the blade to clip more smoothly. Use a slicker brush to fluff dry the leg furnishings so they stand away from the leg for easier scissoring. (*Fig. 16*). Brush the head and eyebrows toward the muzzle to make sure eyebrows lie flat (*Fig. 17*).

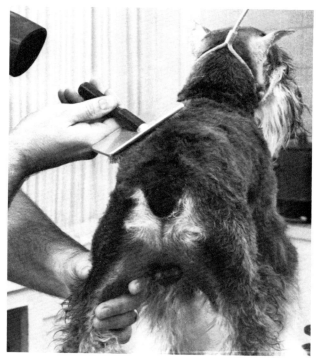

Figure 15.

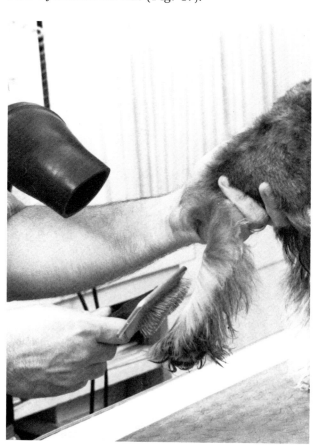

Figure 16.

Figure 17.

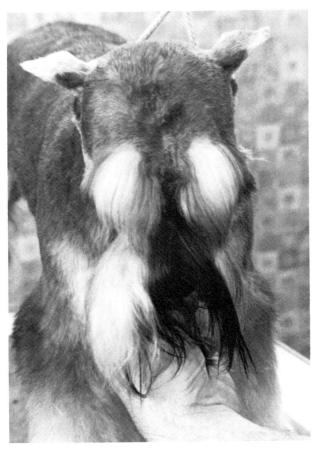

Figure 18.

Figure 18 shows the lay of the eyebrows after brush-drying, and *Figure 19* shows the entire dog, bathed and fluff-dried, ready for finishing.

Finishing the Head

The head should show a rectangular, not cheeky, skull. Thick whiskers enhance the rectangular look. Whiskers are not scissored off to a blunt look. The eyebrows are scissored to accentuate the rectangular shape of the head and the keen expression of the eye.

Repeat the head work after bathing and drying in order to smooth the appearance of the skull and to set the eyebrow line (*Fig. 20*) using a #9 or #10 blade. It helps to back brush the head coat before clipping. Establish the eyebrow line by following the marked color change where the head coat and eyebrows meet. If there is no definitive color change, set the eyebrow line just behind the eye socket. This gives a correct line to the eyebrow in proportion to the dog's head.

With your comb, part the eyebrow to both sides exposing the area between the eyes. Carefully scissor an inverted "V" between the eyes to the stop (*Fig. 21*). With curved scissors, clean out only that area between the eyebrows as is necessary to accentuate the stop (*Fig. 22*) and be careful not to

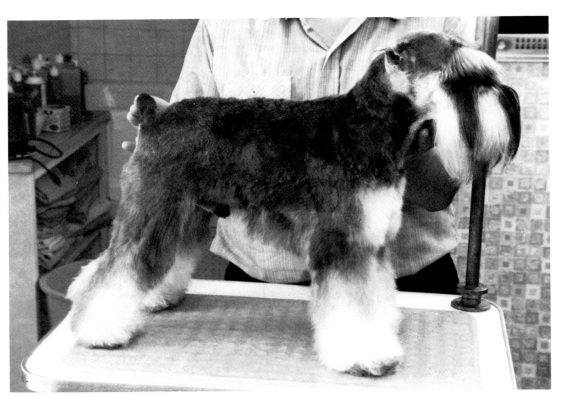

Figure 19.

Figure 20.

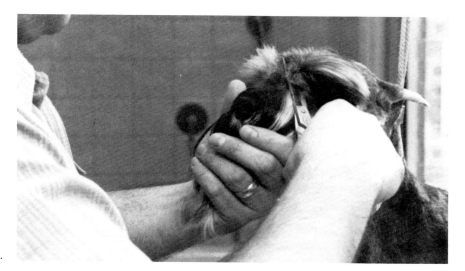

Figure 21.

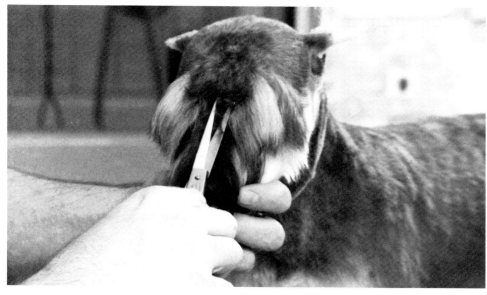

Figure 22.

dig into the coat, leaving a mark. DO NOT SCISSOR OR CLIP UNDER THE EYES. Clean the area above the stop, blending into the skull and defining the eyebrow (*Fig. 23*). Position your scissors at the outside corner of the eye, flat against the skull and cut in a line straight forward. (A tip to advanced groomers: Use a curved scissor for this cut, reversing the position of your scissors and holding them backwards. This gives the cut of the eyebrow a slight arch, and gives the eye a keener expression (*Fig. 24*).) Reverse the scissor in your hand to do the opposite eyebrow, taking care to hold the scissor at *exactly* the same angle as used for the first eyebrow (*Fig. 25*).

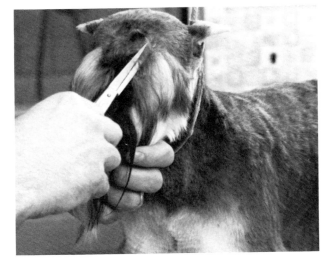

Figure 23.

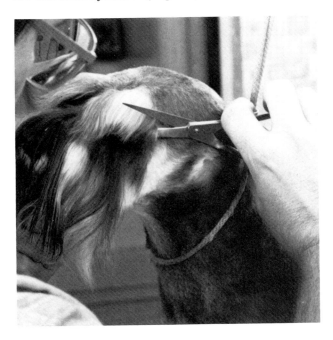

Figure 24.

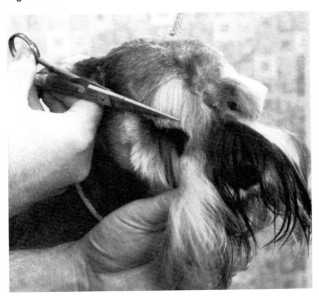

Figure 25.

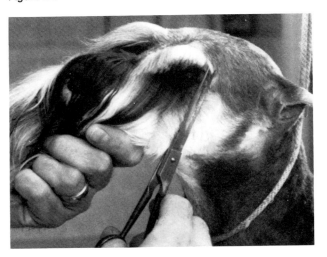

Figure 26.

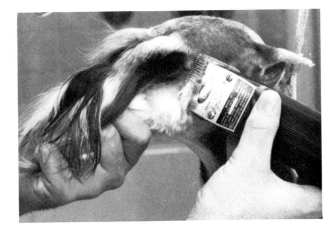

Figure 27.

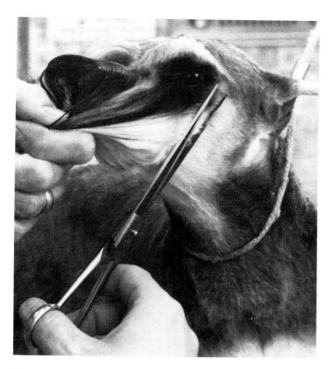

Figure 28.

Some Schnauzers are "skully" behind the eye in which case, the scissors should be positioned slightly out from the back corner of the eye when scissoring the eyebrow. Blend the coat at the back corner of the eye into the head coat (*Fig. 26*).

Clean the cheek area to the back corner of the eye (*Fig. 27*). Clip around the underside of the jaw to the back corner of the other eye using a #10, #9, of #7F blade. These areas, as well as the front of the neck, can be clipped with or against the grain of the coat depending on the sensitivity of the dog.

The positioning of the beard depends on whether or not the dog has a coarse head. The line of the beard is established between the whisker nodule on each cheek and a point directly behind the corner of the mouth. The corner of the mouth is not exposed. Take the beard in your hand and with scissors trim away any unsightly hairs to give a clean beard line. (*Fig. 28*).

Body and Leg Work

The Schnauzer body should be short-backed with the brisket extending at least to the elbow. Ribs should be well-sprung and deep. The overall appearance should be that of a square body.

If the underbelly area was not clipped before the bath, clean this area before continuing the body work. Do not clip higher than the navel unless the dog is badly matted in this sensitive area.

Back brush the entire clipped body area and lightly spray with finishing spray. Re-clip the body coat for a smoother finish using a #7F, #9 or the standard #10 blade depending on the finish desired. Work *with* the grain of the coat. Blend with a #7F blade where the undercarriage furnishings begin and along the angulation line of the rear leg (arrows in *Fig. 29*). To prevent ridging, remember to keep the clipper teeth in line with the direction of the coat growth, especially on the side of the rib cage. The Oster #7 blade works well when blending body lines into the furnishings.

Remove body coat on the rib cage to accentuate depth of rib. Skirting is *never* left up on the sides of the rib cage. Groomers in some parts of the country still leave an apron of coat all the way around the body of the Schnauzer. This practice totally destroys the breed profile.

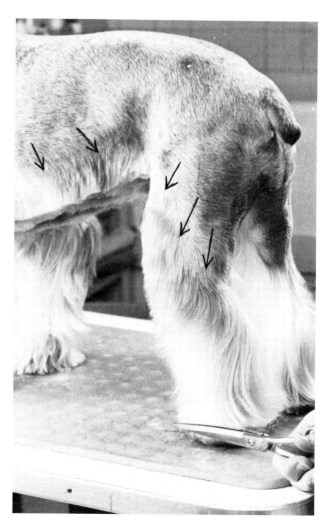

Figure 29.

Comb through the undercarriage coat to be sure all mats are removed before scissoring the furnishings on the brisket (*Fig. 30*). Scissor in the tuck-up line (the high point of the loin area just in front of the rear leg). The line of the undercarriage furnishings comes out of the tuck-up and is scissored to a point at or just below the elbow to accentuate depth of chest (*Fig. 31*). These furnishings are scissored evenly on both sides of the rib cage under the brisket and extend to meet the chest coat between the front legs.

Blend the chest hair with either a #5F blade or a scissors. Eliminate any appearance of a bib; blend into the top of the front legs (*Figs. 32 & 33*). Scissor away any appearance of bulk behind the elbow on the front leg (*Fig. 34*). To neaten the coat swirl on either side below the tail, reverse clip around the swirl with a #7F or #9 blade (*Fig. 35*).

Figure 30.

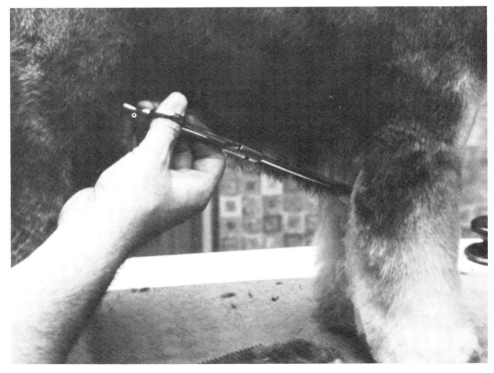

Figure 31.

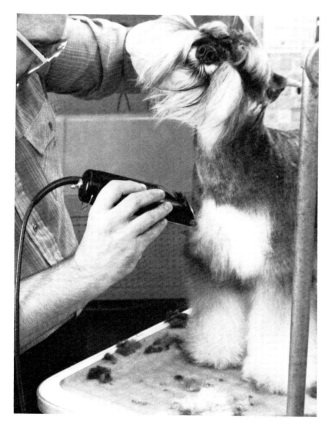

Figure 32.

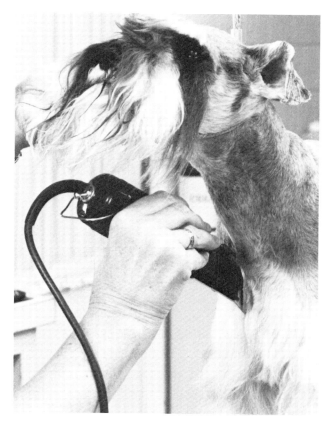

Figure 33.

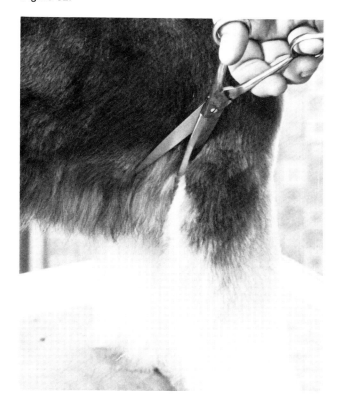

Figure 34.

Figure 35.

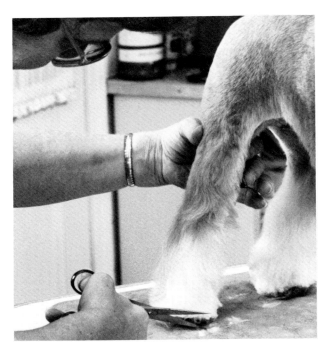

Figure 36.

Scissor a round (not pointed), tight foot (*Fig. 36*). *Do not* expose toenails. Leg coat is scissored in a cylindrical shape down to the foot which is to be covered (*Fig. 37*). It is difficult to scissor a pretty leg on an open coat (*Fig. 38*). Use a vertical scissor technique on an open coat to prevent cross cut marks.

Clipping the Forequarters

The front legs are straight and parallel when viewed from any angle, and are separated by a deep brisket. The elbows should appear to be close to the body allowing the dog to move in a straight line.

Beginning just above the elbow, scissor leg coat straight down on the front and sides to show straight, parallel lines. The clipper work on the body is brought down to just above the elbows to show the muscle tone above the front legs. When looking at the Schnauzer's front from a side profile there should be no hair protruding beyond the line of the furnishings on the front legs. Do not hollow out the forechest hair between the front legs. The hair on the back of the front leg is scissored in close to the elbow, scissoring down a vertical line (*Fig. 39*). This makes the elbow appear close to the body, and gives a squarer appearance when the dog is moving.

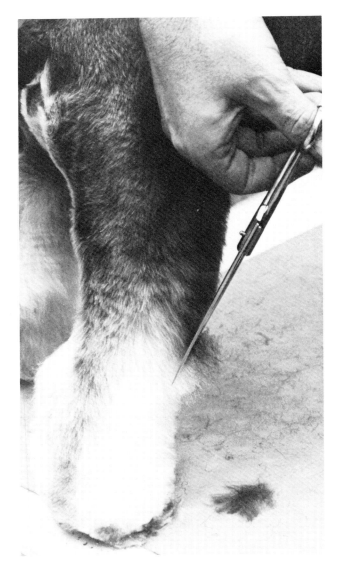

Figure 37.

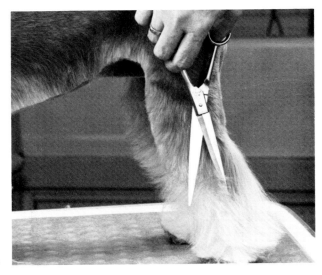

Figure 38.

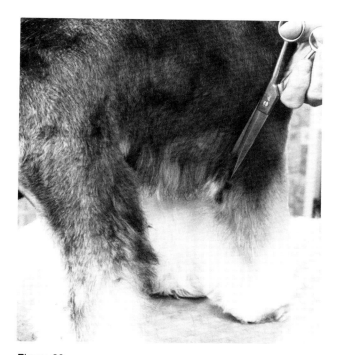

Figure 39.

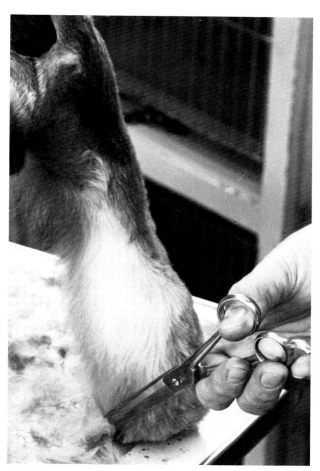

Figure 40.

Clipping the Hindquarters

Hindquarters are well-muscled with enough angulation to show a well let-down hock. Scissor around the rear foot (*Figs. 40 & 41*) and compare the finished and unfinished coat on the legs of this dense-coated dog. Scissor the inside and outside lines of the rear legs to form parallel lines. Notice that the rear legs form a well-arched hindquarter (*Fig. 42*). The leg coat near the top of the arch on the inside rear leg is scissored, not clipped. Scissor

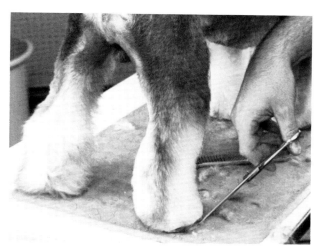

Figure 41.

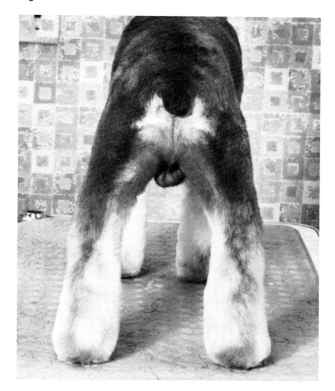

Figure 42.

the coat on the back of the leg below the hock on a slightly outward angle to accentuate angulation (*Fig. 43*).

When doing the leg work on an open-coated Schnauzer, use vertical strokes to eliminate ridges from cross-cut scissoring. Use a *#7* or *#5* blade to blend all lines where short coat flows into longer

coated areas. There should never be any sharply defined lines where body coat and furnishings meet. All lines should flow smoothly.

Figures 44 and 45 show the finished front head work of the Schnauzer with a natural ear and an open, sparse coat. *Figures 46 and 47* show the finished work on the densely-coated Schnauzer.

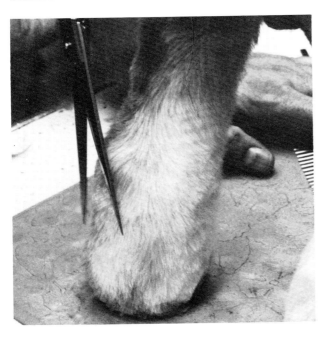

Figure 43.

Figure 44.

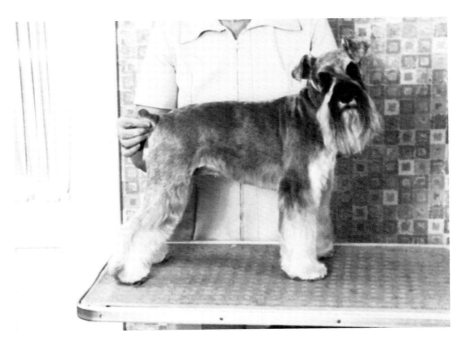

Figure 45.

Figure 46.

Figure 47.

I am particularly indebted to Paul Bryant for his assistance in preparing this chapter. Paul has been an active breeder/exhibitor of Miniature Schnauzers for many years.

17
Grooming the Bichon Frise

The early 1970s showed a rise in the popularity of these small, white, dogs whose gentle and affectionate nature make them particularly appealing. The Bichon is a descendant of the Barbet, or Water Spaniel, as is his cousin, the Caniche (Poodle). Through miniaturization, they were bred down to their present size. Although the original Bichons were divided into four categories, all were native to the Mediterranean area.

This is a very old breed even though it has only recently been popularized in the United States. Because of their dispositions, they were often used in barter for needed goods. They were frequent companions of sailors, and were transported from one continent to another. They were particularly popular in Spain, and it is thought that Spanish sailors first introduced them to the Canary Island of Tenerife. There they became known as the Bichon Tenerife, and this name was retained because of its exotic inference which enhanced its commercial value.

Italian sailors rediscovered the little dogs in the 1300s, and brought them back to the continent where they became the pets of Italian nobility. The "Tenerife" or "Bichon" soon became popular in France, especially in the court of Henry III, where they lived a pampered life. Later during the reign of Napoleon III, there was renewed interest in the breed. However, in the 1800s this aristocratic little dog became a common dog of the streets. There they performed with organ grinders and were found doing tricks in circuses and fairs.

At the end of World War I, four French breeders recognized the potential of the Bichon and began a controlled breeding program. In March 1933, an official breed Standard was adopted by the Société Centrale Canine of France. At that time, the breed was known under two names, "Tenerife" and "Bichon." The president of the International Canine Federation proposed a name based on the characteristics of the dogs and the name "Bichon Frise" was adopted.

In 1934 the French Kennel Club admitted the Bichon to its stud registry. The International Canine Federation recognizes the Bichon Frise as a "French-Belgian breed having the right to registration in the Book of Origins from all countries."

The first Bichon litter whelped in the United States was born in 1956, accepted for entry in the Miscellaneous Class on September 1, 1971, and then admitted to registration in the American Kennel Club Stud Book in October 1972. They were first shown in regular show classifications in the Non-Sporting Group at AKC shows on April 4, 1973.

THE BREED STANDARD

The Bichon is a sturdy, lively dog of stable temperament with a stylish gait and an air of dignity and intelligence. The color is solid white, or white with cream, apricot or gray on the ears and/or body. The head is proportionate to the size of the dog. The skull is broad and somewhat round, but not coarse. It is covered with a topknot of hair. The muzzle, of medium length, is not heavy or snipey. There is a slightly accentuated stop. The

Am. Can. Champion Lily Gatlock of Druid shown winning a Canadian Best In Show. Owner, Ms. Betsy Schley. (Photo - Alex Smith)

dropped ears are covered with long, flowing hair. The ear leather should reach approximately half the length of the muzzle. The eyes are black or dark brown with black rims. They are large, round, expressive and alert. Lips are black, fine, and never drooping. The nose should be black, round and pronounced. A scissors bite is required. The neck is rather long, gracefully and proudly carried behind an erect head. Shoulders should be well laid back. The elbows are held close to the body. The body is slightly longer than the dog is tall, and is well developed with a good spring of ribs. The back inclines gradually from the withers to a slight rise over the loins. The loin is large and muscular. The brisket is well let down. The tail is covered with long flowing hair. It is carried gaily, and curved to lie on the back. The height of the dog at the withers should not exceed 12 inches, nor be under 8 inches. The legs and feet are strong boned, appearing straight, with well knit pasterns. Hind-quarters are well angulated. The feet are tight and round resembling a cat's paw. The coat is profuse, silky and loosely curled with an undercoat.

When groomed, the head is *scissored* to show the eyes and give a full, rounded appearance to the head and body. The minimum length of show coat for an adult is two to three inches.

GROOMING THE BICHON

When the Bichon first made its appearance in the show ring, it was not heavily groomed. However, it wasn't long before famous handlers began shaping a more precise line on the Bichon coat. These trimmed Bichons began to win top honors and now most Bichons appearing in the ring are precisely scissored showing a level top-line without any rise over the loins as was the case when they were first shown in the United States.

They are being selectively bred to show a shorter top-line and give the appearance of a squarer dog.

The pet Bichon is clipped and scissored to exactly the same breed profile as the show dog. The only variations include a slightly shorter beard to keep it out of food and water, and a shorter body coat, scissored or clipped to a length of about one inch.

With the rising popularity of this breed, groomers are seeing more and more of these dogs. A Bichon clip is used for much mixed breed styling as well as for Poodles with tendencies to scratch their faces. An interesting thing to note is the fact that the *body* work for the Poodle and Bichon is similar.

HOME CARE

These little dogs are expensive to purchase and need frequent grooming. The new owner brings in a small ball of fluff, not always realizing that this will develop into a coat needing *much* grooming with complete grooming done about *once a month*.

As the coat grows and develops, daily home brushing is needed to prevent formation of tiny mats which then grow into larger matted areas almost overnight. The groomer must help reinforce any directions the breeder has given for coat care, and take the time to be sure the owner knows how to properly brush and comb. As with the Poodle, the Bichon blows its coat sometime between the ages of eight to sixteen months. A wire slicker brush can be used to clean the coat all the way down to the skin of the pet Bichon. A pet Bichon in longer coat, or a show Bichon must be brushed with a pin brush. The coat must *always* be moisturized when beginning to brush to prevent breakage. Since the Bichon is a double-coated breed (there is a longer, silky outer coat with a soft undercoat), the coat should be layerbrushed for thorough removal of mats. This is done by separating the coat a half an inch at a time, moisturizing that section, then brushing and combing each section until *completely* free of mats.

BATHING

Figure 1 shows a pet Bichon that loves to play in the woods with its German Shepherd companion. It usually takes an hour and a half to brush, comb and totally de-mat this particular Bichon. Before beginning to brush, a small section of coat at a time is moisturized with a de-matting solution. All matted areas are worked through using the small Oster Mat Comb (see Ch. 14). Two sudsings are usually needed to thoroughly remove dirt and whiten the coat. A tearless shampoo is used to prevent irritation to skin or eyes. This Bichon's coat is very dense, and particular attention is paid to forcing water through the coat until every trace of shampoo has been removed (*Fig. 2*). The water should run clear, and the coat should have no slippery feel to it. A rinse of *Final Touch*™ sets up the coat for easier scissoring.

Drying

Always fluff dry the Bichon after the bath as there is no other way to create the "powder puff" look for which this breed is known. In *Figure 3*, the Bichon coat is being dried, beginning with the rear quarters and fluffing toward the head. Short, quick strokes of the brush need not go to the skin, but rather are needed only to move the coat for air penetration. This is particularly important to protect the sensitive skin of the white Bichon. Always begin fluff drying at the shortest area of the coat. Keep a spritzer bottle on hand to re-dampen any area that begins to kink up from air drying too quickly.

Figure 1.

Figure 2.

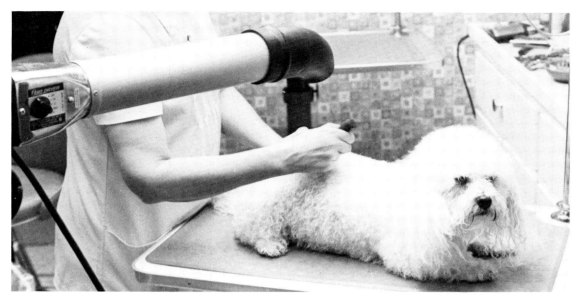

Figure 3.

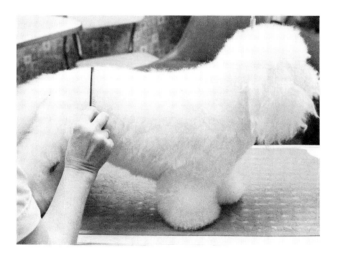

Figure 4.

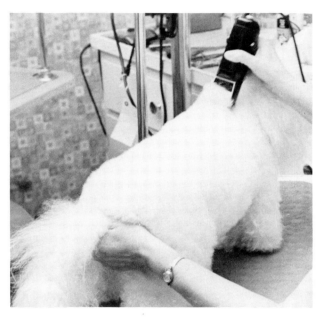

Figure 5.

FINISHING THE BODY COAT

Note: All body work described in this section is also applicable to the body work for the Poodle. The coat receives a final comb-out (*Fig. 4*) to check for any possible mats, and is touched off with a light finishing spray.

Begin clipping the body coat at the withers (*Fig. 5*) but do not clip up on the neck as it will be scissored into the body coat when completing the head. For a one-inch finish on the body work of a pet trim, use a clip-on attachment over a #30 or a blocking blade. For a slightly shorter, but very smooth finish, use an Oster #4F blade. This blade, introduced in 1982, gives the Bichon or Poodle coat

the velvety appearance of being hand scissored. Bichon coat is usually fine, and if your clipper blade begins to jam or pick at the coat, hold the blade up to the light to see if any tiny hairs have caught between the blade teeth. If they have, clean the blade (see Ch. 12).

Continue clipping the back coat over the hindquarters, stopping above the tail. If a blade is used for the body work, the natural lines of the Bichon body will show a rise over the loin area instead of the popular level topline that is hand scissored for

Figure 6.

the show ring. Clip down toward the leg muscle on the rear leg and taper off. Clip down to just above the elbow on the front leg. Clip the rib cage, rolling the clipper down and under toward the stomach area (*Fig. 6*).

The coat around the tail is carefully blended into the base of the tail, taking care not to remove any of the long, tail hair (*Fig. 7*). Use the same clipper as used for the body coat, and come straight out onto the base of the tail for about ½ inch, or hand scissor around the base of the tail. Make sure to leave enough coat to give the base of the tail a plush look.

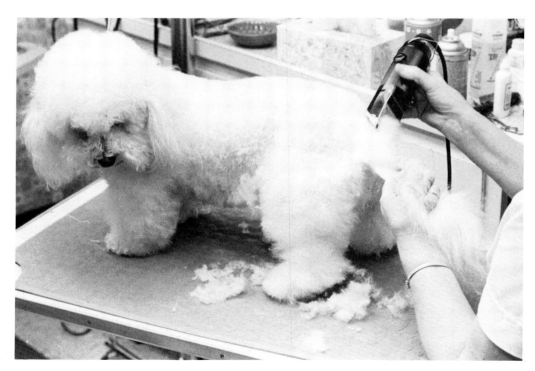

Figure 7.

If the coat is dense blend below the tail area using a clipper (*Fig. 8*); scissor if the coat is thinner in this area (*Fig. 9*). Lift the tail straight up and scissor any straggly hair around the anus to neaten the look of the base of the tail when it lays up over the back (*Fig. 10*).

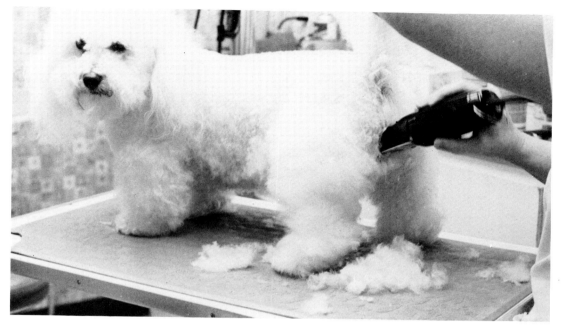

Figure 8.

Figure 9.

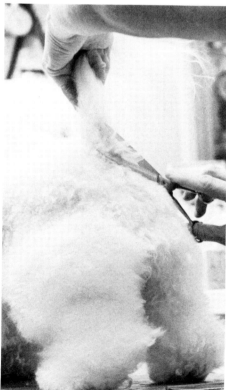

Figure 10.

Figure 11.

Figure 12.

Clip or scissor the chest hair to blend into the top of the front leg (*Fig. 11*). Do not run the clipper down between the front legs as this area looks better if it is hand scissored. Clipping may make it look too bare because of the direction of the coat growth.

Clip the coat on the bottom of the rib cage from between the front legs back to the groin area with the same blade as used on the body (*Fig. 12*). If shorter underbelly coat is desired, reverse clip with the same blade from the groin to between the front legs.

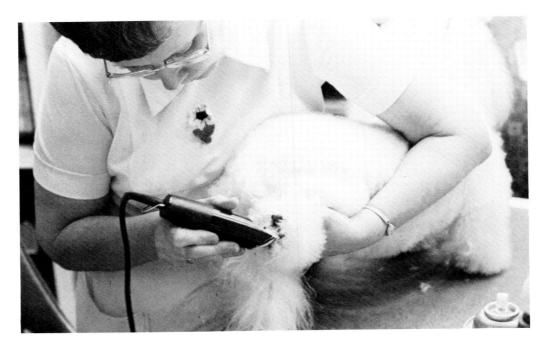

Figure 13.

FINISHING THE LEGS

Begin leg work by removing the hair between the pads on the underside of the foot (*Fig. 13*) using either a small, blunt-tip scissor, or a small blade. Take care not to remove coat along the side of the foot. Scissor coat on the bottom of the foot straight across, level with the foot pads (*Fig. 14*).

With your comb fluff out the coat on the front legs. Begin scissoring just above the elbow at the same depth as the finished body coat, and scissor a straight line down to the grooming table (*Fig. 15*). The legs should look like cylinders when completed, flowing from the body coat with no break, and covering the entire foot.

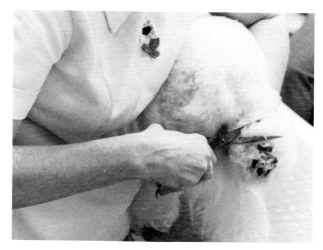

Figure 14.

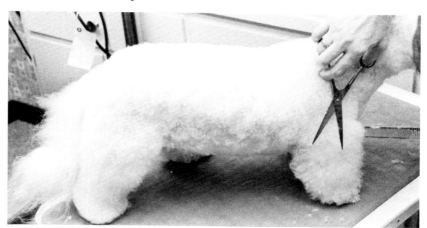

Figure 15.

Rear legs are to be scissored in the same manner, beginning over the hip area and working down the leg (*Fig. 16*). Round off the coat at the very bottom of each leg around the foot but do not expose the toenails (*Fig. 17*). The inside and outside lines of the rear leg are parallel.

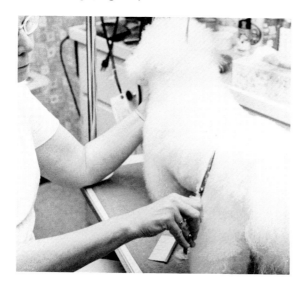

Figure 16.

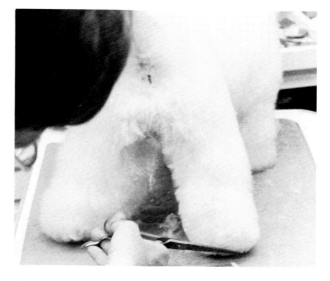

Figure 17.

Since the breed Standard calls for a well-angulated rear leg, scissor in the angulation line (*Fig. 18*). The rear leg lines are pleasing, flowing lines, showing no break from the body lines.

Inside lines of the legs must also be smoothly scissored (*Fig. 19*). It is easy to forget to do these areas, but they will be visible when the dog is moving. To keep the dog from moving on the table while doing leg work, lift the leg opposite the one you are scissoring (*Fig. 20*). When leg work is completed, do a final check and scissor any unevenness on the body coat and legs for a smooth look (*Fig. 21*).

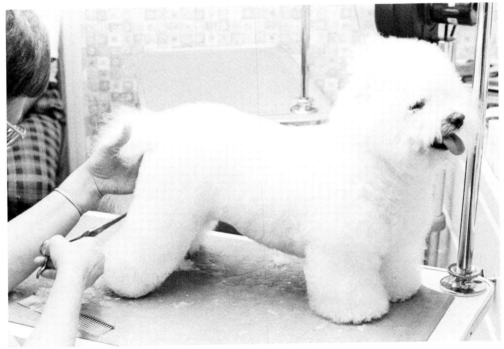

Figure 18.

Figure 19.

Figure 20.

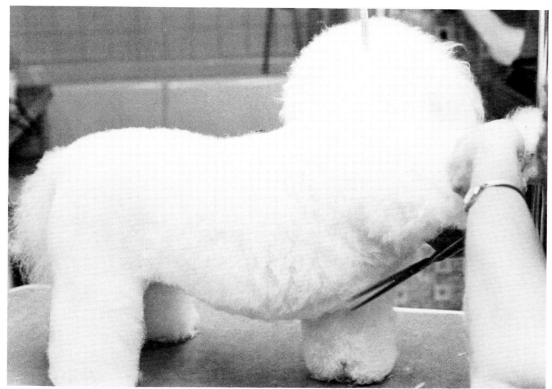

Figure 21.

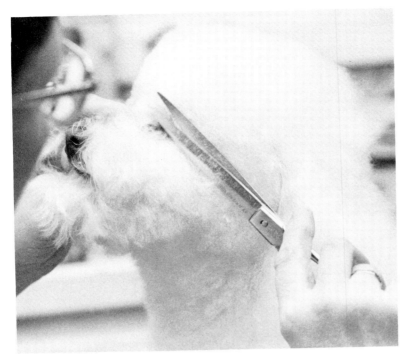

Figure 22.

Figure 23.

FINISHING THE HEAD

Most pet owners do not want as much beard as is customarily left on a show Bichon. If this is their preference, mold the face and beard work accordingly. In these head studies, a shortened beard is shown. For correct head study see the champion Bichon pictured at the beginning of this chapter.

The head is scissored to show the eyes (*Figs. 22 & 23*). Clippers are *never* used on the Bichon face. All grooming of the head is done to create a full, rounded appearance. Remove only such coat from the beard that detracts from the full, rounded look (*Fig. 24*). If preferred, thinning shears can be used to remove bulk if there is no need to shorten the coat. Coat just under and around ear opening should be thinned so ears will hang nicely and blend in with face and topknot.

The total head picture has a domed look; there is no separation line at the top of the ears. Coat at this point is blended into one flowing line into the topknot. Coat of the top of the head is gently rounded. Coat on the back of the head and down the neck continues this flowing line, and is blended into the body coat at the withers.

Comb out the ears, body, and tail to remove loose coat and to check for any uneven spots (*Fig. 25*). Scissor wherever necessary. Add a bow in the

topknot or body coat, and your customers should be pleased with this finished "powder puff."

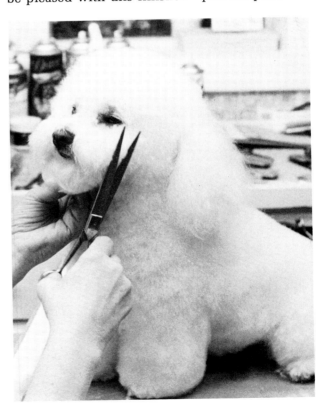

Figure 24.

Figure 25.

18
Grooming the Shih Tzu, Lhasa Apso, Maltese, Yorkshire Terrier

These four breeds share common grooming procedures for the body and leg coat if they have been kept in proper long coat. If not, grooming can be done to the customer's preference, or perhaps finished with one of the mixed-breed styles described in Ch. 22. Finishing the head coat is different for each breed, and is described individually.

THE SHIH TZU

Breed Standard

The Shih Tzu is a lively, alert dog that gaits with his head well up and his tail carried gaily over the back. The head is broad and round, his foreface wide between the eyes. The muzzle is square and short, not wrinkled, and measures about one inch from tip of nose to a definite stop. The eyes are large, dark and round, placed well apart, but not prominent. The ears are large, dropped, and heavily-coated over long leathers. The ear coat appears to blend with the hair of the neck. The teeth are level, or may have a slightly undershot bite. The front legs are short, straight, well boned, muscular, and heavily-coated. The legs and feet look massive because of the wealth of hair. The body between the withers and the root of the tail is somewhat longer than the height at the withers. The chest is broad and deep, the shoulders firm, and the back level. The rear legs are short, well boned, muscular, and straight when viewed from the rear. The thighs are well rounded and muscular. The feet are of good size, firm, and well padded with hair between the pads. Dewclaws on the hind legs are generally removed. Dewclaws on the front legs may be removed if so desired. A heavily plumed tail is carried well over the back. There is a luxurious, long, dense coat, with a wooly undercoat. The topcoat may be slightly wavy, but not curly. The hair on top of the head can be tied up. The average height at the withers is 9 to 10½ inches. The average weight of a mature dog is from 12 to 15 pounds; may be as much as 18 pounds but should not be less than 9 pounds.

Brief Breed History

The Shih Tzu is among a group of dogs whose ancestry is buried in the antiquity of the Orient—the Tibetan Spaniel, the Lhasa Apso and the Pekingese—all of whom bear a superficial resemblance to the Shih Tzu. Ancient Chinese legends speak of a "Lion Dog" playing with a ball, a story that could refer to any one of these small breeds. In Tibet, the lion is an animal that is much respected in the Buddhist religion, adding to the esteem of the small dogs which were bred in the temples of Tibet and given as gifts to the court of China.

History recounts that the breeding of the Shih Tzu was delegated to court eunuchs who vied with one another to produce specimens which would take the Emperor's fancy. Those elected had their pictures painted on wall hangings and tapestries. The eunuchs responsible for their breeding received gifts from the Emperor. The Shih Tzu was highly favored by the royal family during the Ming Dynasty and were given as gifts to those in favor with the royal family. At the time of the revolution, large numbers of these dogs were destroyed and only a few escaped the invaders.

In the early 1930s, an English woman living in China visited a dog show in Peking. There she recognized the Shih Tzu as something other than a Pekingese or an Apso. She was fortunate to purchase a few which she brought to England. These, and a few salvaged by an English officer on duty in China, made up the stock responsible for the continuation of the breed in Europe. They were first shown in England in 1933 and were classified as Apsos. In 1934 the Tibetan Breed Association sorted things out and the Shih Tzu was recognized as a separate breed. At the close of World War II, American servicemen who had become acquainted with the breed in England brought them to the United States.

The Shih Tzu was admitted to registration in the American Kennel Club Stud Book in the miscellaneous group in March 1969, and to the regular classification in the Toy Group in September 1969.

In the short time since he arrived in the western world, the Shih Tzu has become quite popular. He is usually an extrovert and enjoys being the center of attention. His delightful temperament makes him an excellent family companion.

Grooming the Shih Tzu and the Lhasa Apso

The Shih Tzu and the Lhasa Apso are probably the dogs most often stripped in the spring after a winter of playing in the snow. Customers make a valiant effort to keep up with coat care, but it is only the most patient and careful of them who will be able to keep a Shih Tzu or Lhasa in full coat through its life.

These two breeds are so similar in grooming procedure that our illustration will apply to either breed. Head work is shown and described separately. Also, a shorter clip is described.

Often as the customer presents his Shih Tzu for grooming, he will say, "I brush him all the time." From experience, this comment makes me leery. The topcoat may look beautiful, but when I pick up the dog, the lumps underneath tell a different story. The dense, wooly undercoat of this breed gives most owners a hard time. When it mats into a felt jacket there is no other recourse but to strip it. Most owners are shocked when they see their Lhasa or Shih Tzu stripped for the first time. If they laugh and make fun of the dog, you will notice how ashamed the dog feels, so for the sake of the dog's pride, suggest that the owner buy a sweater for the dog to wear until the coat begins to grow out. Also the Shih Tzu or Lhasa is sensitive to temperature changes and the sweater will serve as temporary protection.

If the coat can be saved and the dog can tolerate the de-matting, begin the grooming process by using a tangle removing solution on one section of the coat at a time (*Fig. 1*). Be sure to cover the eyes when using any spray products. Do not use a bladed mat remover because excess coat may be cut

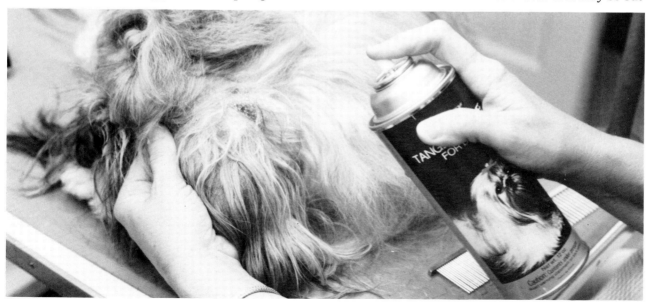

Figure 1.

and removed. Instead, loosen the mats with your fingers or the end teeth of a strong comb. *Figure 2* shows the wooly, undercoat mats being brought to the surface to be brushed away. If the customer has done a good job of coat care, you can brush through the coat with a pin brush (*Fig. 3*) using straight strokes and being careful not to flip the brush at the end of the stroke. Layer-brush with a Universal slicker brush if necessary to remove mats in the undercoat (*Fig. 4*). If the dog can be trained to lie on its side for this procedure, so much the better. If not, begin at the bottom of the rear leg, lift the coat with one hand, and brush a small layer at a time, working your way up the leg. Do the same with the body coat, starting in front of the tail, holding the coat out of the way with one hand, and brushing one layer at a time. Remember to moisturize each layer to lessen coat breakage and help release the mats.

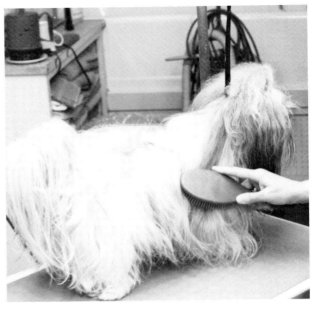

Figure 3.

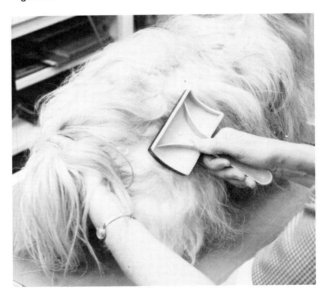

Figure 4.

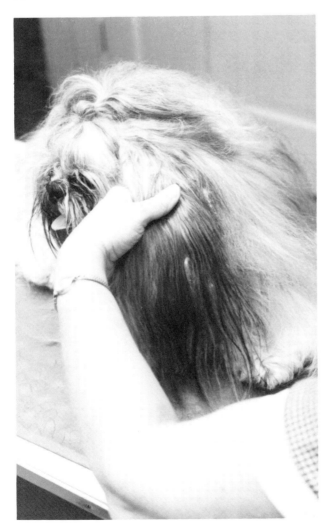

Figure 2.

The muzzle of the Shih Tzu is very short. Examine it for short hairs that may rub against the eyes. A Shih Tzu or Lhasa in show coat has the coat on the muzzle trained to drape from a center part and it is not scissored in the eye area. However, the pet Shih Tzu or Lhasa is free to rub its head on furniture or carpet, breaking coat under the eyes and in the area of the stop. The broken hairs can irritate the eyes, causing excessive tearing or even permanent scaring. Once this coat is broken it takes months to regrow and the best measure is to carefully scissor such a coat at the stop and at the inner corners of the eyes (*Fig. 5*). Use a small, blunt-tip scissor for this delicate procedure.

The ear openings of these breeds are frequently moist and waxy. Use an ear powder to dry out the ear canal and loosen ear hair to make it easier to remove (*Fig. 6*). Afterward use ear wash to remove the powder and clean the ear. Any ear with a discolored core of hair matted into the ear is a difficult job to tackle. Have someone help you steady the head while you loosen the core a little at a time. If the core is filled with a dark, smelly discharge, refer the dog to a veterinarian as it may have to be anesthetized for ear cleaning.

Clean the area under the tail around the anus. You may use thinning shears to thin the coat,

making it easier for feces to drop away instead of catching in the coat where it may harden and mat.

Before bathing, comb through the coat to check for remaining mats. Squeeze the shampoo through the coat of a long-haired breed, rather than vigorously massaging it. You might want to try one of the newer shampoos with a built-in conditioner. If not, thoroughly rinse all traces of shampoo and finish with a conditioning rinse. *Make sure no shampoo or rinse solution is left on the skin or coat as this will cause itching and flaking.*

If a breed such as the Shih Tzu, Lhasa Apso, Maltese, or Yorkshire Terrier is kept in long coat, use a pin brush when drying (*Fig. 7*). Just before beginning to dry, spray the coat lightly with a non-oily conditioner (*Whispering Mist*™ from Gerard

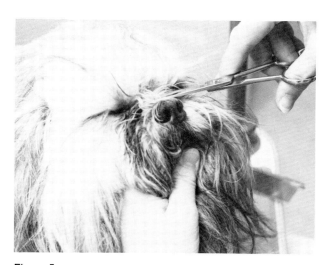

Figure 5.

Figure 6.

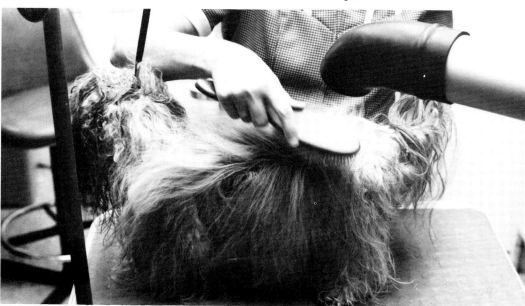

Figure 7.

Pellham does a nice job of preventing the "frizzies"). As the dryer's air current blows the coat, use the pin brush to dry, stroking the coat in the direction it is being blown. Dry one section of the coat at a time, then move the dryer to blow through another section. For the short cut on any pet of these breeds, a soft slicker brush can be used while drying.

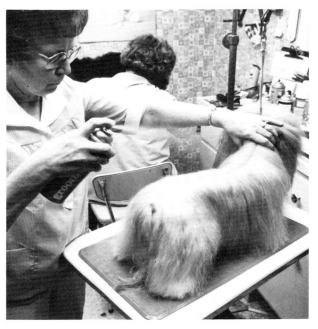

Figure 8.

FINISHING - When the entire dog is dry, place it in a natural stance on the table. Lift the outer layer of long body coat out of the way and scissor a rather large, *round* foot. As you are scissoring, slant the scissor blade under the foot for a smooth edge. Use curved scissors for greater ease in shaping the necessary rounded look and complete all four feet before moving on to the body coat.

Part the back coat from a point between the top of the ears, down the back of the neck, and follow the center of the backbone to the tail. Separate the coat at the top center back using a knitting needle or the end tooth of a comb. It is important that the center part be straight and sharply defined. If the dog twists and turns, you may need help to steady it to make sure the part is straight. When the part is complete, comb the coat down all around and give it a light touch of finishing spray. (*Fig. 8*). While the coat is damp, smooth it down with your hands to help it stay in place (*Fig. 9*).

To do the topknot for the Shih Tzu, part the head coat just above the outer corner of the eye on both sides of the head. Bring the part back to just above the ear set and in a slight curve across the top of the head to the other ear. Gather the topknot into a latex band to hold it in place (*Fig. 10*). Before finalizing the look of the topknot, check to see if there are any tiny hairs floating on the surface of the eye. If so, place a few drops of eye solution in each eye and wipe gently with a tissue.

Figure 9.

To finish the topknot of the Shih Tzu, loosen the coat just above the stop with your fingers or a knitting needle and make a small pouf in the topknot to accentuate the stop. Tie a ribbon in the topknot that matches or is a pretty contrast to the dog's coloring (*Fig. 11*).

Figure 10.

Figure 11.

THE LHASA APSO

Breed Standard

The Lhasa is a gay, assertive dog, wary of strangers. Its size may vary but the average is 10 or 11 inches at the shoulder for the male, and slightly smaller for the female. All coat colors are acceptable but this being the true Tibetan Lion-dog, golden or lionlike colors are preferred. Dark tips on the ears and beard are an asset. The length from the point of shoulders to the point of buttocks is longer than the height at the withers. These dogs have a large rib spring, strong loins, and well developed hindquarters and thighs. The coat should be heavy, straight, and hard, not wooly or silky. It should be of good length and very dense.

A slightly undershot bite is desirable though a level mouth is acceptable. The muzzle is of medium length and should not be square. There are heavy head furnishings with a good fall above the eyes, a heavy beard and whiskers. The skull is narrow, falling away behind the eyes. The skull is not quite flat, but not domed or apple-shaped. The nose is black, and about 1½ inches long. The length from the tip of the nose to the eye is to be roughly one-third the total length from the nose to the back of the skull. The eyes are dark brown, neither very large and full, not small and sunken. Ears are pendant-shaped, and heavily feathered. The front legs are straight, and both front and rear legs are heavily furnished with hair. Feet are well feathered and should be round and catlike, with thick pads. The tail is heavily feathered and should be carried well up over the back in a screw. There may be a kink at the end of the tail. A low carriage of the stern is a serious fault.

Brief Breed History

Beyond the northern boundaries of India lies the mysterious land of Tibet. The intense cold and extreme heat of this climate is hard on man and beast. The history of the dogs of the region is closely connected to the histories of the monasteries where the dogs were revered as holy animals. The name "Apso" is believed to have evolved from a Tibetan word for goat—"rapso."

Two Lhasas were given to a Colonel Kennedy, a medical officer, in 1921. They were brought to England and exhibited at a show in London in 1929. A breed club was formed in 1933.

The Lhasa is a sturdy dog whose coat protects him from all weather conditions. In spite of his size, he is very much a guard dog, just as he was in the temples of Tibet. The Lhasa is a dog that repays any attention given to its coat. Because the hair is long and easily separated, today's exhibitors spend hours preparing the coat, which now normally reaches the ground, for the show ring.

His disposition gives the impression that lurking inside the small body is a much larger dog trying to express himself. He is always playful, and when in the company of other Lhasas, seems to make up games to play. He will play with anyone or anything and makes a charming family companion.

Finishing the Lhasa

The Lhasa shown in *Figure 12* is definitely in need of help. De-matting, brushing, comb-out, bath, and brush dry were done as described for the Shih Tzu. *Figure 13* shows the same Lhasa after being bathed and dried using a pin brush during table drying. Body and head coat are then parted in the center beginning at the stop between the eyes, and continuing to the tail. This particular Lhasa has a lot of broken coat above the stop as can be seen in *Figure 14*. This photo also shows the finishing completed around the feet, and the trimming of excess coat so that it doesn't touch the ground and pick up debris when the dog plays outside. In *Figure 15*, broken coat at the stop and muzzle just in front of the eyes, has been scissored to blend into the beard and head fall.

If the owner of a Lhasa or Shih Tzu cannot keep up with the necessary coat care, the only recourse is a shortened haircut. In *Figure 16*, the groomer is brushing out a short cut on a Lhasa. When the undercarriage is felted with mats, clip a path up the center of the undercarriage to just between the front legs. (*Fig. 17*). The body side coat will hang down and cover the clipped area. Clipping this area as shown eliminates a lot of pain for the dog since the groomer won't need to de-mat the tender areas of the undercarriage.

Figure 12.

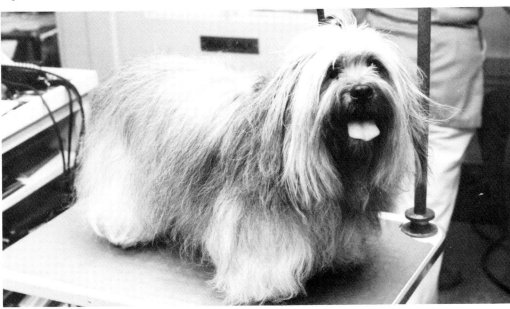

Figure 13.

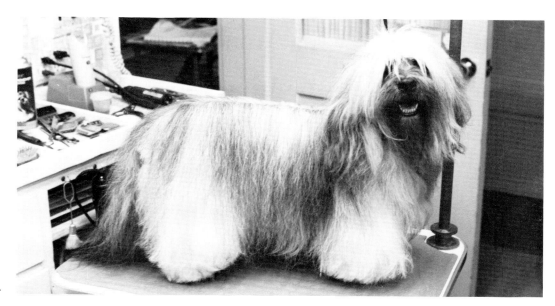

Figure 14.

Figure 15.

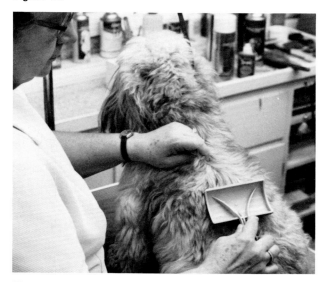

Figure 16.

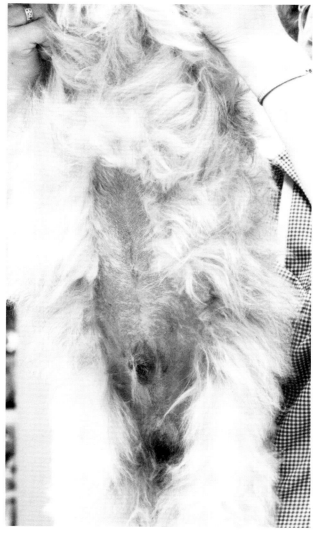

Figure 17.

To create a pretty, short haircut on either the Shih Tzu or Lhasa, use a #4F blade, and begin clipping the skull just behind the eyebrows (*Fig. 18*). Blend at the top of the ears, leaving the full ear coat. Clip the neck and all the body coat with the #4F, blending at the top of the legs and scissoring the leg coat in proportion to the rest of the body.

Shorten the fall over the eyes, so no hair falls forward (*Fig. 19*). Trim the muzzle just in front of the eyes and the stop, so the area at the inner cor-

ners is cleared of any short hairs that could rub on the eyes (*Fig. 20*). Turn the ear back and clip the sides of the face from the back corner of the mouth to the front of the ear (*Fig. 21*). Clean under the ear and continue clipping the neck and the front of the chest. Shape the sides of the beard evenly, beginning close to the back corner of the eye (*Fig. 22*). Even off the beard in proportion to the rest of the head so it conforms to the total look (*Fig. 23*).

Figure 18.

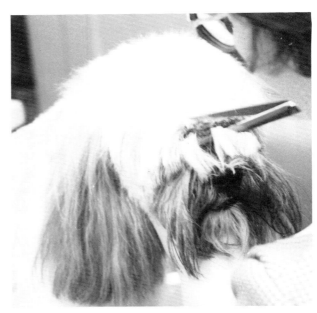

Figure 19.

Figure 20.

Figure 21.

Figure 22.

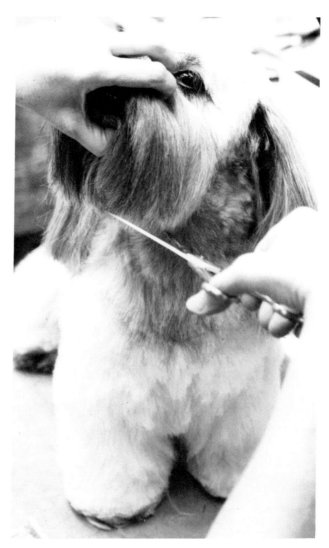

Figure 23.

THE MALTESE

Breed Standard

The Maltese is a toy dog weighing about four to six pounds and covered with a mantle of long, silky, white hair. He is gentle and affectionate, eager and sprightly in action. His head is medium length and in proportion. The skull is slightly rounded on top, with a moderate stop. The drop ears set rather low, and are heavily feathered with long hair that hangs close to the head. The eyes are very dark and round with black eye rims to enhance the gentle, yet alert, expression. The muzzle is of medium length, fine and tapered, but not snippy. Teeth meet edge-to-edge or in a scissor bite. The neck is sufficiently long to give a nice carriage to the head. The body is compact. The height from the withers to the ground equals the length from the withers to the root of the tail. The topline is level and the ribs well sprung. The chest is fairly deep, the loins taut, strong, and just slightly tucked-up underneath. The tail is a long-haired plume carried gracefully over the back; its tip lying to the side over the hindquarters. The front legs are nicely feathered, straight, with strong pastern joints free of any appreciable bend. The hind legs are strong and moderately angulated at the stifles and hocks. The feet are small and round with black toe pads.

The coat is single without any undercoat. It hangs long, flat and silky over the sides of the body, almost touching the ground. The long hair on the head may be tied up in a double topknot or may be left hanging. Any suggestion of kinkiness, curliness or wooly texture is objectionable. The color is pure white. Light tan or lemon color on the ears is permissible, but not desirable.

Even though a small dog, the Maltese seems to be without fear. His trust and affectionate responsiveness are appealing. He is among the gentlest-mannered of all the toy breeds, yet lively and playful as well as vigorous.

Brief Breed History

The Maltese is known as the "ancient dog of Malta" and for more than twenty-eight centuries has been an aristocrat of the canine world. Malta, an island, was settled by the Phoenicians about four thousand years ago. The island was known for its wealth and excellence of craftsmanship in many fields. The people enjoyed a high state of civilization, and it was here that the tiny Maltese lived.

During the time of the apostle Paul, the Roman governor of Malta had a Maltese named Issa. He was very fond of this little dog, and had a painting done that was said to be so lifelike that it was difficult to tell the picture from the actual dog. Ancient authors described the beauty, intelligence and other lovable qualities of the Maltese dogs. Greeks erected tombs to honor their Maltese.

The Maltese breed first came to England during the reign of Henry VIII. By the middle of the 19th century the breed was well established as a pet dog in England, and when dog shows began, Maltese were among the first to be exhibited. By the turn of the century, Maltese were being imported into the United States where their splendid coat and showmanship made quite an impression. It should be remembered that these dogs were once called "Maltese Terriers" and that history records their spirited disposition.

Grooming

All work on the coat prior to finishing the head is the same as that of the Lhasa and Shih Tzu. Head, neck and back coat are center-parted as described for those breeds.

To create a double topknot, use the end of your comb or a short knitting needle to part the head coat just above the back corner of the eye. Part the coat on an upward curve to just in front of the ear set, then curve across the top of the head to the center part. Comb through this coat and gather it in your fingers (Fig. 24). Slip a fine, orthodontics-type latex band around the base of this tuft of hair (Figs. 25 & 26). To shape a small pouf in this topknot, pull forward slightly on this hank of hair. Next, take a small rectangle of clear plastic wrap or netting, measuring about 1 by 1½ inches. Wrap the coat at the latex band rather snugly to control the coat,

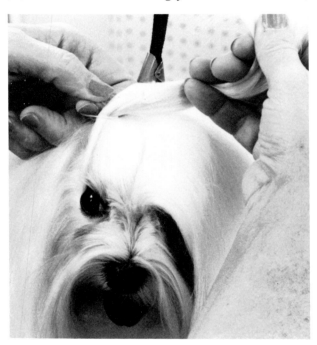

Figure 25.

Figure 24.

Figure 26.

then bend the wrap about ½ inch from the head with the ends of the coat hanging toward the ear (*Fig. 27*). Place another latex band next to the head to hold the bend of the plastic in place. Turn the loose ends of the topknot to the side to blend with the ear and face coat (*Fig. 28*). Fasten a small, prefabricated bow at the front of the plastic (*Fig. 29*). Repeat for the other side of the head. Bows can be seasonally colored and should be bright enough to contrast nicely against the white coat. The

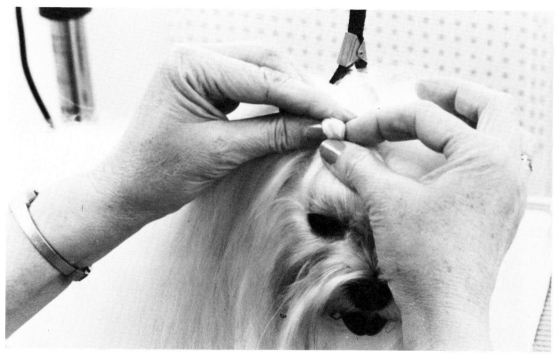

Figure 27.

Figure 28.

Figure 29.

Figure 30. (Photo - D. Walin)   Figure 31.

double topknot is used in the United States, and a single topknot as shown in *Figure 30*, is used in England. (You may want to add an extra charge for doing a double topknot since there is more time involved.) The finished Maltese is shown in *Figure 31*.

THE YORKSHIRE TERRIER

Breed Standard

The Yorkshire Terrier is a toy Terrier whose weight should not exceed seven pounds. The body is compact and well proportioned. The dog's high head carriage and confident manner give the appearance of vigor and self-importance. The head is small and rather flat on top. The skull is not too prominent or round; the muzzle not too long, in proportion to the head. Either a scissors or a level bite is acceptable. Ears are to be small, V-shaped, carried erect and set not too far apart. The compact body has a short back with a level topline. The height at the shoulder and the rump are the same. The forelegs should be straight and should not elbow in or out. The hind legs are straight when viewed from behind, with moderately bent stifles when viewed from the side. The feet are round with black toenails. Dewclaws, if present, are generally removed from the hind legs. The tail is docked to a medium length and carried slightly higher than the level of the back.

The coat quality, texture, and quantity are of prime importance. The blue and tan coat is glossy, fine, and silky in texture. It is parted on the face and from the base of the skull to the end of the tail. The moderately long coat hangs evenly and perfectly straight down each side of the body. It may be trimmed to floor length to give ease of movement and a neater appearance. The fall on the head is long, tied with one bow in the center of the head, or parted in the middle and tied with two bows. The hair on the muzzle is very long. The *tips* of the ears are trimmed short, and the feet are trimmed to give them a neat appearance.

Brief Breed History

The Yorkshire Terrier is a fairly recent breed. Yorkshire, England's largest county, is well known for breeding all types of livestock and Terriers have always been raised in Yorkshire, but their breeders had a particular type of dog in mind when they produced the original Yorkshire Terrier. Among the breeds probably intermixed in the bloodlines are the Waterside Terrier, the old rough-coated Black and Tan English Terrier, the Paisley and Clydesdale Terriers. The Skye Terrier and possibly the Maltese contributed length and silkiness to the coat.

At first, the Yorkshire Terrier was not a particularly small dog. At shows they were divided into two classes: over five pounds and under five pounds. It soon became apparent that the smaller Yorkshires were preferred, and the longer the coat, the better. Continued attempts at miniaturization have resulted in larger bitches, for ease of whelping, and smaller males. Pups from these litters show considerable variance in size with the oversized ones going to the pet market.

Grooming

Show Yorkies must learn to endure having their coat put up in protective wrappers to prevent damage and insure its long, silky appearance. Although a pampered pet, the Yorkie is still a Terrier that enjoys games and walks that allow him to express his ancestral hunting instincts.

Careful de-matting is the name of the game for this fine, silky coat. Yorkies are not particularly pleased when you hit a mat, so watch for a nip or two. They do not intend to hurt but just to let you know they don't like pulling and tugging on their coat. Moisturize the coat well, and, when possible, use your fingers to open mats. Many Yorkie owners

finally come to the conclusion it is better to have a short haircut. The Yorkie looks darling in a #4F bladed trim on the body and head, leaving a beard and lightly scissoring the leg coat.

For the fully-coated Yorkshire, do the pre-work before the bath as described for the other breeds in this chapter. Use a mild, tearless shampoo, and squeeze it gently through the coat. Wrap the Yorkie in a towel and blot out the water (*Fig. 32*). Dry the long coat with a pin brush, brushing through the coat in the direction of the dryer's air current.

Figure 33 shows the Yorkie ready for finishing. Trim around the feet to remove straggly coat. Clip the top one-fourth of the Yorkie ear. No scissoring or clipping should be done on the face even though there will always be wispy bits of coat around the eyes. These can be controlled somewhat by the use of a little mustache wax or hair-setting lotion applied with the tip of the finger. Take care not to get it in the eyes.

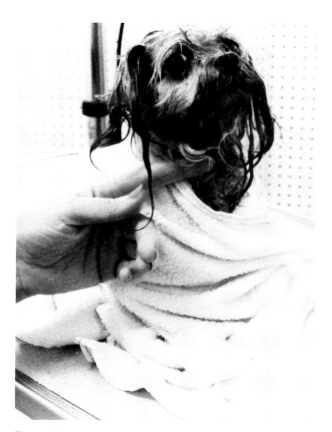

Figure 32.

Figure 33.

To create the single topknot, part the head coat beginning at a point between the outer corner and the center of the eye. Make a circular part upward toward the inner corner of the ear. Repeat on the other side of the head, and across the head from ear to ear. Gather this coat, comb to smooth it, and hold it in your fingers (Fig. 34). Slip an orthodontics latex band around this head coat (Fig. 35). Make a little pouf over the stop (Fig. 36) and finish off with a bow (Fig. 37). Separate the ponytail to lie over the head and down the sides, blending it with the head and beard coat. Small, plaid ribbons are often the best choice to finish off the topknot on a Yorkie.

Figure 34.

Figure 35.

Figure 36.

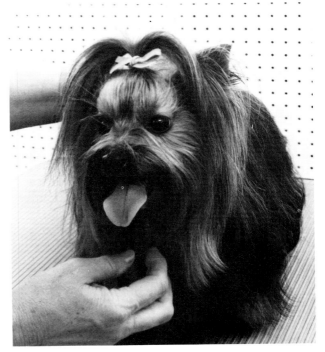

Figure 37.

19
Grooming the American Cocker Spaniel

The Cocker has a well-proportioned head, in balance with the rest of the body. The skull is rounded, but not exaggerated, with no tendency toward flatness. The eyebrows are *clearly defined* with a pronounced stop. The muzzle in front of the eyes is well chiseled. It is broad and deep with square, even jaws. The upper lip is full and of sufficient depth to cover the lower jaw. The teeth are strong and meet in a scissors bite. The eyes are round and full, and look directly forward. The expression should be intelligent, alert, soft, and appealing. The ears are long, hang loosely, are well feathered, and should be set no higher than in line with the lower part of the eye. The neck should be long enough to allow the nose to reach the ground easily. It is muscular, rises strongly from the shoulders, and arches slightly as it tapers to join the head. The well laid-back shoulders form an angle with the upper arms of approximately 90 degrees. This permits the dog to move in an easy manner with considerable reach. The upper points of the withers are set at an angle which permit a wide rib spring. The body is short and compact, giving the impression of strength. The back is strong and slopes slightly downward from the shoulders to the tail. The hips are wide, and the rear quarters well rounded and muscular. The chest is deep, reaching at least to the elbows at its lowest point. It is sufficiently wide for adequate heart and lung space, yet not too wide to interfere with the straight-forward reach of the front legs. The tail is docked and set on in line with the topline of the back, or slightly higher. The front legs are parallel, straight, strongly boned, and muscular. The rear legs are strongly boned and muscled with good angulation at the stifle joint. The hocks are well let down and when viewed from behind, the hind legs are parallel when in motion or at rest. The feet are compact, large, round, and turn neither in nor out.

The coat on the head is short and fine. On the body, it is of medium length with undercoat for protection. The ears, chest, abdomen, and legs are well feathered. The coat is silky, flat or slightly wavy; excessively curly or cottony texture is not desirable.

BRIEF BREED HISTORY

The Spaniel family, from which the American Cocker developed, is one of the oldest in canine history. Models of dogs resembling Spaniels are found in ancient Egyptian tombs.

In works of literature, we are told that the Spaniel was known in England as far back as six centuries ago. Around the 1500s the Spaniels were first divided into land or water Spaniels. Further divisions of the breed gave such designations as Springer, Springing Spaniel, Cocker, Cocking Spaniel, and Cock Flusher. The smallest, most compact member of the family became known as the Cocker, primarily because of their ability to hunt woodcock.

The English Springer Spaniel evolved in the early 1800s, and was probably the branch of the family from which the Cocker developed. In 1866,

Spaniel classes were divided into large and small Spaniel, including the Cockers. By 1874, the Cocker was shown as a Field Spaniel, and no longer designated as a separate breed.

In 1880 a black Cocker Spaniel was exported from England to the United States, and first shown here in 1883. About this same time the founders of the American Spaniel Club became interested in further developing the Cocker which was still not recognized as a separate breed. Spaniels were divided by weight, and the Cocker was in the smaller class. In 1901, size qualifications were eliminated by the American Spaniel Club and breeders began to concentrate their efforts toward better type. Later, the American Kennel Club changed its rules to allow two varieties. In 1920, the American Spaniel Club began holding Specialty shows and the Cockers realized a definite increase in popularity. At the same time, the American Cocker began to undergo a change in type and profile. Breeders selected for a more and more profuse coat, until at the present time the breed is too coated to be considered a hunting breed.

Interbreeding between the American and the English Cocker was discouraged with the founding of the English Spaniel Club of America in 1935. The American Cocker was smaller than the English Cocker, and the field work required of the American Cocker differed in the type of game. The English Cocker was bred to carry larger game, and so developed a larger muzzle and head and a rangier body. Finally in 1946, the American Spaniel Club recognized the English Cocker as a separate variety. In 1946, they dropped any jurisdiction over the English Cocker, allowing the two breeds to be developed separately. The American Cocker was not shown in Britain until in the 1960s and was first registered in Britain in 1968.

From 1940 to 1956, Cockers outranked all other breeds in registrations in the American Kennel Club. In 1984 it once again achieved top ranking in registrations. For a while, overbreeding and indiscriminate selection led to the development of some temperament problems, but American breeders have made valiant efforts to re-introduce the correct stable temperament.

The Cocker is capable of considerable speed, combined with great endurance. He is usually easily trained, with good manners, and a willingness to obey. He loves his family and under ordinary circumstances is very adaptable. His size is ideal for a family dog and he loves human companionship although he needs gentle and considerate handling.

GROOMING THE AMERICAN COCKER

The mature American Cocker has an abundant, silky coat. When properly cared for, it has a luxurious look. However, most Cockers are a matted mess when brought in for grooming, and frequently have to be clipped short all over. Lack of knowledge, or lack of time on the part of the owner contributes to the Cocker's matted coat. Again it is the job of the groomer to instruct the owner of a new puppy as to coat care even though the seller may have already done so. By the time the puppy is old enough to groom all those instructions have probably been forgotten and even with more reinforcement from you, the groomer, chances are the Cocker's coat will not be adequately cared for from one appointment to the next. The length of time between appointments determines whether or not the Cocker goes home with a very short haircut.

Pre-bath Body Work

Final finishing has a smoother look if excess body coat is removed before the brush-out and bath. Use an Oster #7F blade to do the body work. Begin clipping slightly up on the neck, and clip in a continuous stroke to the tail. Go back to the neck again, and begin working down the shoulders, tapering off above the elbows (*Fig. 1*). Work with the lay of

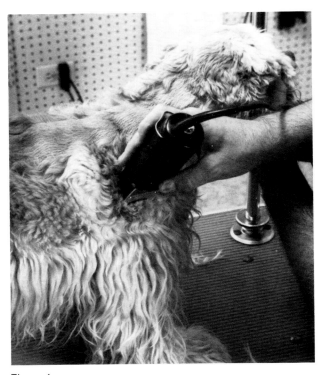

Figure 1.

the coat to the point where the coat hangs straight from the body. Clip the tail with the same blade as used for the body, beginning at the base and working toward the tip (*Fig. 2*). Clip top, sides and underside of the tail; scissor the tip. Use a #10 blade to clean the underbelly and inner flanks of the rear legs. If the undercarriage is badly matted, clip a section up the middle to a point between the front legs. Leave enough coat on the sides of the brisket and the front of the chest to hide the bare area.

Pre-bath Head Work

Begin clipping the head from a point behind the pronounced eyebrow using a #9 or #10 blade depending on the blade used for the body coat. Complete the crown and back of neck with the same blade, tapering off to blend where the neck meets the body at the withers. Clean the top of the muzzle, clipping an inverted "V" at the stop to emphasize the stop and enhance the expression (*Fig. 3*). Clip the sides of the muzzle down to the edge of the lip using a #10 blade (*Fig. 4*). Clean the sides of the head to the front of the ear opening and toward the throat area using the same blade as used for the top of the skull (*Fig. 5*). Clean the lower lip

Figure 3.

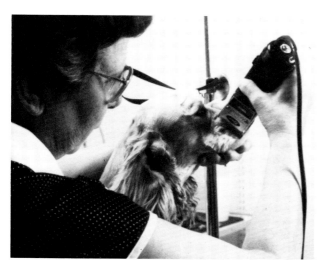

Figure 2.

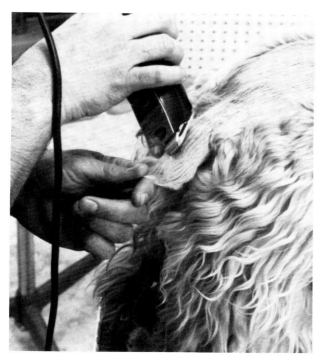

Figure 4.

Figure 5.

and underjaw area. Lift the upper lip out of the way and stretch the lower lip to facilitate cleaning the flew (*Fig. 6*). Clip the neck and throat area working with the lay of the coat. Clip a U-shape from a point directly under the ear to approximately 1½ inches above the sternum (breast bone). The edges of this area are blended at finishing so no defined line is present (*Fig. 7*).

Pre-bath Ear Work

Clip the top one-third of the ear (including the feathering) using a #10 or #15 blade. Begin at the top of the ear, placing the thumb of your other hand at the point where you want to stop clipping (*Fig. 8*). Clip from the center toward the outside edges and to the same point on both the top and underside of the ear (*Fig. 9*). Clean around the base of the ear on all sides where it joins the head (*Fig. 10*). Clean carefully around the ear opening with a #10

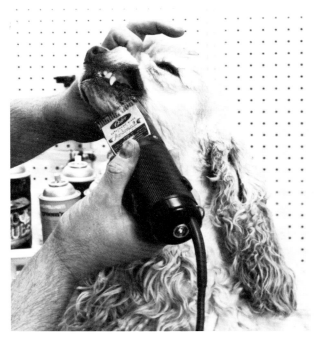

Figure 6.

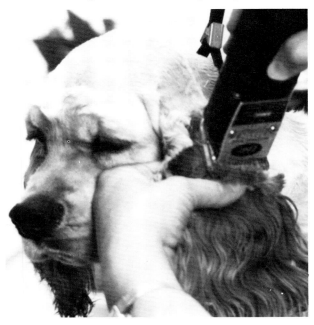

Figure 8.

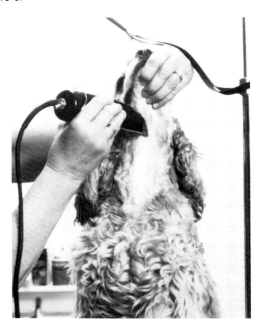

Figure 7.

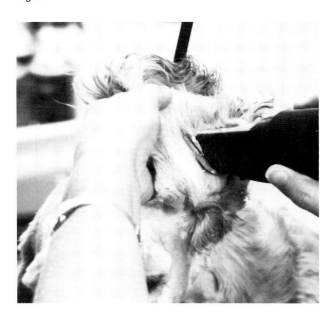

Figure 9.

blade and a small, blunt-tipped scissor to rid the opening of any straggly hair (*Fig. 11*). Finalize the pre-work on the ears by scissoring the edges of the clipped area of the ears. Hold your scissors at a 45 degree angle to clip closely without nicking the ear leather (*Fig. 12*).

Figure 10.

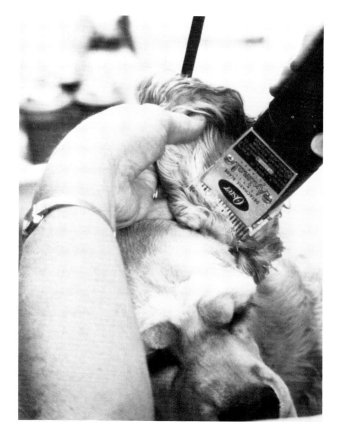

Figure 11.

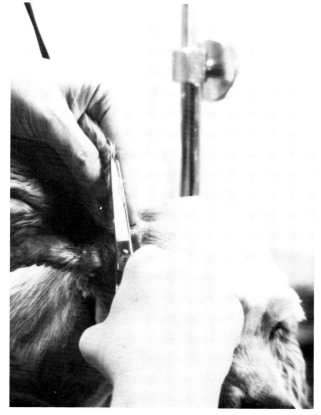

Figure 12.

Ears are usually matted. Thoroughly moisturize them with tangle remover solution and allow a few minutes for the solution to soak into the mats.

Use an *Oster Mat Comb*® to break open the mats (*Fig. 13*). Brush and comb through the ears finalizing with a deep-tooth comb to be sure all mats are removed (*Fig. 14*).

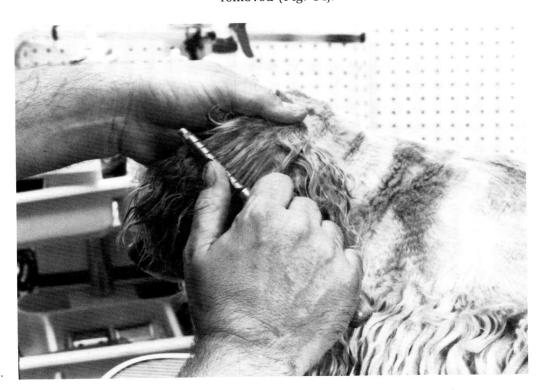

Figure 13.

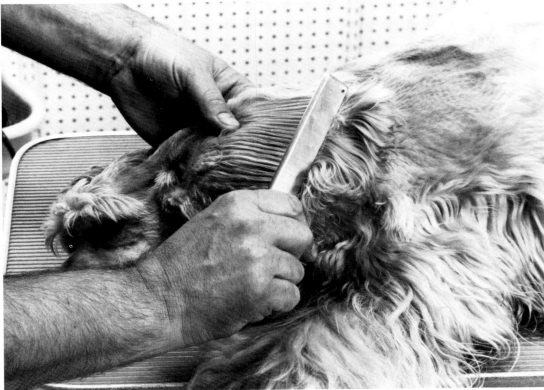

Figure 14.

Pre-bath Leg Work

Remove mats from between pads of the foot. Since Cockers love to roam in brush and fields, check for chewing gum, small pebbles, weeds, or

Figure 15.

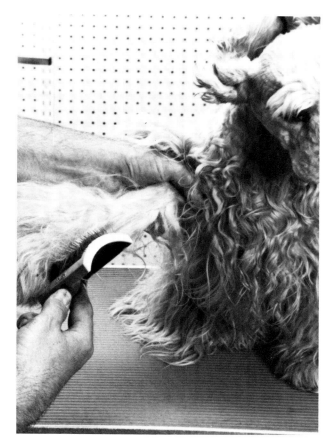

Figure 16.

stickers that might be in the foot or leg coat. Cut the toenails and if the Cocker gives you a hard time during nail clipping, de-matting or any other part of the grooming process, you may want to restrain him with a device such as the Oster Haunch Holder shown in *Figure 15*. As previously discussed in other chapters, de-mat the legs using an *Oster Mat Comb®*, Universal slicker, and a strong, wide-tooth comb in sequence (*Fig. 16*). Work through all the body feathering in the same way.

BATHING AND DRYING

For the most luxurious finish, bathe and brush dry the fully coated Cocker. A short-clipped Cocker can be crate dried in a controlled temperature.

Final Finishing

Reclip the body coat using the same blade as for body pre-work. (*Fig. 17*). When blending the side of the body into the feathering, use a slightly longer blade than the one used on the body coat.

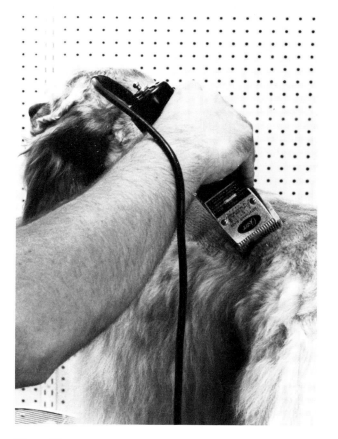

Figure 17.

Figure 18.

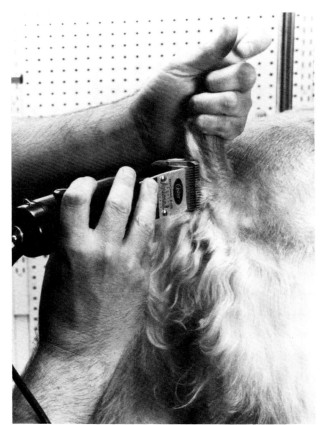

Figure 19.

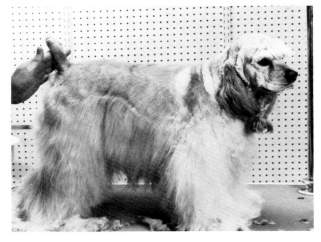

Figure 20.

In *Figure 18*, a #5F blade is being used for blending after a #7F was used on the body coat. Finish and blend around the tail with the same blade, (*Fig. 19*) or use thinning shears. We see the finalized body and blending work in *Figure 20*.

Figure 21.

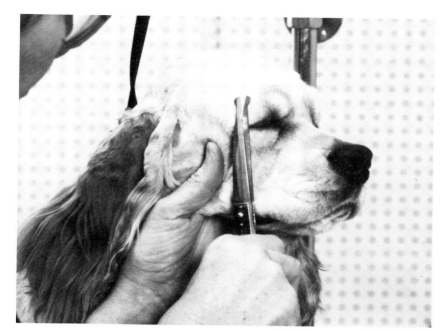

Figure 22.

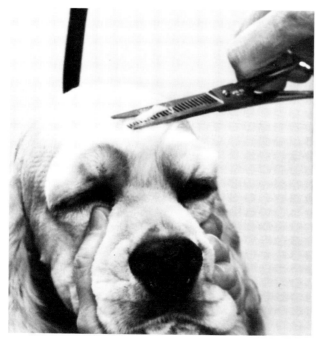

Figure 23.

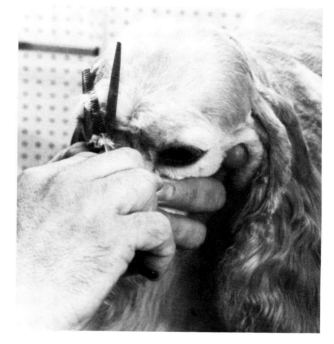

Figure 24.

To finalize the head work, begin by reclipping the headpiece as done for the pre-work (*Fig. 21*). Using the same blade gives the head coat a smooth finish, and eliminates any blade ridging. If you have problems with ridges showing, check your blade to make sure there is no matter or loose coat plugged between the teeth of the blade. Carefully scissor at the outer corner of the eye for a smooth line, blending into the cheek area (*Fig. 22*). Use thinning shears to blend the crown into the skull. The puppy shown has a well-rounded head and a pronounced eyebrow. *Figure 23* shows blending this area into the coat on the topskull. The mature Cocker could use a higher crown to give a better look to the stop, however, the owners preferred to have the eyebrow area blended down (*Fig. 24*).

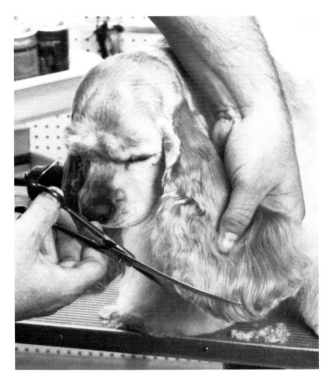

Figure 25.

Figure 26.

Figure 27.

The feathering on the ear of the Cocker is left natural. However, the owner of a pet may want to have the feathering shortened somewhat to keep ears out of food and water (*Fig. 25*). Use long, curved shears if you have them. *Figure 26* shows the finished ear, hanging close to the head, neatly trimmed to the customer's preference.

To complete the leg work, begin by scissoring the leg coat flat across the bottom level with the pads (*Fig. 27*). Place the dog in a natural stance on the grooming table and comb all the leg coat down into place. Scissor a large, rounded foot, using curved shears (*Fig. 28*). After the foot has been shaped, scissor a rounded bottom of the leg coat and edge of the foot (*Fig. 29*). Use your straight

Figure 28.

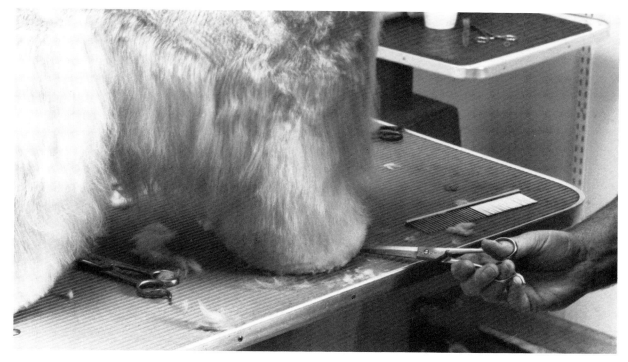

Figure 29.

shears to scissor a clean, defined line at the bottom edge. Lightly scissor coat along the sides and back of the front leg to enhance the look of the leg (*Fig. 30*). The scissoring of the hock area on the rear legs should show and define angulation at the hock. The rear legs of the Cocker are to have the appearance of a well-let-down hock, and this can be emphasized by rounding off the back leg coat below the hock joint (*Fig. 31*).

Figure 32 shows the difficult, seven-month-old Cocker puppy after finishing. He shows promise of developing into a nice specimen of the breed. *Figures 33 and 34* show the finished mature Cocker.

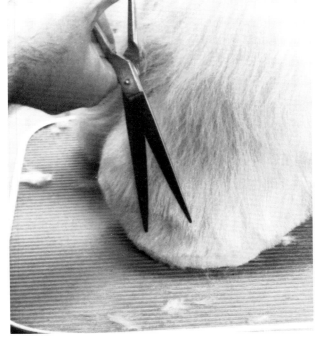

Figure 31.

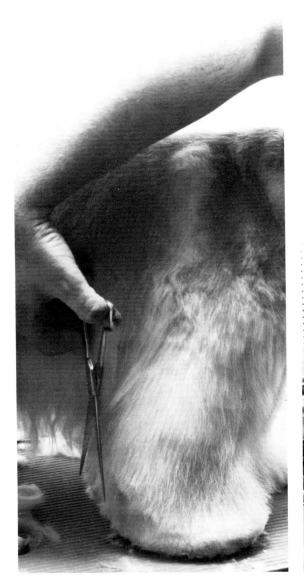

Figure 30.

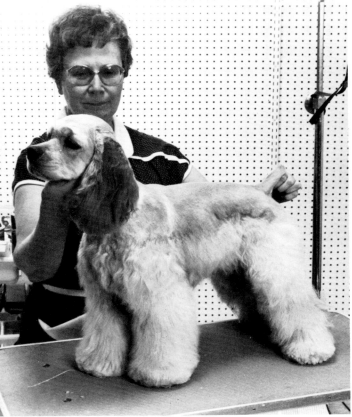

Figure 32.

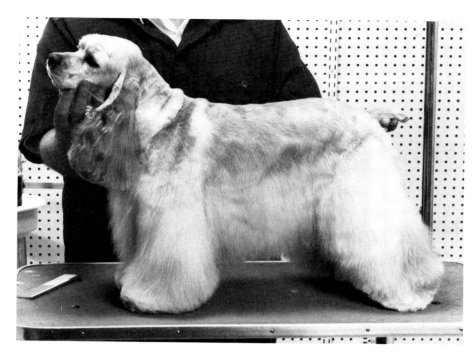

Figure 33.

Figure 34.

20
Grooming the Short-Legged Terriers

It is possible that the West Highland Terrier, the Cairn Terrier, and the Scottish Terrier all originated from the same stock in Scotland. In condensing the breed standards for these particular dogs, only those things that influence the lines and methods of grooming are mentioned. For a complete breed standard of these breeds, consult the AKC Standard of the Breed. The Westie and Scottie are illustrated using photos of champions to better present a correct breed profile.

THE CAIRN TERRIER

Brief History and Description

The modern Cairn is believed to be an attempt to preserve some of the characteristics of the "Earth Dogs" from the Isle of Skye. However, a 15th century writer noted that there was a small dog used for hunting fox and badger in Scotland. Whether the Cairns claim their origin in Scotland or on the Isle of Skye, it is plain that these terriers were noted for their courage when routing out otter, foxes, and other small game from among rocky crevices and cairns; hence the origin of the name Cairn Terrier. The word "Terrier" is derived from the Latin word "terra," meaning "earth." The small terriers were able to go down into holes and burrows and worry at the fox or badger until it emerged for the hunter to kill it.

The Cairn was registered as a separate breed by the British Kennel Club in 1910. Prior to that time it was shown as a Skye Terrier. They were first registered in the United States in 1913. The Cairn has ranked among the top 15 breeds in England for many years.

The Cairn is a small dog equally suited to indoor or outdoor living, is people oriented, and good with children. They still have well developed hunting instincts which might cause problems if they decide to dig for a mouse or a mole in the flower bed. Farmers who own these little dogs have little problem with rodents.

Condensed Breed Standard

The Cairn is an active, hardy, small terrier in the short-legged class. He moves freely, has a strong, but not heavy build, and stands well forward on his front legs. His head is shorter and wider than any other terrier and well furnished with hair that lends a foxy expression. The skull is broad and strong. The jaws are strong and powerful with large teeth and a scissors bite. The eyes are set rather wide apart, dark hazel in color, medium sized, and rather sunken with shaggy eyebrows. The ears are small, pointed, carried erect, set wide apart on the side of the head and *are free from long hairs*. The tail is well furnished, though *not feathered*, carried gaily but not turned down toward the back. The body is compact with well-sprung ribs and strong hindquarters. The back has a level topline, is of medium length, and the whole body gives the impression of strength and activity. Front legs are straight and should not be out at the elbows. Front feet are larger than hind feet. The legs must be covered with hard coat. The pads of the feet should be thick and strong, and the dog should be well up on his feet. The outer coat is hard and weather resistant. It is a double coat with profuse, harsh outer coat, and short, soft, thick, furry undercoat. The Cairn may be any color except white, and dark ears, muzzle and tail tip are desirable.

Grooming

Cairns are protective and loyal to their families. This characteristic is one that groomers should note. It is better to let a Cairn walk on lead to the grooming area than for the groomer to try to take him from the owner's arms, at least until the dog knows the groomer well. They do show affection for a groomer they like and trust.

The Cairn is not bothered by cold weather, being protected by a thick, wooly undercoat and a long, harsh topcoat that is weather resistant. The Cairn's coat has a shaggy appearance when fully grown out, and should be bathed with a shampoo that does not relax the coat or remove its natural oils. Facial coat and leg furnishings should be handled gently during grooming since they do not regrow rapidly if damaged.

Cairn owners can do a great deal to keep their dogs tidy at home. Groomers should be sure to emphasize the coat should be thoroughly moistened with a good conditioner before brushing. Toenails should be kept short and filed to keep the pads tight which will prevent the foot from splaying. A little trimming around the feet keeps them neat in appearance.

The Cairn owner who wants a neater, trimmed appearance, should be cautioned that if the coat is cut too closely it may lose its proper texture. If you must give the Cairn a clip, cut down the harsh outer coat no further than where it emerges from the dense, wooly undercoat. Do not clip into the undercoat. The Cairns I have clipped in this manner did not lose the texture of the harsh, outer coat as it grew back in.

Usual grooming times are spring and fall when the coat is undergoing seasonal changes. The coat should be plucked, removing only dead coat, and allowed to regrow from underneath. However, most groomers have neither the time nor the expertise to do this type of grooming.

I have never seen a Cairn coat matted to the point of no return. Applying a liberal dose of moisturizer, and using a Universal Slicker brush and a good strong comb will remove mats and dead undercoat and prepare the coat for a protein bath. Do not use a rinse that might soften the coat.

The coat may be brushed dry, which will relax it a bit, or the Cairn can be crate dried, though it may take some time to completely dry the undercoat. The coat can be finger-dried on the table, then sprayed lightly with a conditioner and combed out. During cold weather check the undercoat for dampness before releasing the dog.

Finishing

Figure 1 shows the Cairn as it usually looks when coming in for grooming. Clean the under-

Figure 1.

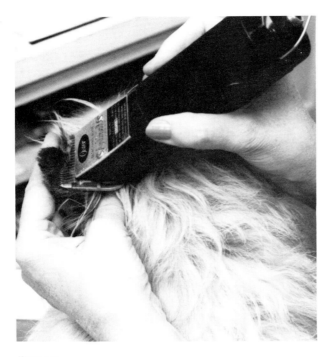

Figure 2.

belly, under the tail, between the pads, and inside the ears as described in previous chapters.

Remove any straggly hairs from inside and outside the ears with a #10 blade or thinning shears. Since the outside ear coat should have the appearance of velvet, do not clip them with a close blade (*Fig. 2*). Trim the edge of the ears for a neat appearance.

For a longer, more natural appearing coat on the Cairn, use a clip-on attachment over an Oster #30 blade or with a blocking blade. Rake through the coat, always working *with* the lay of the coat (*Fig. 3*). Blend into leg coat at shoulders and hindquarters.

To shorten the head coat, comb up a section, hold the coat erect between your fingers, and scissor a small section at a time (*Fig. 4*). Shorten the head coat only enough to be in proportion to the amount of coat left on the body, but remember, the distinguishing feature of the Cairn is its head coat, so the head should always look well-coated (*Fig. 5*). Neaten the back of the head to blend into

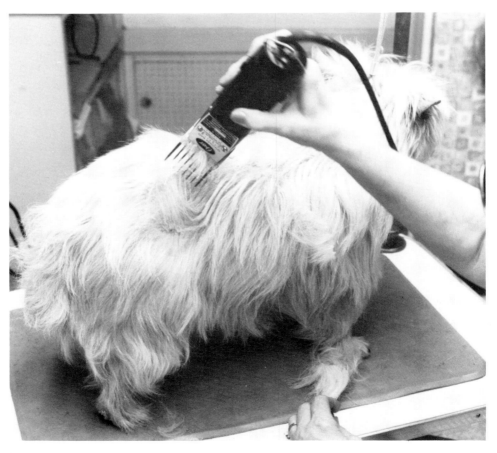

Figure 3.

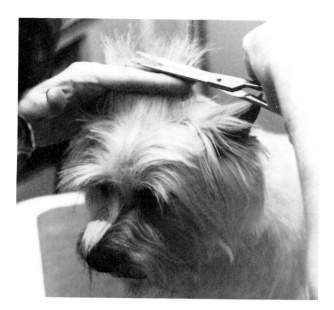

Figure 4.

the body coat. If necessary for sanitary purposes, scissor a little at the inner corners of the eyes. The finished head should be well-coated and rather shaggy looking (*Fig. 6*).

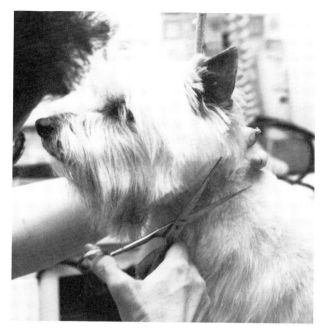

Figure 5.

Scissor the tail to resemble half a fat carrot with the tip slanted toward the head (*Fig. 7*).

Figure 6.

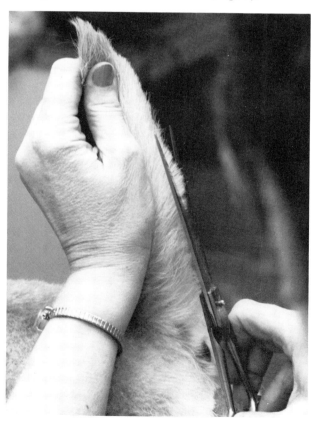

Figure 7.

Figure 8 shows a Cairn whose body work was done with a clip-on attachment over a #30 blade. The hindquarters were blended with thinning shears and straight scissors. The same was done over the front shoulders and down over the elbows.

Front chest coat was raked with the same attachment rather than clipped. It was blended where necessary with thinning shears. Leg coat was lightly scissored to give a better line, and feet were trimmed for a neat appearance.

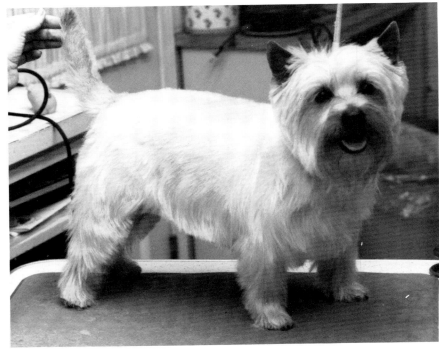

Figure 8.

Figure 9.

Figure 9 pictures another Cairn whose owner wanted a shorter clip. The head piece is considerably shortened. The entire body coat was hand scissored just above the dense undercoat. The coat over the elbows, on the turn of the rib cage, and on the muscular area of the hindquarters was also blended with thinning shears. Leg coat and tail were scissored shorter in keeping with the proportions of the body coat.

Figure 10.

In *Figure 10*, the hindquarters are shown from the rear. The rear was scissored and blended to leave all parts coated, so that nothing would have a bare appearance.

Remember, the pictures and instructions in this section are *not* correct to the Cairn's profile, but rather, one groomer's version developed to be in accord with the owner's needs and desires. This is one breed that (as far as pet grooming is concerned) should be finished in deference to the owner's wishes.

THE WEST HIGHLAND WHITE TERRIER

Brief History and Description

The West Highland White Terrier is said to have been developed by the Malcolm family at Poltalloch, Scotland. These dogs stem back to the same roots as the Cairn and other Scottish Terriers.

In early days, Westies were sometimes buff or reddish in color, but Colonel Malcolm decided to perfect and breed only the white Westie strain to make them more distinguishable from rabbit and other game when hunting. The Malcolms were the first recognized fanciers and breeders of the ancestors of the Westies we now know. The lineage of their dogs probably went back to the time of King

Champion Sno-Bilt's Puzzle—Multiple Best In Show winning Westie bred, owned and handled by Jodine Vertuno. (Photo - Booth)

James I, who asked for some "earth-dogges" out of Argyllshire.

The Westie is all terrier, with spunk, determination and devotion to its family all crammed into a small body. They have all the desirable qualities of a pet: faithfulness, understanding, gaiety, and devotion. They are hardy and need no special pampering.

Condensed Breed Standard

The West Highland White Terrier is a small, well-balanced, hardy-looking terrier that exhibits self-importance and good showmanship. The dog should be neatly presented with considerable hair left around the head to act as a frame for the face to yield a typical Westie expression.

He is strongly built with deep chest and ribs, good straight back, and powerful hindquarters. The Westie coat should be about two inches long, white, with heavy undercoat and should not show any tendency to curl. The skull is broad, in good proportion to the powerful jaw, slightly domed, and with a definite stop. The muzzle is slightly shorter than the skull, tapering to a large nose. The jaws are level and powerful with large teeth in proportion to the size of the dog. A level or slight scissor bite is correct. The ears are *small, erect,* wide apart and terminate in a *definite point.* They are never cropped. The hair on the ears is *short* and *velvety,* and the ears are trimmed free of fringe at the *tips.* The eyes should be very dark, set wide apart, and looking from under *heavy eyebrows* with a piercing expression. Black pigmentation should be present on lips, eye rims, pads of the feet and toenails, with a grayish pigmentation of the skin. The neck is muscular, flowing into a strong body. The ribs are deep and well arched in the upper half of the rib cage and give the appearance of a *flatter* side profile. The hindquarters are strong and wide across the rump. Both the front and rear legs are short and muscular. The front legs should be straight and thickly covered with short, hard hair and the elbows held close to the body. The hind legs are short and sinewy with well bent hocks. The feet are round, strong, thickly padded and covered with short, hard hair and with the hind feet being *smaller* than the front feet. The tail should be relatively short and when held erect, *should not* extend above the top of the skull. It should be covered with hard hairs, *no feathering,* as straight as possible, carried upright but not curled over the back. The tail set should be high enough so the spine does not slope down to it. The tail must never be docked.

Faults in the breed include an open coat, any color except white, light colored eyes, overshot or undershot bite, and a muzzle longer than the skull and not in proportion. Such things as round, broad or large ears, or ears set too closely together are very objectionable. Movement that appears stiff or stilted is incorrect.

The temperament of a well-bred Westie is alert, gay, courageous, and self-reliant but friendly. It would be a serious fault if the Westie shows excess timidity or is overly belligerent or quarrelsome.

Figure 11.

Grooming

Westies look the best and most characteristic when they are kept as natural looking as possible. Their outer coat is hard and stiff and can be kept so by proper brushing and dry cleaning with a spray whitener, rather than by too much washing. Some people think a white dog is difficult to keep clean, but just a little time each day can keep them looking very well.

In *Figure 11*, Ch. "Puzzle's" headcoat is fluffed by combing, allowing the coat to fall naturally in place. *Figure 12* shows the face furnishings being shaped to give the proper "dish" shaping to the furnishings of the head. Notice the small, well set ear, and compare it to the ear on the pet quality Westie also shown in this section. The blending of the back of the head should look natural where the furnishings on the skull meet the neck coat. In *Figure 13*, the left side of the head has been finished, the right side has not. The rear shaping of the coat on the champion is shown in *Figure 14*. This same type of profile can be achieved on a pet quality Westie by using a clip-on attachment over a #30 blade, or blending carefully with thinning shears. Take particular note of the nice draping of the furnishings just above the hock. Also, there is no bunching out of the coat over the muscling of the hindquarters.

Figure 12.

Figure 13.

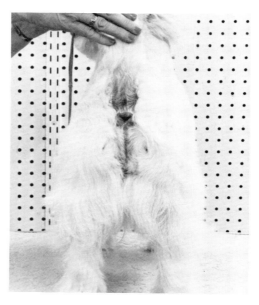

Figure 14.

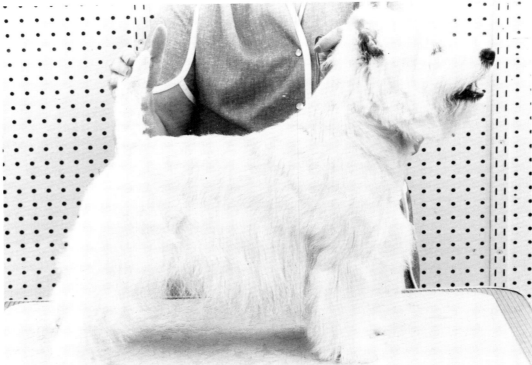

Figure 15.

In the complete side profile (*Fig. 15*) the chest coat shows a slight bib of coat. The front legs are well under the shoulder which gives the body a compact look. The apron of furnishings flowing off the rib area give the proper look of *flatness* that the breed Standard calls for; there is *no* rounding of rib spring indicated. There is a slight tuck of coat behind the front elbow, to emphasize the muscling of the front shoulders. The coat lays smoothly over the rear, and flows off in a natural drape of furnishings. If the pet Westie is fortunate to have good furnishings, try to convince the owners to allow you to clip and shape the Westie to its proper breed profile.

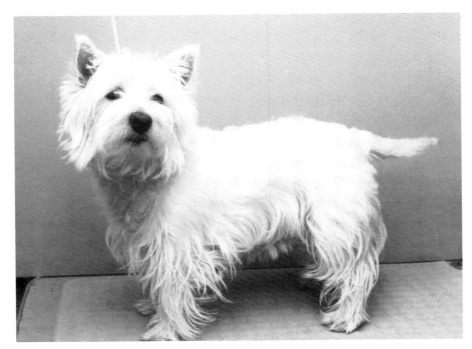

Figure 16.

Figure 16 presents a "before" photo of a typical, pet-quality Westie. "Angel" has a fair amount of coat, though not of the hard quality of a show-type coat. The back coat, and the coat extending down the side of the body to where it hangs straight down, was clipped with a #4 skip-tooth blade, and skimmed just above the undercoat (*Fig. 17*). It was blended off at the turn of the ribs to give the Westie a *flat-sided* appearance.

Figure 18 shows the use of a #1½ clip-on attachment over a #30 blade. Use this attachment to blend the upper thigh area, along the sides of the rib cage, and over the front shoulder and elbow area to give a nice fall of coat. It is especially useful for those who are not proficient in the use of thinning shears.

The Westie tail should be compact in appearance with *no* indication of feathering. Use a #4F blade, hold the tail straight out, and clip the top of the tail from base to tip. Scissor the balance of the tail to about the same depth, in the shape of a fat carrot (*Fig. 19*).

Figure 17.

Figure 18.

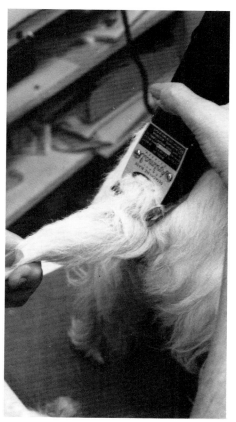

Figure 19.

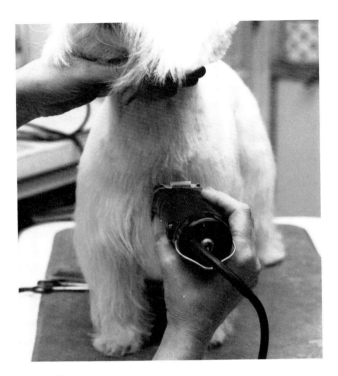

Figure 20.

Figure 21.

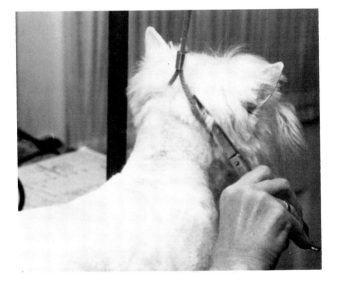

Figure 22.

The chest coat is blended and shaped to give the indication of an inverted "V" beginning at or just below the sternum (breast bone) (*Fig. 20*). The coat on either side of the bib flows from the shoulder into the leg coat. If you are proficient with the thinning shears, use them to blend in this area.

Trim the headpiece to give it a rounded, dish appearance (*Fig. 21*). Notice that in this case, the Westie had large ears. Except for the owner's pref-

erence, the head coat should have been allowed to grow longer to give a fuller appearance to the head and hide more of the ear but many Westie owners prefer shortened clips so the dog does not need grooming as often. *Figure 22* indicates the area of blending at the back of the head and upper neck. Use thinning shears to give a more natural line and refer back to the rear head work on the champion Westie.

THE SCOTTISH TERRIER

Brief History and Description

In early times, a great many different terriers existed in Scotland, all of which were known as "Scottish Terriers." Among these, as we have already indicated, were the Cairn, the origins of the Westie, the Dandie Dinmont, and the Skye Terrier. Fanciers of the Scottie as we now know it believe that this breed is the original Highland Terrier. Terriers of the type now known as the Scottish Terrier were bred on the Isle of Skye, and were first exhibited as Skye Terriers, though they in no way resembled the terriers we now know by that name. The fairly isolated areas of the islands of Scotland produced some close interbreeding that established certain types among the dogs bred there. This led to different areas each claiming that their type of terrier was the true Scottish Terrier.

The Scottish Terrier Club was formed in Scotland in 1882, when a committee of representatives drew up a Standard for the breed, which has changed very little from that time. The American standard was adopted by a small committee in 1925; the only difference in the two standards being the weight limit allowed.

Most people know the Scottish Terrier as a black dog largely because that seems to be the most

Condensed Breed Standard

The skull is long, medium width, slightly domed, and covered with short, hard hair. The skull is not quite flat, as there is a slight stop or drop between the eyes. The muzzle is in proportion to the length of skull. The nose is of good size and black. The jaws are level and square. The nose projects over the mouth a little, giving the impression that the upper jaw is longer than the lower. The teeth should be evenly placed, with a level or

Champion Dana's Sunday Edition owned by breeder-judge, Nancy Fingerhut. (Photo - Ritter)

prevalent color. However he can be any of the following colors: steel or iron grey, brindled or grizzled, black, sandy, or wheaten. Any white markings are objectionable and allowed only to a slight extent on the chest.

The Scottie is a strongly built dog, with a keen temperament. The Scottie is friendly with the people he knows, but may be on guard with strangers. It is not the type of dog to antagonize because the strong jaws are capable of inflicting deep wounds.

A Scottie puppy should be worked with every day so it will readily accept combing and brushing. Pet fanciers who feel that this is the breed they want to own, should look carefully for a puppy that has a stable temperament.

scissors bite. The eyes are set wide apart, small and almond-shaped. The eyes, with a piercing expression, should be dark brown or nearly black, and are set well under the eyebrow. The *small, prick ears* sit well up on the skull, are *pointed*, and covered with *short, velvety hair*. The thick, muscular neck is of medium length, and should not appear short and clumsy. The body is moderately short, well ribbed, with strong loins, deep flanks, and muscular hindquarters. The chest is broad and very deep, coming well down between the front legs. The front and rear legs are short and very heavily boned in proportion to the size of the dog. The front legs are straight or slightly bent, but with the elbows held close to the body. The stifles are well bent and the rear leg is straight from the hock to the heel. The feet are round and thick with strong nails, and front feet that are larger than the rear. The tail is docked and is about 7″ long, carried with a slight curve, but not over the back. The Scottie coat is rather short, about 2″ in length, with a dense undercoat, and a very hard and wiry outer coat.

Grooming

Grooming the headpiece of the pet Scottie requires totally different lines than those described for the Cairn, Westie, or Schnauzer.

Begin the headpiece work by clipping the skull with a #9 or #10 blade. Clip from just behind the eye socket back to between the ears, working with the lay of the coat. Do not clip the tufts of hair in front of the ears. (Examine the head study in *Figure 23.*) The side of the cheek behind the eye is clipped about 1 to 1½ inches toward the ear. Do not clip too far. The balance of the distance to the ear is blended with thinning shears to prevent a bald appearance in front of the ears.

Figure 23. (Photo - Worline)

The amount of tufting left in front of the ear toward the top of the skull varies on each Scottie. (*Fig. 24*). The length of the coat in the tuft can minimize the height of a large ear, and can shorten the appearance of the distance between the ears. The tufting is shaped into somewhat of a fan-shaped triangle. The tuft is the longest at the inner corner of the ear and tapers off at a point somewhat between the midpoint of the inside of the ear and the outside, lower edge of the ear where it meets the skull. The coat at the longest point of the tuft can sometimes reach almost to mid-ear. There should be no fuzziness at the outer edge of the ear where the ear meets the side of the skull. If the ear is large in proportion to the head, a small amount of coat may be blended at the base of the backside of the ear to minimize the size of the ear.

Beginning at the nodule on the underside of the jaw with a #9 or #10 blade, clip with the lay of the coat down the front of the neck in a pronounced "V" shape ending at, or just above the breastbone. Blend the edges of the "V" with thinning shears to promote the flat appearance of the chest (*Fig. 25*).

To complete the head work, both the beard and eyebrows are shaped to give a triangular appearance. The beard should be trimmed from the outer corner of the eyebrow and eye socket to the back corner of the mouth. To create the triangular appearance of the beard, lift the coat on the upper muzzle and move the beard on the lower jaw to just forward of the back corner of the mouth. This helps the beard lay flatter and enhances the rectangular look of the head. Clean between the eyebrows at the stop with blunt pointed scissors or thinning shears and be careful not to dig into the coat causing bare spots.

To do the neck and body work, use a #5F, and clip the back and sides of the neck, continuing down the center of the body to the tail with the same blade (*Fig. 26*). The Scottie being used in these photos is a young, pointed male just under a year old. His coat has been hand stripped, so is obviously of the proper hard texture. Using a #5F to do the body work for a pet Scottie does less damage to the texture of the coat and gives a more "coated" look. Clip about one-third of the distance down the side of the body, *no further* than to where the coat changes direction and grows downward at the turn of the rib spring. At that point blend the body and furnishings with thinning shears so side of body has a flat appearance. Blending at the shoulder area and over elbows and hips can be

Figure 24. (Photo - Worline)

Figure 25. (Photo - Worline)

Figure 26. (Photo - Worline)

done with a #1½ clip-on attachment over a #30 blade.

The chest coat is allowed to drape between the front legs to give the appearance of a very deep chest. The skirting on body coat can be thinned or shaped with thinning shears rather than scissors to give a more natural look. Trim around the feet to give them a tidy appearance.

There is definite indication of the muscular build of the shoulders and hindquarters (*Fig. 27*). The coat is kept tight and flat over these areas. The tail is scissored with no appearance of feathering. Its shape is that of half a carrot.

Figure 27. (Photo - Worline)

21
Grooming the Wire, Welsh & Lakeland Terriers

The Wire, Welsh and Lakeland Terriers have somewhat similar body profiles, therefore the body work is similar. However, finishing the head coat for each causes problems for some groomers. Of course, we cannot expect to create the same look on a pet as on the hard coat of a show dog. But we can use blades and thinning techniques that give a coated look and do not completely break down the coat's texture. (For the grooming of a purebred show dog read the complete breed standards or consult the parent club, professional handlers, or breeders.)

Separate breed histories, descriptions and condensed breed standards defining the desired outline, coat, and head shape are given for all three dogs. The grooming is handled as one unit since only the head is done differently in a pet.

THE WIRE FOX TERRIER

Brief History and Description

The Fox Terrier is found wherever the English language is spoken as it is an ancient breed of English origin. The Smooth Fox Terrier probably stemmed from the smooth-coated Black-and-Tan, the Bull Terrier, the Greyhound, and the Beagle. The Wire Fox claims as ancestors the old rough-coated Black-and-Tan working Terriers of Wales. Wire Fox pedigrees will often include many Smooth Fox Terrier ancestors.

The original Standard of the breed drawn up in England in 1876 was so complete that no changes have been made. The American Fox Terrier Club adopted it in 1885 and later added some amplification to clarify measurements.

The Wire Fox Terrier is to resemble the Smooth in all respects as the breed Standard except for a "broken" (rough, harsh) coat. The texture of the coat should be hard and wiry, and in no way wooly nor silky. The coat should not be too long, so as to give a shaggy appearance, but should show a marked difference from the Smooth. The Wire Fox show dog needs to be frequently plucked and trimmed. From time to time, the coat is completely taken down to allow it to regrow strong and hard.

Condensed Breed Standard for the Smooth and Wire Fox Terrier

The skull should be flat and moderately narrow, gradually decreasing in width to the eyes. Not much stop is apparent. They should not be cheeky. The ears should be V-shaped and small, of moderate thickness, and drooping forward close to the cheek. The jaws should be strong and muscular. The area in front of the eyes is moderately chiseled. The muzzle gradually tapers toward the nose, which should be black. The eyes and their rims should be dark in color, deep-set, full of fire and intelligence, and close to circular in shape. The teeth form a nearly level bite with the upper teeth just barely overlapping the lower teeth. The skull and foreface are very nearly the same in length. The neck should be clean and muscular, without throatiness, of fair length, and gradually widening to the shoulders. The well laid back shoulders should be long and sloping. The chest is not broad. The brisket should be deep, yet not exaggerated. The loin should be very muscular and very slightly arched. The front ribs are moderately arched, and the back ribs deep and well sprung. The hindquarters are strong and muscular with long and powerful thighs. The stifles should be well curved, turning neither in nor out. The hocks are well bent, well let down, and perpendicular to the ground. They are parallel to each other when seen from behind. The tail is set rather high and carried gaily, but not over the back or curled. The front legs must be straight when viewed from any direction, with strong bones down to the feet. The coat should be smooth, flat, hard, dense, and abundant. *The belly and inner thighs should not be bare.* The dog must present a generally gay, lively, and active appearance.

THE LAKELAND TERRIER

Brief History and Description

The history of the Lakeland is obscure, though its origin was in the English Lake District, an area known for its fox hunting, not so much for sport as for necessity to protect the flocks of sheep. The Lakeland is believed to be a blend of Border Terrier, Bedlington, and Fox Terrier. He has also been known as a Patterdale, Cumberland, and Fell Terrier mixture. An English hunter is believed to have developed the Lakeland by interbreeding the old English Hard-Haired Black-and-Tan Terriers with Bedlingtons to produce dogs with better hunting instinct. The Lakelands were courageous dogs that would enthusiastically go after fox and badger making them highly desirable to hunters, farmers, and ranchers. The English Kennel Club first recognized the breed in 1928.

The Lakeland is an ideal family dog, well-suited to rough and tumble games, but responding well to firm handling. He has good manners and is not prone to tearing things up when left alone as are some of the other Terriers. He has a gay, friendly, somewhat cocky attitude toward life.

Condensed Breed Standard

The head is well-balanced and rectangular in appearance. The skull is flat and moderately broad, the cheeks almost straight-sided, and the stop is barely perceptible. The muzzle is broad and straight to the nose, and there is little chiseling under the eyes. The powerful jaws have teeth that meet in either a level or slightly scissors bite. The small, V-shaped ears are folded just above the top-line of the skull. The inner edge of the ear lies close to the cheek with the flap pointing down. The eyes are set fairly wide apart, are dark in color, slightly oval in shape, and with good expression. The neck has a good reach, looks refined but strong, with clean lines and a slight arch. The withers are noticeably higher than the level of the rest of the back. In overall body proportions, the Lakeland gives a square-built appearance. The chest is moderately narrow and extends to the elbows, which are held close to the body. The ribs are well-sprung, and the hindquarters are broad and muscular. The front legs appear straight when viewed from any side, are strong boned, and with no appearance of a bend at the pastern. The hind legs are strong and well angulated. The hocks are well let down and perpendicular. The nails are strong and dewclaws are to be removed. The tail set is high on the body and the tail is docked so that its tip is approximately level with the skull. The tail is held upright with a slight curve toward the head. The Lakeland coat is double, with a hard outercoat and soft undercoat. The muzzle and legs are well furnished, but not profusely so.

WELSH TERRIER

Brief History and Description

The Welsh Terrier is considered one of the quieter Terriers. He is a good companion, excellent with children, and of a size that fits well with most family situations. When brought into the family between the ages of six weeks to three months, he is easy to train and soon established into the routine. The Welsh Terrier has a great deal of natural curiosity stemming from his hunting background. With proper training this curiosity can be correctly channeled.

These long-legged Terriers are native of Wales. They are most certainly descended from the old Black-and-Tan Terrier common in Britain in the 18th and 19th centuries. Some describe him as a miniature Airedale, but he differs in proportions and other details. He was first considered as a show breed toward the end of the 19th century and around 1901, classification was offered for the Welsh at Westminster.

Condensed Breed Standard

The skull should be flat and slightly wider between the ears than the Wire Fox Terrier. The jaws are powerful, clean, deep, and give a punishing bite. The Welsh Terrier head has a more masculine look than the Wire Fox. The stop is not too defined, with good length of muzzle from the stop to the end of the black nose. The ear is to be V-shaped, small, not too thin, set on fairly high on the skull, carried forward and close to the cheek. The eyes are small, not too deeply set, but not protruding, dark hazel in color, expressive and indicating courage. The neck is of moderate length and thickness, slightly arched and sloping gracefully into the shoulders. The back should be short with a well-ribbed chest.

GROOMING THE WIRE, WELSH, AND LAKELAND TERRIERS

In viewing the picture of a champion Wire Fox Terrier (*Fig. 1*), certain determinations can be made as to how to adapt this look into a pet trim. The body coat should not be clipped too closely since this is a coated breed. The best results would be obtained using a #5, #5F, #4 or #4F blade. The choice would be made based on the density of the coat. The skull and sides of the cheek would be finished using a #7F or a #9. The leg coat would be scissored keeping in mind that the front legs hang straight from the body, so there should be no blousy lines of coat at the shoulders or elbows. The

Figure 1. Champion Illsan's Brandy Alexandra, bred, owned and groomed by professional groomer, Sandy Bamberger. (Photo - Debbie Barthowink)

The chest has good depth and moderate width. The shoulders are long, sloping and well set back. The hindquarters should be strong, with well muscled thighs of good length. The hocks are moderately straight, well let down, and with a good amount of bone. The tail is set on moderately high, but not carried too gaily. The front legs are to be straight, muscular, and possessing a fair amount of bone. The pasterns should be upright and powerful. The feet are to be small, round, and catlike. The coat is to be wiry, hard, very close, and profuse; color should be black and tan, or black grizzled and tan, free from black penciling on the toes. The coat should be strong, with a healthy sheen.

rear legs look muscular, but again the line is a smooth flowing continuation of the body coat. (The head work is discussed later in this chapter.)

In grooming these three terriers, removing body coat before bathing insures a better final finish. Use a blade one size shorter than the one you use for final finishing. Remember, dirty coat always lies flatter and closer to the body, and there will be more resiliency and spring to the coat after bathing.

A #7F blade is used to quickly remove excess coat (*Fig. 2*). It is not necessary to do a smooth clip at this point as you are only removing some of the coat to facilitate cleaning during the bath. Remove

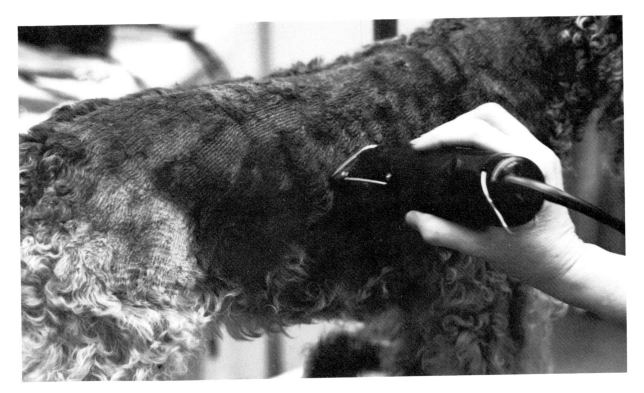

Figure 2.

excess coat over the hindquarters, blending off the muscle of the upper thigh at its thickest point, and carefully cleaning around the rear. If the coat under the tail seems sparse, use a longer blade for that area (*Fig. 3*).

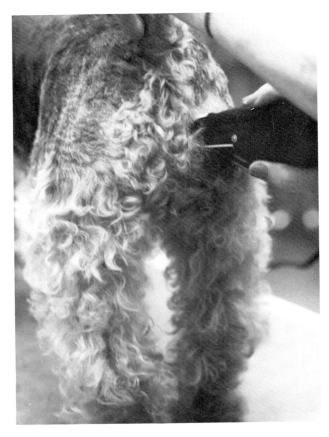

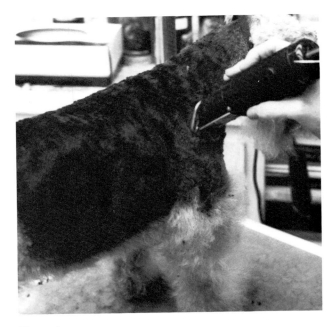

Figure 3.

Figure 4.

De-mat, brush using a slicker brush, and dry as previously described. Fluff-dry the furnishings. Back brush all the body coat and use a light finishing spray before final clipping. Reclip all the body work. *Figure 4* shows a Welsh Terrier coat being finished using a #5 skip-tooth blade for a textured look. Blend smoothly off the front shoulders, over the elbow area, and off the front of the chest.

Figure 6.

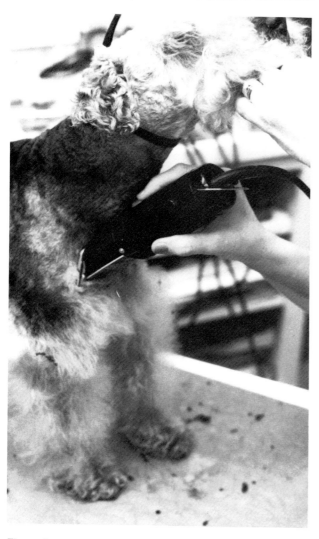

Figure 5.

No appearance of bib coat is left on the chest (*Fig. 5*). Keep in mind that the front legs hang straight from the body. The finished front of the chest and leg scissoring is shown in *Figure 6*. The scissoring of the front legs should emphasize that these legs are very straight, and that the elbows are close to the body, so there is a nice flowing line off the front shoulders. The undercarriage is scissored to conform to the dog's body.

Figure 7.

The ears of all three terriers are similar in shape and should be clipped leaving a light coating of hair. A #10 blade, or one of similar depth, leaves a nice finish (*Fig. 7*). Always clip from the base to the tip of the ear, supporting it with your fingers. Work from the center to the outside edges. Trim the edges of the ear neatly, scissoring at a 45-degree angle to avoid nicking the ear leather (*Fig. 8*).

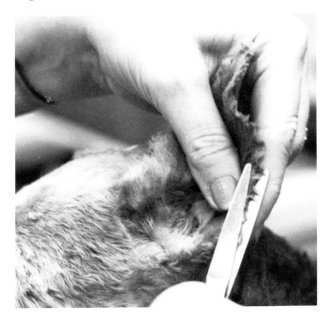

Figure 8.

Finishing the Head Coat

Wire Fox - The head coat is clipped with the lay of the coat, beginning just behind the eye socket, and working toward the back of the skull. The Wire Fox has the smallest eyebrows of the three Terriers. They are shaped with thinning shears to appear as an extension of the head coat. *They do not stick up*, but form a small triangle exposing most of the eye, narrow at the outer corner, with a small amount of fullness at the inner corner. The area between, in front of, and under the eyes is blended with thinning shears to maintain a long, lean rectangular head shape. There should be no dished-out area under the eyes, and no bushy whiskers sticking out to break the lean look. The mustache and goatee are shaped separately. The mustache on the upper muzzle overlays the goatee only slightly. It is thinned and shaped with thinning shears to lie down and forward. (See photo of champion.) The goatee begins forward of the back corner of the mouth, and is only a little longer than the depth of the under jaw.

The Lakeland Terrier - His head is a medium rectangle, not as lean as the Wire Fox nor as broad through the skull as the Welsh. *Figure 9* shows the

Figure 9.

skull of the Lakeland being clipped with a #9 blade. (For a more coated look, use a #7F.) The Lakeland's headpiece shows a full fall (the extension of the eyebrow coat down over the muzzle), giving an almost level line from the top of the head extending to the end of the muzzle at the nose. The fall is not of the thickness of what you would see on a Kerry Blue or a Wheaton Terrier. It is thinned and shaped to continue the line of the skull. Use either thinning shears or a #5 skip-tooth blade, clipping toward the nose to even off the top of the eyebrows. Scissor only lightly to open up the indication of the eye at the outer corner of the eyebrows. Thin and shape the furnishings of the muzzle to give the effect of a rectangular box, using the side of the head as the outer line (*Fig. 10*). (See *Fig. 15* for the finished Lakeland.)

Figure 10.

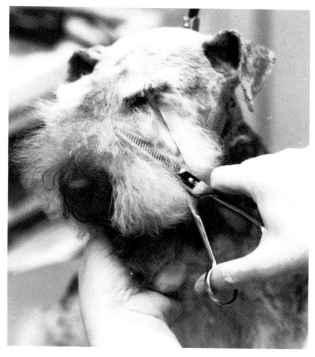

Figure 11.

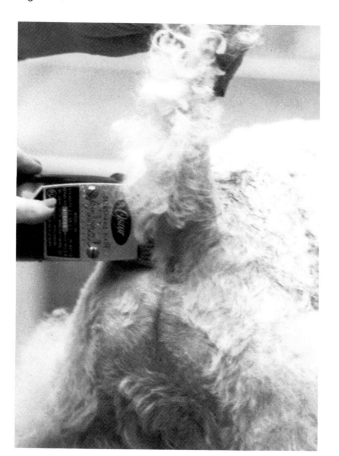

Figure 12.

Welsh Terrier - The eyebrow is a more defined triangle, however, it does not resemble that of a Schnauzer. The area between the eyes is not cut down, but rather the area between the eyebrows and down the nose is thinned to give the indication of a stop. Blend the area in front of the eyes (*Fig. 11*). The muzzle furnishings are thinned and scissored to maintain the boxy, rectangular look of the head. Neaten the back line of the whiskers from the back corner of the eye to just behind the back corner of the mouth. Work the goatee on the bottom jaw separately, usiing thinning shears to shape, and moving the back line of the goatee slightly forward of the mustache on the upper jaw. The whiskers of the Welsh and Lakeland are never left long and straggly. Rather, they are nicely shaped within the imaginary box and should not appear bulky.

Finishing the Tail

To finish the tail do not clip closely or shave with a blade, but rather leave a nicely coated appearance. Clean around the rear base of the tail with a #7F blade. If you don't trust yourself to do an even job using scissors on the rest of the tail, use a #5F or #4F blade to get a coated look (*Figs. 12-14*). The tails of the Wire Fox and the Lakeland are set on rather high. The Welsh tail is set a little further back

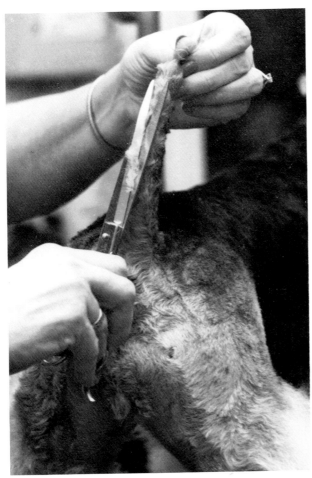

Figure 13.

Figure 14.

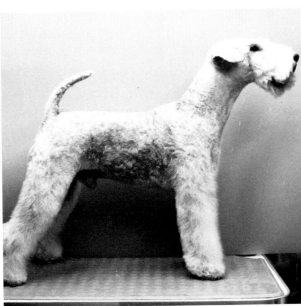

Figure 15.

on the rump, and does not curve toward the head as much as the other two. In all three cases, the very tip of the tail should be trimmed in the direction of the head when viewed from a side profile. The body coat directly in front of the tail should be blended so that it does not lay up the tail.

Figure 15 shows the finished Lakeland Terrier. Overall, he is a good pet example of the breed; he has nice reach of neck, making it easy to achieve a graceful arch.

These three terriers, together with the Westie, Scottie and Cairn, are present at every major dog show. Take a camera, use a fast film that doesn't need a flash, and take pictures of the heads of the champions of these breeds to help you remember what they *should* look like when you are finishing them at your shop.

22
Mixed Breed Design Grooming

When groomers are asked "What breed do you most enjoy grooming?" invariably the answer is "Mixed-breeds," for, with them groomers are challenged to show their creativity and skill. There is no defined profile to follow, so the groomer depends on her "eye" to bring out the best features of each mutt.

The groomer encounters many different types of coat textures from the super soft, silkiness of a Maltese mixture to the rough, hard coat where the Terrier has left its mark. Every mixed-breed requires a slightly different technique to properly handle the body structure and coat requirements.

You may groom the same dog a number of times with a slightly different touch each time, until you find the clip that is most flattering to the dog, or one that particularly suits the owner. Sometimes, you need take only one look at the dog to immediately "see" the finished trim.

Frequently, the groomer is faced with a cute dog so badly matted that there is no choice except to clip it short. Carefully open the coat on the back by scissoring a slit in the mats to see if there is any growth of coat under the matted layer. If you find coat free of mats under the matted layer, use the longest blade you can get under the mats, and give a soft, overall, short clip leaving at least some covering of coat.

For the mixed-breed that is not badly matted, styling is usually the choice of the groomer. Occasionally, the owner has had the dog groomed in a pleasing style at some other shop. In that case, try to determine what the owner wants, and do the best you can. If possible, ask the owner to sketch what he wants on paper. Sometimes, it is best to *insist* that the owner give *you* the chance to develop a style.

In finishing the coat, always consider the texture. A coat with a strong Terrier background has more body when shampooed with a protein-based shampoo. A coat with more Poodle background needs a cleansing shampoo and finishing rinse that does not rob the coat of its natural oils and sets the coat up for finishing.

Another consideration is the dog's environment. A dog that spends 90 percent of its time in the house can get by with a shorter clip than one that is exposed to weather.

As with any other breed, your first step is thorough de-matting, brushing and bathing. Then clip the underbelly, clean the ears, and check under the eyes for any accumulated matter. The paws need careful attention, particularly on outdoor dogs. Also, check the toenails to be sure none are broken or irritated. Except for the smaller lap dog, most mixed-breeds are not groomed on a regular basis.

Some mixed-breed coats present particularly difficult problems, such as the one heavily influenced by a sporting breed background. Cocker-Poodle mixes fall into this category. The coat is often long, soft, and without much texture. This type of coat can be lifted between the fingers in much the same way as a beautician would do, and scissored to whatever length the owner would like. Another method would be to use a clip-on attachment over a #30 blade for a shorter, yet very coated look. For a still closer trim, use a #4F blade. Anything shorter on that type of coat would not have a particularly pleasing finish.

A series of "before" and "after" photos of various mixed-breeds are presented here.

COCKER/POODLE/TERRIER MIX — Groomer, Paul Bryant

FIGURES 1 AND 1A

Coat texture - Straight, soft, Poodle-type coat with intermixed Terrier guard hairs.

Color - White, with grizzled, gray-brown color patches on back and tail, and shaded gray-brown ears.

Head - Head piece was parted and hand scissored from the center part to each ear, and from just above the eye socket to leave a soft coating of hair on the head. The eyes were enhanced by scissoring close over the inner corner and graduating in length at the outer corner to blend in the head coat down into the beard.

Body work - The body work was done with a #4F blade, blended at shoulders and hips into scissored leg coat. Blended off sides at turn of rib cage, and scissored to conform to the body structure.

Legs - Scissored, tubular in shape on front legs with a slight suggestion of paw. Rear leg scissoring conforms to shape of leg with slight angulation shown.

Tail - The tail was left full and natural, with slight scissoring at base of tail to clean away straggly coat.

Figure 1.

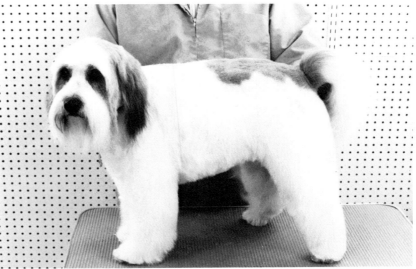

Figure 1A.

SCHNAUZER/BEAGLE MIX — Groomer Paul Bryant

FIGURES 2 AND 2A

Coat texture - Soft and sparse.

Color - Dark grey, shaded to light silver.

Head - All head coat clipped with a #9 blade. Top of skull, cheeks, under throat area, and back of neck worked in the direction of the lay of the coat. Schauzer-type eyebrows were scissored. Ears were clipped with a #10 blade from the base to the tip.

Body work - Body coat was clipped with a #7F blade following the direction of the coat growth. Chest was so sparse it was scissored to give a more coated look. Undercarriage was scissored to leave a short apron, similar to the type left on the undercarriage of a Schnauzer.

Legs - The coat on the legs was so thin, the hairs were merely tipped to give more symmetry.

Tail - Coat on the tail was very thin. It was left natural, with only straggly tips scissored.

Figure 2.

Figure 2A.

COCKER/POODLE MIX — *Groomer, Paul Bryant*

FIGURES 3 AND 3A

    Coat Texture - Soft, Poodle-type coat.

    Color - Cream.

    Head - A soft, short, topknot-type effect was scissored to give a "Bonnet" look. The eyebrow coat was combed forward and scissored in an arch over the eyes, blending into the ear coat and the beard. No earset was indicated. The ears were left full and untrimmed.

    Body work - The body coat was removed using a medium, clip-on attachment over a #30 blade. Entire body, chest, and undercarriage were worked with the lay of the coat to the same depth. No apron was left underneath.

    Legs - Length of leg coat scissored in proportion to the body coat. Scissor blended at shoulders and hip area.

    Tail - Flag-type tail, shortened slightly.

Figure 3.

Figure 3A.

"HEINZ 57" MIX — Groomer, Dorothy Walin

FIGURES 4 AND 4A

Coat texture - Texture of coat changed with each color change.

Color - Predominantly black, grizzled with grey, and phantom marked with white.

Head - The skull from behind the eye socket, back of neck, cheeks, throat, and front of neck all clipped with a #7F blade working with the lay of the coat. Although the eyebrow coat showed Schnauzer influence, the eyebrow area was scissored short to emphasize the white, triangular patches over the eyes. The stop was blended with thinning shears. A full beard was left from the back corner of the eye to the back corner of the mouth. The dog sometimes wears a bandanna around his neck to play up his hobo image.

Body work - Body coat was clipped with the lay of the coat using a #5F blade. Furnishings on the chest and undercarriage were scissored to a medium length.

Legs - Front legs were scissored slightly fuller than the rear legs to hide protruding elbows. The rear legs scissored in proportion to the amount of body coat.

Tail - Tail was left completely natural, only lightly scissored directly above the anus.

Figure 4.

Figure 4A.

YORKIE/POODLE MIX — Groomer, Dorothy Walin

FIGURES 5 AND 5A

Coat texture - Yorkie-type outer coat, with soft, poodle-type undercoat.

Color - Saddle of deep brownish-black color. Ears, light brown and grizzled with same color as saddle. Legs, a tawny, beige-brown, shading into deeper color at shoulders and hips.

Head - All head coat clipped with #4F blade, beginning at a point directly above the eyes, working back over the crown and down the back of the neck. Clipped over side of skull only to a point directly in line with the back corner of the eye then blended into a full beard. Top of muzzle just in front of eye, scissored in a V-shape, and blending up between eyes to head coat. Head coat feathered and blended at top of ears. Ears left full and natural. Orange, velvet ribbons tied in hair at top of ears.

Body work - All body work, including chest and brisket area, done with the #4F blade. Owner's request was for body and legs to be left fairly long and cuddly.

Legs - Scissored tubular in shape, with feet covered. Scissor blended at hips and shoulders for smooth, flowing line.

Tail - Tail coat left full, but shortened so it would not drag.

Figure 5.

Figure 5A.

DACHSHUND/CAIRN TERRIER MIX —
Groomer, Dorothy Walin

FIGURES 6 AND 6A

Coat texture - Body coat crisp and wiry. Legs of softer texture.

Color - Deep orange-brown on body, shading to light cream on head and legs.

Head - Used #9 blade to do skull, beginning behind the eyebrow area. Head coat feathered into ear coat and ears left natural. Throat and front of neck clipped with a #7F blade, clipped with the lay of the coat and blended into chest coat where neck and body met. Eyebrows were combed upward, eyes were covered, eyebrows were sprayed and scissored to form a halo effect. Area in front of eyes and along top of muzzle cleaned and shortened with thinning shears.

Body work - All body work done with a #4F blade. Coat blended at shoulder and hip area. No skirting.

Legs - Legs were scissored and blended where legs and body meet. Feet were left uncovered.

Tail - Tail scissored to carrot shape. Coat on tail was shortened and blended into body coat at base of tail.

Figure 6.

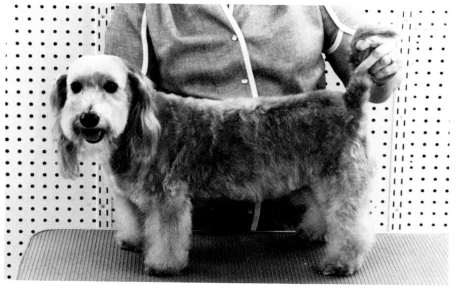

Figure 6A.

POODLE/CAIRN/WIRE FOX TERRIER MIX — *Groomer, Dorothy Walin*

FIGURES 7 AND 7A

Coat texture - Dense, fuzzy undercoat, with longer Terrier-type topcoat.

Color - Coat when grown out has cream-brownish tone. When clipped, cream undercoat color comes through. Tail and ears grizzled with brown.

Head - Head was scissored round and full to compliment round, black, button eyes. Care was taken to leave long, black eyelashes at outer corners of eyes. They were combed forward and held out of the way while scissoring around the eye area. Ears left full and natural and blended into topknot in Bichon style.

Body work - Body left full and plush in appearance by using a clip-on attachment over a #30 blade. After clipping, entire body coat was hand scissored to give smooth, plush appearance. Clip-on attachment was used to clip about an inch at base of tail to give the tail a more defined look.

Legs - Bichon-type, scissored legs.

Tail - Tail left natural, except for light shaping at base.

Figure 7.

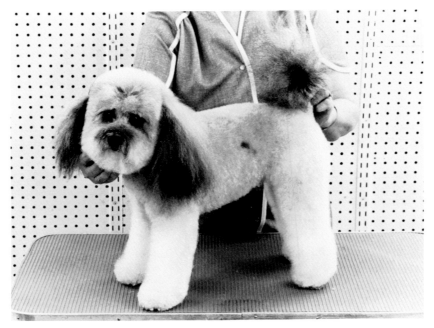

Figure 7A.

23
Problem Dogs

At some point, every professional groomer encounters the dog that is absolutely determined not to be groomed. To a great extent this behavior is the result of one of two causes: improper socialization as a puppy, or a trauma situation that has caused fear.

SOCIALIZATION

If a puppy is to accept the many facets of his environment, he must be exposed to them during early puppyhood, from three to twelve weeks. During this period, he should be introduced to adults, children, other animals, *and his future groomer*. It's smart thinking on the part of those groomers who invite customers with young puppies to leave them at the grooming shop for a visit while the owner is shopping. You might have to put up with some whining and barking as the puppy experiences the stress of being away from familiar people, but if you handle him gently, talk to him frequently, and walk him around the grooming area, he should soon quiet down. It's easy to enjoy a young puppy (they are all so cute) but the young puppy that won't respond to your attentions may become an adult dog that has personality problems.

When a puppy has not been properly socialized to his surroundings, children, mailmen, other animals and even the grooming shop, the dog reacts in one of two ways—aggression or cowardice. Either reaction could lead to someone getting hurt.

Dogs are group-oriented under normal circumstances. Humans are included in their group and are accepted as another dog. This might explain the fact that a dog may risk his life to save the life of a human, if that human is within his group. Within every dog's life there exists a dominance order. This type of order is established within a litter, kennel, household, or in the wild.

Anyone who has ever raised a litter of puppies becomes aware of the dominance factor within the litter; there always seems to be a leader of the pack. Some puppies are placid and do not initiate trouble, and sometimes one sits quietly by until the others are through eating or playing. He is the one most likely to whimper if the others get too pushy when playing or eating. He is also the puppy most likely to appeal to an elderly couple who sees his quiet ways, takes him home, and proceeds to spoil him rotten. He comes to the grooming shop expecting to be treated the same way, and can turn into a real problem.

The dominant puppy in a litter should have an owner who loves, yet trains the dog with patience to understand its place in the family circle. If the dog doesn't receive this type of training, he will be pushy in every situation, for example, jumping on his owner or a guest even though commanded not to do so. This dog might even bite its owner given certain circumstances. When such dominance is evident in a puppy, the owner must do something to change the dog's position in the family circle so that the dominance factor is passed to the owner or another adult. One method is to spay or neuter the dog. It takes a number of months for total hormonal changes to take place after a spay or neutering, and during that time, obedience training, correctly taught and faithfully practiced, helps bring about submission on the part of the dog. Meanwhile, the groomer of this dog has to deal with the possible aggression and dominance that this dog displays. Your confidence in handling the animal, using certain techniques we discuss, can turn the dominance factor to your advantage in most cases. A dog that growls and snaps at every tug of the comb or brush must be retrained to accept a certain amount of discomfort in order to experience pleasure when the grooming session is over. Whenever an aggressive dog gets pushy, you have to command the situation with a sharp, confident "No" or "Stop it," and an appropriate restraining hand. On occasion, unruly puppies can be stopped from misbehaving by holding them by the scruff of the neck, giving them a quick shake together with a firm "No." They are so astonished at being reprimanded, you can usually get the upper hand. This is also the method a mother dog would use for discipline in the wild.

Every dog has social distances within which he accepts or rejects certain objects and people:

a. Home Range - The farthest area he goes from his home and bed.
b. Territory - Usually within the home range. The area he protects.
c. Flight Distance - When a stranger enters the dog's territory and reaches the flight distance of the dog, the dog will retreat or flee if possible.
d. Critical Distance - If a stranger passes the flight distance and forces the dog to a point where he can't flee, the dog may attack.
e. Social Distance - A dog that has been socialized to adults, allows a strange adult to enter within social distance, but the adult may not be able to get close enough to touch the dog and no contact is made.
f. Personal Distance - The dog allows familiar adults and children into his personal distance. The dog allows petting and holding.

Be aware of the body language a dog uses. Bristling of the back hair, flattening of the ears, showing of the teeth or curling the lip, or holding the tail stiffly erect, are all indications of aggressive behavior. If you note such behavior, be particularly aware that a bite may not be far behind. Discuss these and any previous behavior problems, with the dog's owner and help them determine how to handle the dog.

A dog that is passively submissive shows some or all of the following body language communication:

a. As you approach, the dog may look away, lower its face and head. His tail may be down, but he seems relaxed.
b. If you touch the dog he may freeze in position or shrink away.
c. If the dog exhibits extreme signs of submissiveness, he will roll over showing his abdomen or may urinate a small amount.

Since the abdomen is the most vulnerable part of the dog, rolling over on the back and exposing the abdomen indicates complete submission. Occasionally, a groomer sees this type of behavior when taking a dog on leash from its owner, or when removing a dog from the crate.

We can understand the dog's feeling better if we relate them to our own feelings when faced with unpleasant or uncertain situations. Most of us are apprehensive about going to the doctor or the dentist. We react this way because at some time a visit has caused us pain. When faced with the possibility of a shot or of having a tooth pulled, the palms of our hands begin to sweat and our pulse rate speeds up dramatically. If we feel pain, we let the doctor know, and he tries to alleviate the situation.

Consider the dog's dilemma. He comes to a strange grooming shop for the first time, badly matted and feeling out of sorts in general. There he is placed in a cage, forced to experience strange new sights and sounds, and then subjected to pain of varying degrees as his knots and snarls are removed. Then he is thoroughly soaked, soaped and then dried with a noisy apparatus that blows hot air in his ears. Is it any wonder that he objects strenuously at times in the only way he knows, by growling and biting. I am constantly amazed that the dogs are as patient as they are!

GROOMING A "NEW" OR PROBLEM DOG

We have already discussed the necessity of properly socializing the young puppy. What do we do about the dog that has already experienced a traumatic situation at some other grooming shop, and comes in with a chip on his shoulder, ready to take on anyone who comes near him? What about the older dog with advanced disease or arthritic problems? Is there a time when the wise groomer refers the dog's owner to a veterinarian to completely anesthetize an unruly dog before grooming?

Inexperienced groomers may be uneasy with a difficult dog, and the dog immediately picks up on this through a highly developed sense of smell. Any dog that acts as though it is going to be problematic should only be groomed by someone who knows what to do.

There are certain measures the groomer should take when confronted with a new dog that comes to the shop for the first time. First, make sure the dog is on leash. Should the owner forget his leash, supply one from the shop. Keep a supply of 4 foot and 6 foot leashes with leather handles and various sized collars on hand, so that no new dog or dog with questionable behavior is put into a holding crate without a leash to use in removing him from the crate. If the owner is holding the dog, ask that he put on the collar and leash. At this point, it is important that the owner be questioned as to any recent trauma that could affect its behavior. Also it is important to note if the dog is deaf or blind in one or both eyes.

Next, have the owner place the dog on your grooming table for a quick orientation to the groomer for that particular dog. When working with a new dog, it is best to have one person in charge of the dog for the entire procedure. Approach the dog and watch for reactions. Does he back away, or does he allow you to come within his flight distance (the area around the dog in which he allows the approach of a person or another dog before reacting) without signs of aggressive behavior. Stay in front of the dog where he can see you, talk gently to him, then ask the owner to leave the room. The dog may become agitated without the "security blanket" of the owner's presence, but it is important that the dominance factor be transferred from owner to groomer. Make sure the grooming noose is sufficiently taut so the dog cannot bite. Many times a dog is quieted simply because of the grooming noose. He seems to know that the noose restrains him, and allows a stranger near. Watch for curling of the lip or flattening of the ears. Slowly bring up your closed hand to within sniffing distance so the dog can establish your scent. Never reach for a strange dog with an open hand. It may react thinking you are going to strike.

After a few minutes on the table to get acquainted, the dog should be transferred to the holding crate. Leave the collar and leash attached to any strange dog, or to any dog you have previously noted has a problem coming out of the cage. A chain leash prevents the dog from chewing the leash while crated.

When it is time to remove the dog from the crate, pick up the leash and as you open the crate door, shorten and raise the leash with one hand, and as you pull the dog forward if it is reticent, keep your one hand up in the air with the leash taut so the dog cannot lower its head, and scoop the dog up with the other arm. Keep the head controlled with the leash until you put the dog on the table and fasten the grooming noose. At this point, if the dog seems aggressive, use a humane muzzle to prevent biting. Always place a large dog in a crate from which the dog can be walked out. Again, leave the collar and leash in place, and loop the leash over the top of the crate door. When time to remove the dog, raise the leash, keeping it out away from your body at arm's length, open the crate door keeping control of the head with your arm and walk the dog to the grooming table. Hopefully, you will have someone available to help with the lifting of a large dog. If not, you will need some steps to get the dog on the table. If you are working totally alone, do not accept a dog for grooming that you cannot lift comfortably. If you must take a large dog, arrange for the owner to remain and assist.

Make sure the grooming post is securely fastened to the grooming table. Use a post and grooming noose strong enough to hold any dog. Make sure the muzzle, if one has to be used, is securely fastened. Watch for signs of hyperventilation and remove the muzzle at the first signs of stress. Never allow sufficient slack in the grooming noose for the dog to reach around and bite. Conversely, the noose should not choke the dog.

Always position hands and body out of reach of the dog. Begin your work on the rear portion of the dog's body. If a dog gives you a hard time with brushing and combing on the rear legs, chances are he will be twice as aggressive when you work closer to the head.

Should the dog somehow free himself and jump from the table, or if he escapes from the crate, make sure all grooming shop doors are closed and perhaps locked so that no one can enter or leave the shop until the situation is under control. The dog will probably retreat into a corner or under some object where it is difficult to get him out. Every shop should have an emergency loop snare to use in just such a situation. If the dog gets into a corner without surrounding obstacles, take a crate with its door open and push it as close to the dog as possible. The dog will be scared and traumatized by this time, and may enter the crate as a refuge. After he has been retrieved, do not do anything further with him until he has had time to stabilize. If he continues to show signs of agitation, contact the owner and discuss the situation. It may be necessary to make a new grooming appointment. Perhaps the owner should contact the veterinarian to discuss the use of tranquilizers to be given before bringing the dog to the shop. However, some dogs have adverse reactions and are worse than ever when tranquilized and some cannot be tranquilized because of other medications being used. In some cases, one groomer must restrain the dog physically, while the other does the work. The owner should be charged accordingly.

If the dog quiets down after a period of rest, allow a different groomer to approach the dog and watch for visible reactions. The fact that one groomer may succeed with a difficult dog where another has failed does not cast aspersions upon the first groomer. Another groomer's voice or appearance may be more acceptable to the dog. Even the perfume used in various cosmetics may influence the dog's behavior.

No method of control should ever be used maliciously. If you become angry with the dog's unruliness, you must not strike the dog with your hand or a grooming tool to vent your anger. However, if the dog is continuously snapping at your hand, you might let him strike at a metal comb held transversely across his muzzle.

Should you attempt to recondition a dog that has been badly traumatized in some way and shows aggressive behavior while still in the owner's possession? The choice to accept an unruly dog *must* rest with the groomer. Don't allow an owner to bully you into accepting a dog if you feel uncertain about your ability to handle him. The dog may have given other groomers a bad time. Such animals should be groomed under a veterinarian's supervision.

Should you decide to try to rehabilitate an aggressive dog, you might want to try a method that has worked successfully for us a number of times. In one particular instance, a customer brought in a dog that had recently come from the humane society. The dog was in obvious need of grooming, but when anyone other than the owner came near, the dog bared his teeth and snarled. I really wasn't anxious to risk my hands to those teeth, however, the customer was adamant. She told us of the veterinarian's recommendation of our shop, and pleaded with us to try to help. I requested that she spend some time reconditioning before we attempted to

groom the dog. She agreed, and appointments were made for her to bring the dog and leave it at the shop three times per week. Each time the dog came in, we took a crate and set it out on the floor of one of the grooming areas where there was quite a bit of traffic. When the customer came, she put the dog in the crate and left. For the first two weeks of the dog's visits, he rushed at the bars snarling and snapping whenever anyone went by. We totally ignored the dog's bad behavior, and just spoke its name quietly when we were near. Each time the dog came, I spent some of my lunch hour sitting near the crate talking to the dog. He either ignored me completely by sitting off in the corner looking in a different direction, or came at me snarling. By the end of the third week, I suggested that the dog could never be socialized to others because of previous trauma, but the owner wanted to try a little longer because the dog didn't seem quite as aggressive when coming into the shop. One day, in the middle of the fourth week, I sat down to talk to the dog as before. Imagine my surprise when the dog came over to my side of the crate and sat quietly watching me. I carefully brought my closed hand near the side of the crate, and saw no signs of aggressive behavior. I spoke the dog's name, and as I was praising and talking to the dog, there was a slight wag of the tail. I didn't push my luck that day, but spent a little extra time talking to and praising the dog. The next time the owner came in, I mentioned I would try to let the dog out of the crate to see if we had made any real progress. This would be the final week of trying to work with him. During lunch, I asked everyone to leave the grooming room and closed the door. I sat quite close to the front of the cage and talked quietly to the dog for a few minutes, then I carefully opened the crate door. The dog came out immediately, climbed into my lap, and leaned his weight against me. He must have decided I belonged in his group. I gently set him on the floor, got to my knees and stood up, lifting him to the grooming table. He showed no signs of aggression and allowed me to place his head in the grooming noose with no trouble. The dog stood quietly, but he was still on guard. I picked up a brush, and continuing to talk to him, began to brush his rear legs. His ears flattened a couple of time, but he let me work. When I called the other groomers back into the room, they couldn't believe their eyes. I asked them to be as quiet as possible because the dog still reacted fearfully whenever anyone else came close, but I was able to complete a minimal grooming that day. We scheduled another appointment for the following week and gradually socialized the dog to one of the other groomers who was also able to groom the dog without trouble. Patience does pay off unless the dog is a real psychotic.

With experience, every groomer acquires certain reflexes and learns to read the body language a dog uses to let you know he's going to be a problem. Gather complete information about each new dog before you attempt grooming. Confidence, ability, and watchfulness come after handling many types of dogs. There *are* some aggressive dogs that the prudent groomer refuses to service. After all, your hands are your livelihood, and a bad bite can lay you up from work for some time.

GROOMING A YOUNG PUPPY

Puppies must be taught to accept human contact, laying the groundwork necessary for grooming throughout its life. They must also be taught to accept new situations without fear. This is facilitated by loving praise at each new experience. Acceptance is reinforced by praise, and the experience becomes pleasurable in the puppy's mind.

Some puppies need their first grooming experience as young as six weeks of age. Poodle puppies in particular, do much better if the first clipping of the feet is done as early as possible. With my own poodle litters the first clipping of face, feet and tail is done at four weeks—impossible for a grooming shop because the pups haven't been immunized. One Poodle owner routinely brought her puppies in for first clipping at six weeks, right after their first puppy shots. We did them in the evening when no other dogs were present, and covered the grooming table with a freshly washed towel for additional protection. She found this to be to her advantage because the puppies were easier to sell when freshly bathed and trimmed.

The young puppy should be allowed to investigate the clipper to satisfy his curiosity before it is turned on. When he no longer seems interested, you can pass the turned off clipper over his body. Do this until he no longer reacts fearfully, then turn on the clipper. Just hold it in your hand to allow the puppy to become conditioned to the new sound. Let the puppy sniff the clipper if he wants to. Move the clipper around to different sides of his body without actually touching him. Keep talking quietly to him during the entire procedure. Try to make eye contact in a friendly way. Stroking the side of his face with one finger, and along the neck below the ears may help him relax. If you are work-

ing with a Poodle puppy, begin clipping a rear foot. If he starts to struggle, lay the clipper down and speak to him until he quiets down. You may have to use a sharp "no" if he is pushing his advantage. First groomings may take quite some time, and must be done quietly and with sincere love of the animal. You have to make him understand by the gentleness of your hands and the tone of your voice that this is something that brings him pleasure and praise. *The first grooming will forever stamp pain or pleasure on the puppy's mind.* Make sure the owner compliments and praises the young puppy excessively whenever it is groomed. This reinforces good behavior in the puppy, in the same way that praising a child for taking out the garbage may make him more willing to do it next time.

GROOMING THE ELDERLY OR DISABLED DOG

Older dogs present particular problems because many have arthritic joints, which causes them pain if they must stand for long periods of time. Moving the dog's legs for combing and brushing may also cause pain. Crotchety dispositions can be expected in elderly dogs. Don't be surprised if the dog you have done for years without any difficulty becomes irritated and nippy. Be kind enough to pad the grooming table with towels for the elderly dogs. Also, allow the dog to sit for as much of the grooming as possible. Dogs that have cervical spinal degeneration or injury may sit every time you raise their head. Pain along the spinal column causes the dog great discomfort if you move the legs beyond a tolerable range. Another groomer may have to assist by supporting the dog while you complete certain functions. Additional problems may result from diminished sight or hearing. When you remove a blind dog from the crate, always speak to it by name. Allow it to smell your closed hand. Do not unnecessarily startle a blind or deaf dog. If the dog is both blind and deaf, tap the crate with your fingers so the dog can feel the vibration and be aware that someone is there. Use special care when working on the feet of an older dog. Frequently warts or misshapen nails will cause problems. Poodles may have reddened and sore areas between the toes. If clipping is questionable, leave the foot groomed like a terrier with a soft covering of hair all over.

The body of the older dog may present problems. Lumps, abscesses, draining warts and tumors under the skin must be carefully cleaned. If you are removing a lot of body coat on an older dog, feel the underlying skin and body carefully for any protrusion the clipper might accidentally nick. One way to remember where they are is to place a small piece of masking tape at each location. Then you can clean around the area taking special care not to accidentally remove a wart or skin tab.

Keep a reassuring hand on an older dog at all times. Be aware of their movements. The last thing you want is for a blind or elderly dog to accidentally fall off the table. Some cannot be restrained in a grooming noose because of trachea problems.

Always finish them as quickly as possible. Be careful of exposure to drafts. Do not crate dry, as the hot air during crate drying may cause breathing difficulties. Keep the older dogs in crates that are elevated off the floor to avoid drafts. Older dogs or dogs prone to epileptic seizures should be worked straight through and sent home. The less time spent in the grooming shop, the less trauma involved.

Common sense, gentleness and wisdom are the attributes most helpful to the groomer facing a problem dog.

24
Conventions, Dog Shows & Certification

"Hi, friend!" You hear that greeting whenever groomers gather at conventions and seminars. Of course, it's fun to see people from various parts of the country with whom you have so much in common. Some groomers come to *learn*, others to play. Many have saved their money for a year just for the privilege of attending a nationally recognized convention or seminar. It is a privilege to take advantage of the knowledge of those who participate in giving demonstrations. Most of them have many years of experience in the business and can offer tips that enhance the profession and your abilities.

Manufacturers and distributors regularly attend these shows. Often, they offer discounts that are available only at the show or for a limited time. If you have grooming supply needs, a show is a place you can often strike a hard bargain for a needed dryer, grooming table, shampoos, scissors, etc. A salesman may give you a special price because he does not want to pack up and take back the items in his booth.

The prime importance of visiting every booth is to keep abreast of all that is new in supplies to make grooming easier, better, more professional, and more efficient. Many manufacturers now use well-known professional groomers in their booths to answer questions and demonstrate products.

The temptation to indulge in merrymaking and taking in the sights of a new place is natural. However, it is important to try for enough sleep to be clear-headed and able to absorb all available information. Many seminar and convention sponsors now schedule open time for the manufacturers' booths in the morning, knowing full well that the groomers will straggled in around ten o'clock or later. Speeches and demonstrations usually take place in the afternoon when everyone is more alert and ready to participate.

Bring a hardbacked note pad to every seminar. Record notes on presentations, products you are interested in, names and addresses of those you want to contact further, and any questions you may want answered.

There are booths where representatives of various trade publications can take your name and business location for a free subscription to their magazine. (It is vitally important to avail yourself of trade papers.) Trade magazines keep you informed of coming events around the country so you can schedule your travel plans well in advance. Local grooming associations usually have someone available to give information on membership. Many states now have active grooming groups that have excellent annual conventions. If you cannot travel to one of the national shows, your local grooming group is the place to actively participate.

MIDWEST CONVENTIONS

No one grooms in this area for long before becoming aware of the educational contributions of the All American Grooming Contests conducted by Jerry Schinberg of J. & G. Associates. These contests, held in Chicago or a neighboring suburb, were begun in August, 1973, and have been held in the Chicagoland area every August since that time. The first show was a one day show with 50 contest entrants and some 200 people from 7 states in attendance. There were nine booth representatives. Demonstrations were given by Mario Migliorini on a Westie and by Shirlee Kalstone grooming a Shih Tzu while contest scores were tallied.

Contestants were judged on a point-scoring system by nationally known judges such as Shirlee Kalstone and Mario Migliorini and by well-known local groomers such as Robert Hoyt, Herman and Irene Kellman, and Mae Vestgard. Entry fees were $15.00 per dog. Prizes were $30.00, $15.00 and $5.00 respectively for 1st, 2nd, and 3rd place. The Best Groomed Dog received $50.00, the Winners Competitive Grooming Class was also awarded $50.00 and the best Jr. Groomer received a trophy. The Best Groomed Dog award that first year was won by Judy Jiskra of Babette's Poodle Salon in Toledo, Ohio.

The August 1985 All-American Midwest Professional Dog Grooming Contest & Seminar attracted more than 500 participants, including 90 grooming entries in eight categories. Forty three exhibitors presented their products, many with well known groomers demonstrating the newest techniques. Manufacturers are aware of the rising interest in seminars and conventions.

Contestants were divided into two groups; "A" division for those groomers who had previously won a first placement in any previous grooming contest; and "B" division open to all contestants with no previous first place win. Judges for the 1985 contest included Rhonda Gran CMG, owner of Comb and Collar (Ft. Wayne, ID); Shirlee Kalstone, author and organizer of the East Coast Groomerama show; Elizabeth Paul CMG, multi-contest winner; and Dottie Walin CMG, author-educator. Best Groomed Dog and Best All-Around Groomer titles were judged and awarded by Judy Breton Fulop, guest judge from Danville, California. Best All-Around Groomer in Division A competition went to Jacquelyn Bowman (The Silver Leash, Hartland, WI). Competing in five classes, she won four first placements and one second place. Jacquelyn has been awarded the coveted title of Best All-Around Groomer and placed with the Best Groomed Dog *Three* times at the Chicago show. Best Groomed Dog in the 1985 show was awarded to Betsy Schley for her lovely presentation of a Bichon in the Miscellaneous Breeds Class. The award for Best All-Around Groomer and Best Groomed Dog in the Division B classes went to Linda Suter (From Head To Tail, Elmhurst, IL). The judging at this show, and what has become an accepted way to conduct judging, was done by one judge in each class.

Figure 1. Meg Conley Serafino was recently awarded the title of Best All-Around Groomer in Division "A". She also had the Best Groomed Dog. Meg is shown here with Bob Davidson from the Pet Chemicals Co. All-American Midwest Grooming Contest. (Photo - Jerry Shinberg)

Figure 2. The author shown here judging the Miniature Poodle Class "A" competition at a recent All-american Midwest Grooming Contest. (Photo - Val Penstone)

Figure 3. Mrs. Tsujihara from Tokyo, Japan executed a very pretty Continental show clip. Both show and pet trims were allowed in competition at the First International Grooming Contest to give greater flexibility and variety to the competition. All contestants had to be previous first place winners at major contests in this country and abroad. (Photo - D. Walin)

WEST COAST CONVENTIONS

Another long-running combined industry trade show and grooming contest is held on the West Coast in early summer each year. In its first year, 1971, 393 businesses attended the show. At the 1983 show held in Anaheim, California, there were 738 establishments represented. The National Retail Pet Stores and Groomers Assn. (NRPSGA) and Bay Area Pet Industries (BAPI) are two sponsors of major grooming contests on the West Coast. The 1983 winner of the Best All Around Groomer award in NRPSGA's grooming contest was Judy Henigan from Judy's Grooming in Los Angeles, California. A Best of winners class held at the 1985 NRPSGA's show in Long Beach, California was won by multi-contest winner, Elizabeth Paul from Florida.

EAST COAST CONVENTIONS

A more recent entrant into the seminar field has been the International Groomerama, renamed in 1984 to Inter-Groom. This show heralded the first International Grooming Contest at its 1984 gathering held in Newark, New Jersey. All com-petitors at this contest had been previous first place winners at various shows in the United States and abroad. Classes were divided so international competitors did not compete against American groomers until the Best In Each Class and Best In Show. Five classes were offered- Poodles, Terriers, Hand-Stripping, All Other Purebreds, and Mixed-Breeds. Class judges included Paul Bryant from Illinois, John Nash from New Jersey, Margaret Smith from England, Jetty van der Hulst from Holland, and the author from Wisconsin. Mrs. Smith, owner of Margaret's Canine Grooming Salon, holds the coveted title of England's "Groomer of the Year" for both 1981 and 1982. Jetty van der Hulst owns The Dog's Beauty Shop in The Hague and is a member of the Groomer's Committee of Dibevo, the Dutch pet trade association. Jetty is a multi-contest winner in Europe.

International guests have been featured at each year's show. In 1984, these guests included Mr. and Mrs. Masahiro Tsujihara of Tokyo, Japan. Mr. and Mrs. Tsujihara are licensed by the Japanese Kennel Club as instructors of pet and show grooming throughout Japan. They are Directors of the Sepia Pet Grooming School.

The highlight of the 1984 Groomerama was the International Contest. Four of the five winning placements were awarded to American groomers. The fifth went to an English entrant. The placements were as follows:

Best Groomed Poodle in Show - Elizabeth Paul from Florida.

Best Groomed Terrier in Show - Maureen Stapelton from Wisconsin.

Best Groomed Hand-Stripped Dog in Show - Peter Young from England.

Best Groomed Other Purebred in Show - Loretta Vogt from New Jersey.

Best Groomed Mixed Breed in Show - Jacquelyn Bowman from Wisconsin.

The award of International Groomer of the Year, chosen from among the five finalists previously mentioned, went to Elizabeth Paul and her beautifully groomed black Standard Poodle. Elizabeth is a multi-contest winner whose other wins include National Dog Groomers contest in 1983 and Best All Around Groomer and Best In Show in Chicago in 1981 and 1982, and Best of Champions winner at the west Coast WWPSA show in July, 1985. Elizabeth's prizes at the Groomerama included $1,000.00 in cash and numerous product prizes. The runner-up winner was the English contestant, Peter Young, with a hand-stripped West Highland White Terrier. Peter's prizes included $250.00 in cash and other product prizes.

What a difference in winners' awards when compared to early shows in our industry. Each year the shows get bigger and better as many more groomers avail themselves of this educational and fun experience.

Figure 4. Peter Young of England was the winner of the category of Best Groomed Hand-Stripped Dog in Show, and the eventual Reserve Winner in the final judging.

GROOMING ORGANIZATIONS

Many states now have active grooming organizations. Large metropolitan areas are the seed beds of state and local organizations. Some feature various types of contests. One such, conducted by Margaret Migliorini, featured variations on the theme of the Clown Clip. Groomers and their pouches were encouraged to be costumed alike. Margaret, as Ringmaster, awarded prizes for grooming and costuming. There is fun as well as education in attending seminars and conventions.

One other organization should be mentioned. The National Dog Groomers Association of America was organized in 1969. Representing groomers from a cross section of America, they have con-

ducted various types of seminars and contests in different locations around the country.

HOW TO PREPARE FOR CONTESTS

As skills increase, Professional Groomers are challenged to enter local or national contests and compete with their peers. Preparation to enter a contest is begun many months in advance of the actual competition.

Search for a dog to use in the category in which you want to compete. It should have the best of dispositions and the finest coat condition possible. Confer with the dog's owner to find out if the dog would be allowed to travel with you. You may have excellent dogs to choose from, but if the owner declines, you are out of luck.

Figure 5. Maureen Schaefer shown here as the winner of the Best Groomed Terrier (clipped category).

Get used to the idea of appearing before an audience by volunteering to appear before a local grooming group, or to give a talk and demonstration for some local civic organization. If you get the "willies" appearing before the public, you can be sure the butterflies will fly twice as high in a contest.

When you locate an owner who agrees to let you take his dog, your conditioning of the dog requires care for months before the contest. Plan the dog's appointments so the last grooming is six-to-eight weeks before the contest. Give extra care at no cost to the owner to keep the coat in prime condition. If there is to be a pattern, it should be set and reset until the proportions are as perfect as you can make them. Next, begin timing yourself every time you do the grooming pattern you have chosen. You can find out the time available for the class you wish to enter by contacting the sponsoring organization. You must be able to do the entire finished grooming in the allotted time with some time to spare to go over the coat for any uneven clipping or scissoring.

Prepare your wardrobe ahead of time. Wear a nice pair of dress slacks and a clean, fresh groom-

THE COMPETITION

Begin by competing in a small show where the pressure is not as great. Always test all equipment before going into the ring. Be sure to have extra blades of those you most often use. Combs should have no rough spots that might tear into the coat when the judge goes over your dog. If the dog has any sensitivities or problems, call them to the judge's attention during the prejudging examinations.

The dog you bring into the ring must be *completely* de-matted, scrupulously clean and fluff-dried. Nails should be cut and ears properly cleaned. *Every* mat should be removed. If you should miss a mat under the legs, at the bottom of a leg, under an ear, or anywhere else, you may lose out altogether. This is particularly true in a class

Figure 6. Shown in this photo are the five finalists in competition for the title of International Groomer of the Year, and Shirlee Kalstone, Show Coordinator. The flags in the background are those of the nations represented at the show.

ing jacket or apron. Comfortable shoes are a must, but should not be open-toe or sandals. Your hair should be clean and attractive. The judge gets a visual impression of the total picture, and that includes *you*, as you present your dog to the judge for inspection.

"A" competition. As you are doing your work, if you accidentally nick the dog, and the judge either notices when it happens or finds it when examining the dog, it will be marked against you.

During the actual competition, try to ignore everyone around you. Carry a small travel clock in your grooming case, and note the time limit for your class. Work straight through your entire pattern, then go back and smooth any rough parts. If you spend too much time on one particular part, you may not have enough time to finish.

The judge's decision is final and every judge sees patterns and proportions in a different way. Essentially, your dog is in a beauty contest, and it is up to you to make sure he has the best possible chance of winning. There can only be a few winners in each class, but a true professional is a sportsmanlike loser as well as a gracious winner. You may have to compete in many contests, improving your skills each time, until you are at last privileged to step into the winner's circle.

CONTEST JUDGING

As difficult as it may be to be a contestant, there is even greater stress on the judge. Ringside spectators always pick favorites. The only problem is that those who are at ringside cannot see what the judge sees. Each judge carries a clipboard on which to make notations. Any type of fault is recorded. Some things that can prevent your placing in competition are: nicks or abrasions in the dog's skin; nicks between the underpads of the feet; mats anywhere in the coat; uneven pattern lines; incorrect pattern proportions; or incorrect breed profiles. Be sure you know the correct breed profile if you are competing in one of the Terrier classes or for any other purebred dog other than the Poodle.

Unfortunately, there are no classes to teach proper procedure to judges. There is strong feeling in the industry that judges should be taught *how* to judge. Often judges are chosen from among previous winners. That may be all right, unless the judge is asked to do a class in which he hasn't the experience to know the correct breed profile. When grooming contest judging first began, judging was primarily based upon scissoring techniques. There was a great deal of animosity toward the idea of judging by a correct breed profile. The argument was that these were only pets that were being groomed and judged. Competition is far more sophisticated now, especially in the larger shows, and groomers are aware that they are judged on correct profiles as well as grooming techniques. Dog owners are now more knowledgeable and more of them demand correct grooming for their pets.

Every judge should try to make you feel at ease in the ring. You are asked to stand your dog and present him to the judge. Visual first impressions of the overall appearance of the dog can weigh heavily in the judge's mind. If you have ever attended a conformation dog show you have a better grasp of this fact. Practice standing the dog you intend to use in front of a mirror to get a better concept of what the judge sees. Try to smile and

Figure 7. Notice the breed profile on this fine champion example of the Bedlington Terrier. A groomer proficient in the use of scissors could duplicate this look if given a Bedlington with good coat to work on. (Photo - Karen Walin)

look as though you are enjoying the whole procedure, even if you are dying inside.

The judge will ask to use your comb. He should use the same routine with every dog examined. Beginning at the front of the dog, and making its acquaintance, the judge closely examines the head, ears, neck, chest and front legs. He will comb through all the coat to check for uneven scissor marks or mats. Underpads of all the feet are examined for nicks or uneven and unkempt hairs. Pattern lines are scrutinized for proper placement and smoothness of lines. When all these things have been checked, the judge will ask you once again to pose your dog for a final visual impact. The judge then steps to one side and makes any notations about your grooming that will either put you in contention for a placement or eliminate you from consideration. The contestant has the right to question the judge after the competition for any comments and constructive suggestions. If you don't place, ask the judge to critique your work and offer suggestions that may help you the next time you enter.

One of the most difficult classes to judge is the creative grooming class where the contestant is allowed to execute any type of clip. The main criteria for judging this type of class is the uniqueness of the trim, its suitability to the dog, and the smoothness and flow of the lines. Even though the trim may be very different, it must still be well done with good lines and proportions throughout. Even in the mixed-breed classes, the smoothness and execution of a trim that brings out the best features of the dog is the main criteria.

Judges usually serve one or two apprentice judging assignments. Most begin in the "B" classes or judge at minor shows. They are well-known people in the industry and have shown their expertise in a variety of ways.

DOG SHOWS

For as long as I have been involved with grooming, I have encouraged groomers to attend dog shows as often as possible. If the groomer lives anywhere near a large metropolitan area, chances are that a local breed club sponsors a dog show in the area. So much can be learned from attending. Champions of record are excellent examples of the breed from which we train our eyes to learn a correct breed profile. Watching various professional handlers and breeder/exhibitors gives valuable tips on coat preparation and care. Scissoring and finishing techniques teach us a lot. Always wait until the dog's handler or agent is relaxed and not hurriedly preparing to go in the ring to ask questions.

A valuable tool for the professional groomer is a good camera. Many 35mm. cameras are nearly

Figure 8. A groomer should spend time at the dog shows learning to properly execute the head piece of the various terriers. The head work on many breeds seems to be the most difficult for many groomers to do correctly. Shown here is a side profile of the headpiece of a champion Wire Fox Terrier. (Photo - Karen Walin)

foolproof, and with the advent of fast film speeds, photos can be taken indoors under almost any lighting condition without the need of flash attachments. You can also take pictures of your work in the shop and keep a scrapbook for owners.

CERTIFICATION

Professional Pet Groomers' Certification, Inc. had its beginnings in 1979 and 1980. Many of us had felt for a long time that there was a need for a national testing of groomer abilities on a regulated basis by a not-for-profit organization. Margaret Migliorini was instrumental in calling a meeting in Chicago to discuss the proposal of a nationally accredited testing organization. The first meeting, held on May 31 and June 1, 1981, brought together interested parties and association representatives. Jerry Shinberg from Illinois and Miriam Langman from Pennsylvania together with Margaret had prepared some of the groundwork. At the first meeting, officers and a board of directors was elected. Another meeting was scheduled for Chicago in August, 1980 to be held in conjunction with the Midwest Grooming Contest. Pam Lauritzen and the author were asked to begin preparation of the first guidelines for Poodle Certification Guidelines. The first certification for Poodle grooming was held in October 1980 in conjunction with the Iowa State Professional Dog Groomers annual convention. The Iowa group also hosted the first Sporting Breed certification, and the first Terrier and Master Groomer Testing was done in Atlanta, Georgia in the spring of 1983. Certification workshops and testings are now performed in major cities across the country.

The organization functions under properly adopted and rigid bylaws and standards. The Code of Ethics is designed to require the highest standard of professional conduct on the part of the certifiers. At this point in the history of professional grooming, testing is strictly voluntary, though there may come a time when it will become mandatory as in other professions.

Those who are tested are expected to show a reasonable degree of proficiency, but are not expected to do work on the caliber of show grooming. Certifiers watch to see that applicants handle their dogs gently but confidently. They require proper use of grooming instruments, correct clipper work, neat scissoring, correct balance and proportion and correct breed profiles.

The final achievement desired is the designation of Certified Master Groomer (CMG). The groomer who achieves that status has passed three hands-on testing procedures: the Non-Sporting Group; the Terrier Group; the Sporting Breed Group. The final test is a written Master Groomer exam of a hundred or more questions.

As of the writing of this book, there are over 500 groomers in various parts of the country and even Alaska who have been tested and have completed various parts of the program. Over 100 have been tested and have received the coveted title of Certified Master Groomer, signified by a CMG after their name.

For those groomers interested in furthering their image as a professional, I can think of no better way to show your community your expertise than by preparing for and taking the necessary testing. The information that you have passed such testing, provided to your local newspapers, lets people know you care about your professional abilities and image.

A word of caution. Other groups have tried to copy and publicize a certification program of their own. I am not referring to grooming schools that give a graduation diploma. Be aware that the Professional Pet Groomers Certification, Inc. is the *only* independent testing group receiving *national* recognition at this time.

Figure 9. This overall view is from the first public grooming demonstration presented by the author. The location was the Yorktown Shopping Center in a Chicago suburb, and the sponsor was Pet Foods Institute. An entire weekend was devoted to various aspects of dog ownership, with "Pets and People" the theme. The author demonstrated grooming techniques for various breeds, among them the Welsh Terrier, Schnauzer, and Poodle. The public was allowed generous time for questions and answers. (Photo - D. Walin)

Groomer's Dictionary

AKC - American Kennel Club

Almond Eye - An eye of almond shape, set in surrounding tissue.

Angulation - The angles formed by a meeting of bones; the shoulder and upper arm in the front and the stifle and hock bones in the rear.

Apple headed - Showing a roundness of topskull humped toward the center of the skull.

Apron - Longer hair on the chest.

Back of the dog - Generally referred to as the area around the backbone between the withers and the loin.

Bad Mouth - Crooked or misaligned teeth; a bite that does not conform to breed standard specifications.

Balanced - The proportions and relationships of the separate parts of the dog to its whole—the balance of head and body.

Barrel hocks - Hocks that turn out, causing the feet to toe in.

Bat ear - An erect ear, broad at its base, rounded in top outline with the opening pointing directly to the front as in the French Bulldog.

Beard - The long hair growth on the underjaw.

Beauty spot - A distinct spot of colored hair surrounded by a blaze of white on the topskull between the ears.

Best In Show - An award given to the dog judged to be the best of all the breeds at a "match" or "pointed" dog show.

Bird dog - A sporting dog specifically trained to hunt birds.

Bitch - A female dog.

Bite - The position of the upper and lower teeth in relation to each other when the mouth is closed.

Blanket - The color of the coat on the back and upper part of the sides between the neck and the tail.

Blaze - A white stripe of hair in the center of the face running up between the eyes.

Blocky - Used to describe a square shape of the head.

Bloom - The sheen of the dog's coat when in prime condition.

Blow coat - The exchange of immature puppy coat for the final, adult coat, usually found during the period from nine to fifteen months of age.

Bobtail - A naturally tailless dog, or one with the tail docked very short. Often used as the name for an Old English Sheepdog.

Bodied up - A well developed, mature dog.

Brace - Two dogs of the same breed, when shown in conformation, having the same physical characteristics. May be unrelated but must be of the same breed and variety.

Breastbone - Bone in the forepart of the chest. (Pointer)

Breed - Purebred dogs more or less uniform in size and characteristics as bred by man.

Breeder - A person who breeds dogs.

Breed Profile - The correct visual impression of the appearance of each purebred dog when properly groomed.

Breed Standard - The correct structural requirements for each purebred dog, approved by each parent club, and published by the American Kennel Club. It refers to such things as body structure, correct bite, coat texture, size, etc.

Brick-shaped - Rectangular—as seen in the head of a Lakeland Terrier.

Brindle - A mixture of black hair interspersed with hairs of a lighter color such as tan, brown or grey.

Brisket - The front part of the dog's body below the chest, between the front legs, closest to the ribs.

Broken-haired - A roughed up, wire coat.

Broken-up face - A receding nose, together with a deep stop, wrinkle and undershot jaw. (example: Bulldog or Pekingese)

Brood bitch - A female used for breeding.

Brushing - A gaiting fault where the pasterns are so close the legs "brush" in passing.

Burr - The inside of the ear.

Butterfly nose - A parti-colored nose, dark and spotted with flesh color.

Buttocks - The rump area or hips.

Button ear - The ear flap folding forward, the tip lying close to the skull so as to cover the opening, and pointing toward the eye.

Camel back - An arched back resembling a one-hump camel.

Canine teeth - The two upper and two lower sharp, pointed teeth next to the incisors commonly referred to as fangs.

Canter - Describing a gait with three beats to each stride. Slower than a gallop.

Carpals - Bones of the pastern joints.

Castrate - To remove the testicles of the male dog.

Cat foot - The short, round, compact foot like that of a cat. The foot with short, third digits.

C.D. (Companion Dog) - A suffix used with the name of the dog that has been recorded a Companion Dog by the A.K.C. as a result of having won certain minimum scores in Novice classes at a specified number of A.K.C. licensed or member Obedience trials.

C.D.X. (Companion Dog Excellent) - A suffix used with the name of the dog that has been recorded a Companion Dog Excellent by the A.K.C. as a result of having won certain minimum scores in Open classes at a specified number of A.K.C. licensed or member Obedience trials.

Character - The expression, individuality or general appearance and deportment as considered typical of the breed.

Cheeky - Cheeks predominant, rounded, thick and protruding.

Chest - The part of the trunk or body enclosed by the ribs.

Chiseled - Referring to a cleanly cut head, particularly under the eyes.

Choke collar - A leather or chain collar fitted to the size of the dog's neck in such a manner that the degree of tension exerted by the hand, tightens or loosens the collar. Used primarily in the training of dogs to obey obedience commands.

Chops - Jowls or pendulous flesh of the lips and jaws such as found in the Bulldog.

Clip - A prescribed method of trimming the coat of some breeds such as the Poodle.

Clipping - When pertaining to the gait of a dog—the back foot strikes the front foot.

Cloddy - Low, thickset, comparatively heavy dog. Often used to describe an older, obese dog.

Close-coupled - Comparatively short from withers to hip bones.

Coarse - Lacking refinement.

Coat - The dog's hair covering.

Cobby - Short bodied and compact.

Condition - The health of an animal based on the general condition, appearance and deportment.

Conformation - The form and structure, make and shape, and arrangement of parts as they relate to specific, breed standard demands.

Congenital - Hereditary, inherited, referring to conditions that are present at birth.

Coupling - The part of the body between the ribs and pelvis; the loin area.

Coursing - The sport of chasing the hare by Greyhounds.

Cow-hocked - When the hocks turn toward each other.

Crabbing - Another term to describe movement of the body of the dog at an angle to the line of direction. Commonly called "side-winding".

Crank tail - A tail carried down and resembling a crank.

Crest - The upper arched portion of the neck.

Cropping or cropped ears - The surgical cutting or trimming of the ear leather done to cause the ears to stand erect.

Crossbred - A dog whose sire and dam are representatives of two different breeds.

Crossing over - Unsound gait which starts with twisting elbows and ends with legs crisscrossing and toeing out.

Croup - The back part of the back above the hind legs.

Crown - The highest part of the head: the topskull.

Cryptorchid - The adult dog whose testicles are abnormally retained in the abdominal cavity.

Cushion - Fullness or thickness of upper lips such as in the Pekingese.

Cynology - The study of canines.

Dam - The female parent. (Not a swear word!)

Dappled - Mottled marking of different colors.

Debilitating - A problem causing lack or loss of strength.

Dewclaw - An extra claw or functionless digit on the inside of the leg; an imperfectly developed fifth toe.

Dewlap - Loose, pendulous skin under the throat.

Dish-faced - When the nasal bone is so formed that the nose is higher at the tip than at the stop.

Disqualification - A decision made by a judge or by a bench show committee following a determination that a dog has a condition that makes it ineligible for any further competition under the dog show rules or under the standards for its breed.

Distemper teeth - Teeth discolored or pitted as a result of distemper or other disease or deficiency.

Dock - To shorten the tail by cutting.

Dog - A male dog; also used collectively to designate both male and female.

Dog show - A competitive exhibition for dogs at which the dogs are judged in accordance with an established standard of perfection for each breed.

Dog Show-Licensed Conformation - An event held under A.K.C. rules at which championship points are awarded. May be for all breeds, or for a single breed (Specialty Show).

Domed - Evenly rounded topskull; convex instead of flat.

Double coated - An outer coat of harsher hair resistant to weather and protective against brush and brambles with an undercoat of softer hair for warmth and waterprooofing.

Down-faced - The muzzle inclining downwards from the skull to the tip of the nose.

Down in pastern - Weak or faulty pastern set at a pronounced angle from the vertical.

Drive - The solid thrusting of the hindquarters indicating sound forward motion.

Drop ear - An ear folded and dropping downward or forward as contrasted with erect or prick ears.

Dry neck - The neck skin neither loose nor wrinkled.

Dudley nose - Flesh colored.

Dutch Trim - A popular pattern trim used in finishing pet Poodles. The trim includes lengthwise and cross stripes in the Poodle coat.

Ear Set - The manner and point at which the ears are attached to the head.

Elbow - The joint between the upper arm and the forearm.

Elbows out - The elbow turning out from the body; not held close.

Emphasis - Something that attracts the eye to certain features while subordinating others.

Entropian - The turning inward of the edge of the eyelid.

Entrusted - Invested with a responsibility.

Epilepsy - Disease characterized by various symptoms such as loss of consciousness, spasms of the muscles, loss of bladder control. A genetic or acquired condition.

Even bite - Meeting of front edge of teeth with no overlap of upper or lower teeth.

Ewe neck - Concave curvature of the top neckline.

Expression - The general appearance of all features of the head when viewed from the front as being typical of a particular breed.

Eyeteeth - The upper canines.

Faking - The artificial changing of a dog's appearance with the object of deceiving the onlooker as to the actual merits of the dog.

Fall of hair - Hair overhanging the face.

Fancier - A person especially interested or active in some phase of the sport of purebred dogs.

Feathering - Longer fringe of hair on ears, legs, tail or body on sporting and hunting breeds.

Feet east and west - Toes turned out.

Fetch - The retrieval of game or an object by the dog. The command to do so.

Fetid breath - Having an offensive odor.

Fiddle front - Forelegs out at the elbow; pasterns close, and feet turned out.

Field trial - A competition for hound or sporting Breeds in which dogs are judged on ability and style in finding or retrieving game or following a game trail.

Flag - A long tail carried high. Usually referring to one of the pointing breeds.

Flank - The side of the body between the last rib and the hip.

Flat sided - Ribs insufficiently rounded as they approach the sternum or breastbone.

Flat withers - A fault that is the result of short upright shoulder blades that unattractively join the withers in an abrupt manner.

Flews - Upper lips pendulous, particularly at the inner corner.

Floating rib - The last or 13th rib which is unattached to other ribs.

Flying ears - Any characteristic drop ear or semi-prick ear that because of high placement on the head, causes the ear to "fly" when the dog moves its head or changes expression.

Flying trot - A fast gait in which all four feet are off the ground for a brief second. Because of the long reach, the oncoming hind feet precede the imprint left by the front foot.

Fontanel - One of the spaces, covered by a membrane, between the bones of the fetal or young skull.

Forearm - The bone of the front leg between the elbow and the pastern.

Foreface - The front part of the head in front of the eyes. The muzzle.

Foxy expression - A pointed nose with a short foreface.

Frogface - Extending nose accompanied by a receding jaw, usually undershot (example: Boston Bull Terrier).

Front - The dog's body when viewed head-on, including forelegs, chest, brisket and shoulder line.

Frontal bone - The skull bone over the eyes.

Furnishings - The long hair on the foreface, body and legs of certain breeds.

Furrow - A slight indentation or median line down the center of the skull to the stop.

Gait - The pattern of footsteps at various rates of speed, each pattern distinguished by a particular rhythm and footfall. The two gaits acceptable in the show ring are walk and trot.

Gay tail - The tail carried up.

Gazehound - Greyhound or other sight-hunting hound.

Genealogy - Recorded family descent.

Genetic - Pertaining to, or produced by genes.

Granular - An irregular, roughened surface; looking grainy.

Grizzle - Bluish-gray in color.

Groom - To brush, comb, trim or otherwise make a dog's coat neat.

Groups - The breeds divided to facilitate judging.

Guard hairs - The longer, smoother, stiffer hair which grows through the undercoat and normally conceals it.

Gun dog - A dog trained to work with its master in finding live game and retrieving game that has been shot.

Gun shy - When a dog fears the sight or sound of a gun.

Hackles - Hair on neck and back raised involuntarily in fright or anger.

Hackney gait - Lifting the front feet high like a hackney horse causing wasted action. An incorrect gait for a Poodle but the correct gait for the Miniature Pinscher.

Handler - The person, either professional or amateur, that shows a dog in the conformation ring or at a field trial.

Hard mouth - A dog that marks or bites the game he retrieves.

Harefoot - A foot whose third digit is longer, hence, an elongated foot.

Harlequin - Patched coloration usually black on white as found in the Harlequin Great Dane.

Harmony - The effect achieved when all elements work together to promote a final, pleasing result.

Haw - The third eyelid or membrane in the inside corner of the eye.

Heat - The seasonal period of the bitch.

Heel - The command to the dog to stay close to the handler.

Hernia - The protrusion of an organ or tissue through an opening in its surrounding walls.

Hindquarters - Rear assembly of the dog (pelvis, thighs, hocks and paws.)

Hip Dysplasia - An abnormality of hip development producing pain, disability and the gradually increasing deformity of the hip joint.

Hock - The collection of bones of the hind leg forming the joint between the second thigh and the metatarsus—the dog's true heel.

Hock well-let-down - Hock joint close to the ground.

Hydrocephalic - Indicating an accumulation of fluid within the cranium, often causing great enlargement of the head.

Inbreeding - The mating of closely related dogs of the same standard breed.

Incisors - The upper and lower front teeth between the canines.

Inguinal - Pertaining to the groin.

Interbreeding - Breeding together dogs of different varieties.

Inverted - To turn inward—or upside down.

Irritant - A biological, chemical or physical agent that causes a negative response.

Jowls - Flesh of lips and jaws.

Kink tail - A sharply bent tail.

Knee joint - Comon reference to the stifle joint.

Knuckling over - Faulty structure of carpus (wrist joint) allowing it to double forward under the weight of the standing dog; double-jointed wrist, often with slight swelling of the bones.

Layback - The angle of the shoulder blade as compared with the vertical.

Lead - A strap, cord or chain attached to the collar or harness for the purpose of restraining or leading the dog.

Leather - The flap of the ear.

Lesion - Any pathological or traumatic injury to tissue or organs of the body.

Level bite - When the front teeth of the upper and lower jaw meet exactly edge to edge.

Level gait - The dog moves without the rise or fall of the withers.

Line breeding - The mating of related dogs of the same standard breed, within the line or family, to a common ancestor such as breeding a dog to his grandam or a bitch to her grandsire.

Lippy - Pendulous or heavy lips that do not fit tightly.

Litter - The puppy or puppies of one whelping.

Liver - A deep reddish-brown color.

Loaded shoulders - When the shoulder blades are shoved out from the body by overdevelopment of the muscles.

Loin - Region of the body on either side of the vertebral column between the last ribs and the hindquarters.

Luxating Patella - A knee joint that pops in and out; dislocated.

Mane - Long and profuse hair on top and sides of the neck.

Merle - A coloration—usually blue-gray with flecks of black.

Moving close - When the hocks turn in and the pasterns drop straight to the ground and move parallel to one another, the dog will "move close in the rear." This action places severe strain on ligaments and muscles.

Moving straight - A term descriptive of balanced gaiting in which angle of inclination begins at the shoulder or hip joint and limbs remain relatively straight from these points to the pads of the feet, even as the legs flex or extend in reaching or thrusting.

Muzzle - The part of the head in front of the eyes, the nasal bone, nostrils and jaws. The foreface. Also a device attached to the foreface primarily used to prevent biting.

Necrosis - Death of tissue, single or groups of cells in a localized area such as the head of the femur in the hip.

Oblique shoulders - Shoulders well laid back. The ideal shoulder should slant at forty-five degrees to the ground, forming an approximate right angle with the humerus at the shoulder joint.

Occiput - Upper back point of the skull.

Out at the elbows - Elbows turning out from the body as opposed to being held close.

Out at the shoulders - With shoulder blades loosely attached to the body, leaving the shoulders jutting out in relief and increasing the breadth of the front.

Overshot - The front teeth (incisors) of the upper jaw overlap and do not touch the front teeth of the lower jaw when the mouth is closed.

Pads - Tough, shock absorbing projections on the underside of the feet.

Paper foot - A flat foot with thin pads.

Parti-colored - Variegated in patches of two or more colors.

Patella Luxation - Commonly called a slipped stifle (the knee joint of the dog).

Pastern - Commonly recognized as the area of the foreleg between the carpus or wrist and the digits. Comparable to the human wrist.

Pigeon breast - A chest with a short protruding breastbone.

Plume - A long fringe of hair hanging from the tail as in Setters.

Pompon - A rounded tuft of hair on the end of the tail when the coat is clipped. Term used in Poodle grooming.

Predisposed - Having a tendency to disease.

Prick ear - Usually carried erect and point at the top.

Professional Handler - A person who shows dogs for a fee.

Progressive Retinal Atrophy - The advancing or going forward of the destruction of nerve tissue controlling sight.

Proportion - Proportion requires that all parts be related to one another in size, length and bulk.

Puppy - A term used in showing dogs to refer to all dogs under twelve months of age.

Purebred - A dog whose sire and dam belong to the same breed, and are themselves of unmixed descent since recognition of the breed.

Put down - To prepare a dog for the show ring; referring to a dog unplaced in competition. Also refers to a dog put to sleep by artificial means.

Rangy dog - Long bodied - usually lacking depth of chest.

Rat tail - The root thick and covered with soft curls; devoid of hair at the tip or having the appearance of being clipped.

Rhythm - Rhythm in grooming is created when the eye moves smoothly and easily, connecting points of interest without jerking from point to point.

Ring tail - Carried up and around almost in a circle.

Roach back - A convex curvature of the back toward the loin.

Rose ear - A small drop ear which folds over the back so as to reveal the burr.

Rudder - The tail.

Ruff - The thick, long hair growth around the neck.

Saddle - A black marking over the back like a saddle.

Scissors bite - A bite in which the outer surface of the lower incisors touches the inner surface of the upper incisor.

Screw tail - A naturally short tail twisted in a spiral manner.

Second thigh - That part of the hindquarter from the stifle to the hock.

Self color - One color or whole color except for shadings.

Semi-prick ears - Ears carried erect with just the tips leaning forward.

Septum - The line extending vertically between the nostrils.

Shelly - A shallow, narrow body, lacking the correct amount of bone.

Sickle-hocked - Inability to straighten the hock joint on the back reach of the hind leg.

Sickle-tail - Carried out and up in a semicircle.

Sire - The male parent.

Skully - Thick and coarse through the skull.

Slab-sided - Flat ribs with too little spring from the spinal column.

Slew feet - Feet turned out.

Sloping shoulder - The shoulder blade set obliquely or "laid back."

Snipy - A pointed, weak muzzle.

Soundness - The state of mental and physical health when all organs and faculties are complete and functioning normally, each in its rightful relation to each other.

Spayed female - A bitch on which a surgical procedure has been performed on the bitch's reproductive organs to prevent conception.

Splayfoot - A flat foot with toes spreading.

Spread hocks - Hocks pointing outward.

Spring of ribs - Curvature of ribs for heart and lung capacity.

Squirrel tail - Carried up and curving more or less forward.

Standard of the Breed - A description of the ideal dog of each recognized breed to serve as a word pattern by which dogs are judged at shows.

Stern - Tail of sporting dog or hound.

Sternum - Breastbone

Stifle - The dog's knee. The joint of the hind leg between the thigh and the second thigh.

Stop - The step up from the muzzle to skull. Indentation between the eyes where the nasal bone and skull meet.

Strip the dog - The complete or partial removal of coat from the body, head, and leg of a dog.

Swayback - Concave curvature of the back line between the withers and the hipbones.

Symmetry - Pleasing balance between all parts of the dog.

Tail set - How the base of the tail sets on the rump.

Tartar - Hard brownish, or brownish yellow deposits on the teeth.

Terrier front - A straight front such as found on a Fox Terrier.

Thigh - The hindquarters from hip to stifle.

Throatiness - An excess of loose skin under the throat.

Topknot - A tuft of longer hair on the top of the head.

Topline - The dog's outline from just behind the withers to the tail set.

Toxicity - The quality of being poisonous, especially the degree of virulence of a toxic microbe or of a poison.

Toy dog - One of a group of dogs characterized by very small size.

Trauma - A wound or injury. An emotional shock that makes a lasting impression on the mind, especially the subconsious.

Trim - To groom by plucking or clipping.

Trot - A rhythmic two-beat diagonal gait in which feet at diagonally opposite ends of the body strike the ground together; the right hind foot with the left front foot and the left hind foot with the right front foot.

Tuck-up - Characterized by markedly shallower body depth at the loin.

Tulip ear - Ears carried with a slight forward curvature.

Type - The characteristic qualities distinguishing a breed.

Undershot - The front teeth (incisors) of the lower jaw overlapping or projecting beyond the front teeth of the upper jaw when the mouth is closed.

Upper arm - The humerus or bone of the foreleg, between the shoulder blade and the forearm.

Vaginitis - Inflammation of the vaginal tract.

Veterinary Ophthalmologist - An expert in the knowledge concerning the eye and its tissue.

Wirehair - A coat of hard, crisp, wiry texture.

Withers - The highest point of the shoulder, immediately behind the neck.

Wry mouth - Lower jaw does not line up with the upper jaw.

References

BOOKS

American Kennel Club. *The Complete Dog Book.* Howell Book House, 230 Park Ave., New York, N.Y. 10169.

Benjamin, Carol Lea. *Dog Problems.* Doubleday & Co., Inc., Garden City, N.Y.; 1981.

Bergman, Goran. *Why Does Your Dog Do That?* Howell Book House, 230 Park Ave., New York, N.Y. 10169; 1980.

Campbell, William E. *Behavior Problems In Dogs.* American Veterinary Publications, Inc., Drawer KK, Santa Barbara, CA 93102; 1975.

Glover, Harry, editor. *A Standard Guide To Purebred Dogs.* McGraw Hill, New York; 1978.

Jones, Arthur F. and Hamilton, Terelith, editors. *World Encyclopedia Of Dogs.* Galahad Books, New York; 1971.

MAGAZINE ARTICLES

Brody, Jane E. *Five Ways to Fight Fatigue.* Reader's Digest, November 1983.

Hodgkins, Elizabeth M., D.V.M. *Tumors in Dogs.* Groomer's Gazette Magazine, Vol. 5, No. 2 & 3.

McKiernan, Dr. Brendan. *Coping with Heat Stress.* Groom and Board Magazine, May/June 1980.

New Medical Emphasis on Holistic Care. Pet Shop Management Magazine, April 1979.

Tuttle, Jack L., D.V.M. *Ear Problems in Dogs and Cats.* Pet Age Magazine, March 1981.

Walin, Dorothy. *Is the Groomer a Veterinary Assistant?* Pet Age Magazine, March and April 1977.

About the Author

"The Art and Business of Professional Grooming" is Dorothy Walin's first full length book. However, during her grooming and teaching career she has written dozens of articles on grooming and shop procedures for various trade journals. She has also written a series of instructional pamphlets about grooming for Oster Professional Products Division. In addition she has written, directed and narrated the first V.C.R. film on Poodle grooming which was produced by Oster.

Dorothy began her grooming career practicing on the Poodles that had been purchased as pets for her children. As her skills increased, various veterinarians sent clients to her. Finally in 1967 she opened her own shop, The Velvet Bow, in Hinsdale, Illinois.

The ensuing years provided opportunities for Dorothy to take breaks from her role as shop owner and enter that of educator. She taught a course at the local junior high school which covered pet care and careers involved with animals. In conjunction with Pet Foods Institute she participated in a three day weekend show demonstrating grooming techniques and general dog and cat care to the public. In addition she has assisted Oster with grooming seminars and has been testing their products throughout her career.

Upon her husband's retirement in 1982, Dorothy sold The Velvet Bow and moved to the woods of northern Wisconsin. There she has been able to concentrate on the writing of this book which she hopes will help future groomers overcome some of the pitfalls inherent in the professional grooming industry. She continues to participate in grooming seminars and pet industry conventions around the country as a judge and seminar speaker.

Index